NON SANZ DROICT.

A
Midſommer nights
dreame.

As it hath beene ſundry times pub-
likely acted, by the Right Honoura-
ble, the Lord Chamberlaine his
ſeruants.

VVritten by VVilliam Shakeſpeare.

Printed by Iames Roberts, 1600.

Title page of the earliest printed version of *A Midsummer Night's Dream*

William Shakespeare

A
Midsummer Night's
Dream

With New and Updated Critical Essays and a Revised Bibliography

Edited by Wolfgang Clemen

THE SIGNET CLASSIC SHAKESPEARE
General Editor: Sylvan Barnet

A SIGNET CLASSIC

SIGNET CLASSIC
Published by the New American Library, a division of
Penguin Putnam Inc., 375 Hudson Street,
New York, New York 10014, U.S.A.
Penguin Books Ltd, 80 Strand,
London WC2R 0RL, England
Penguin Books Australia Ltd, 250 Camberwell Road,
Camberwell, Victoria 3124, Australia
Penguin Books Canada Ltd, 10 Alcorn Avenue,
Toronto, Ontario, Canada M4V 3B2
Penguin Books (N.Z.) Ltd, 182–190 Wairau Road,
Auckland 10, New Zealand

Penguin Books Ltd, Registered Offices:
Harmondsworth, Middlesex, England

Published by Signet Classic, an imprint of New American Library,
a division of Penguin Putnam Inc.
The Signet Classic edition of *A Midsummer Night's Dream* was first published in
1963, and an updated edition was published in 1986.

First Signet Classic Printing (Second Revised Edition), May 1998
15 14 13 12 11 10 9

Library of Congress Catalog Card Number: 97-62064

Printed in the United States of America

BOOKS ARE AVAILABLE AT QUANTITY DISCOUNTS WHEN USED TO PROMOTE PROD-
UCTS OR SERVICES. FOR INFORMATION PLEASE WRITE TO PREMIUM MARKETING DIVI-
SION, PENGUIN PUTNAM INC., 375 HUDSON STREET, NEW YORK, NEW YORK 10014.

Contents

Shakespeare: An Overview

Biographical Sketch

Between the record of his baptism in Stratford on 26 April 1564 and the record of his burial in Stratford on 25 April 1616, some forty official documents name Shakespeare, and many others name his parents, his children, and his grandchildren. Further, there are at least fifty literary references to him in the works of his contemporaries. More facts are known about William Shakespeare than about any other playwright of the period except Ben Jonson. The facts should, however, be distinguished from the legends. The latter, inevitably more engaging and better known, tell us that the Stratford boy killed a calf in high style, poached deer and rabbits, and was forced to flee to London, where he held horses outside a playhouse. These traditions are only traditions; they may be true, but no evidence supports them, and it is well to stick to the facts.

Mary Arden, the dramatist's mother, was the daughter of a substantial landowner; about 1557 she married John Shakespeare, a tanner, glove-maker, and trader in wool, grain, and other farm commodities. In 1557 John Shakespeare was a member of the council (the governing body of Stratford), in 1558 a constable of the borough, in 1561 one of the two town chamberlains, in 1565 an alderman (entitling him to the appellation of "Mr."), in 1568 high bailiff—the town's highest political office, equivalent to mayor. After 1577, for an unknown reason he drops out of local politics. What *is* known is that he had to mortgage his wife's property, and that he was involved in serious litigation.

The birthday of William Shakespeare, the third child and the eldest son of this locally prominent man, is unrecorded, but the Stratford parish register records that the infant was baptized on 26 April 1564. (It is quite possible that he was born on 23 April, but this date has probably been assigned by tradition because it is the date on which, fifty-two years later, he died, and perhaps because it is the feast day of St. George, patron saint of England.) The attendance records of the Stratford grammar school of the period are not extant, but it is reasonable to assume that the son of a prominent local official attended the free school—it had been established for the purpose of educating males precisely of his class—and received substantial training in Latin. The masters of the school from Shakespeare's seventh to fifteenth years held Oxford degrees; the Elizabethan curriculum excluded mathematics and the natural sciences but taught a good deal of Latin rhetoric, logic, and literature, including plays by Plautus, Terence, and Seneca.

On 27 November 1582 a marriage license was issued for the marriage of Shakespeare and Anne Hathaway, eight years his senior. The couple had a daughter, Susanna, in May 1583. Perhaps the marriage was necessary, but perhaps the couple had earlier engaged, in the presence of witnesses, in a formal "troth plight" which would render their children legitimate even if no further ceremony were performed. In February 1585, Anne Hathaway bore Shakespeare twins, Hamnet and Judith.

That Shakespeare was born is excellent; that he married and had children is pleasant; but that we know nothing about his departure from Stratford to London or about the beginning of his theatrical career is lamentable and must be admitted. We would gladly sacrifice details about his children's baptism for details about his earliest days in the theater. Perhaps the poaching episode is true (but it is first reported almost a century after Shakespeare's death), or perhaps he left Stratford to be a schoolmaster, as another tradition holds; perhaps he was moved (like Petruchio in *The Taming of the Shrew*) by

> Such wind as scatters young men through the world,
> To seek their fortunes farther than at home
> Where small experience grows.   (1.2.49–51)

In 1592, thanks to the cantankerousness of Robert Greene, we have our first reference, a snarling one, to Shakespeare as an actor and playwright. Greene, a graduate of St. John's College, Cambridge, had become a playwright and a pamphleteer in London, and in one of his pamphlets he warns three university-educated playwrights against an actor who has presumed to turn playwright:

> There is an upstart crow, beautified with our feathers, that with his *tiger's heart wrapped in a player's hide* supposes he is as well able to bombast out a blank verse as the best of you, and being an absolute Johannes-factotum [i.e., jack-of-all-trades] is in his own conceit the only Shake-scene in a country.

The reference to the player, as well as the allusion to Aesop's crow (who strutted in borrowed plumage, as an actor struts in fine words not his own), makes it clear that by this date Shakespeare had both acted and written. That Shakespeare is meant is indicated not only by *Shake-scene* but also by the parody of a line from one of Shakespeare's plays, *3 Henry VI*: "O, tiger's heart wrapped in a woman's hide" (1.4.137). If in 1592 Shakespeare was prominent enough to be attacked by an envious dramatist, he probably had served an apprenticeship in the theater for at least a few years.

In any case, although there are no extant references to Shakespeare between the record of the baptism of his twins in 1585 and Greene's hostile comment about "Shake-scene" in 1592, it is evident that during some of these "dark years" or "lost years" Shakespeare had acted and written. There are a number of subsequent references to him as an actor. Documents indicate that in 1598 he is a "principal comedian," in 1603 a "principal tragedian," in 1608 he is one of the "men players." (We do not have, however, any solid information about which roles he may have played; later traditions say he played Adam in *As You Like It* and the ghost in *Hamlet*, but nothing supports the assertions. Probably his role as dramatist came to supersede his role as actor.) The profession of actor was not for a gentleman, and it occasionally drew the scorn of university men like Greene who resented writing speeches for persons less educated than themselves, but it was respectable enough; players, if prosperous, were in effect members of the bourgeoisie, and there is nothing to suggest that Stratford considered William Shakespeare less than a solid citizen. When, in 1596, the Shakespeares were granted a coat of arms—i.e., the right to be considered gentlemen—the grant was made to Shakespeare's father, but probably William Shakespeare had arranged the matter on his own behalf. In subsequent transactions he is occasionally styled a gentleman.

Although in 1593 and 1594 Shakespeare published two narrative poems dedicated to the Earl of Southampton, *Venus and Adonis* and *The Rape of Lucrece*, and may well have written most or all of his sonnets in the middle nineties, Shakespeare's literary activity seems to have been almost entirely devoted to the theater. (It may be significant that the two narrative poems were written in years when the plague closed the theaters for several months.) In 1594 he was a charter member of a theatrical company called the Chamberlain's Men, which in 1603 became the royal company, the King's Men, making Shakespeare the king's playwright. Until he retired to Stratford (about 1611, apparently), he was with this remarkably stable company. From 1599 the company acted primarily at the Globe theater, in which Shakespeare held a one-tenth interest. Other Elizabethan dramatists are known to have acted, but no other is known also to have been entitled to a share of the profits.

Shakespeare's first eight published plays did not have his name on them, but this is not remarkable; the most popular play of the period, Thomas Kyd's *The Spanish Tragedy*, went through many editions without naming Kyd, and Kyd's authorship is known only because a book on the profession of acting happens to quote (and attribute to Kyd) some lines on the interest of Roman emperors in the drama. What is remarkable is that after 1598 Shakespeare's name commonly appears on printed plays—some of which are not his. Presumably his name was a drawing card, and publishers used it to attract potential buyers. Another indication of his popularity comes from Francis Meres, author of *Palladis Tamia: Wit's Treasury* (1598). In this anthology of snippets accompanied by an essay on literature, many playwrights are mentioned, but Shakespeare's name occurs more often than any other, and Shakespeare is the only play-wright whose plays are listed.

From his acting, his play writing, and his share in a playhouse, Shakespeare seems to have made considerable money. He put it to work, making substantial investments in Stratford real estate. As early as 1597 he bought New Place, the second-largest house in Stratford. His family moved in soon afterward, and the house remained in the family until a granddaughter died in 1670. When Shakespeare made his will in 1616, less than a month before he died, he sought to leave his property intact to his descendants. Of small bequests to relatives and to friends (including three actors, Richard Burbage, John Heminges, and Henry Condell), that to his wife of the second-best bed has provoked the most comment. It has sometimes been taken as a sign of an unhappy marriage (other supposed signs are the apparently hasty marriage, his wife's seniority of eight years, and his residence in London without his family). Perhaps the second-best bed was the bed the couple had slept in, the best bed being reserved for visitors. In any case, had Shakespeare not excepted it, the bed would have gone (with the rest of his household possessions) to his daughter and her husband.

On 25 April 1616 Shakespeare was buried within the chancel of the church at Stratford. An unattractive monument to his memory, placed on a wall near the grave, says that he died on 23 April. Over the grave itself are the lines, perhaps by Shakespeare, that (more than his literary fame) have kept his bones undisturbed in the crowded burial ground where old bones were often dislodged to make way for new:

> Good friend, for Jesus' sake forbear
> To dig the dust enclosed here.
> Blessed be the man that spares these stones
> And cursed be he that moves my bones.

A Note on the Anti-Stratfordians, Especially Baconians and Oxfordians

Not until 1769—more than a hundred and fifty years after Shakespeare's death—is there any record of anyone expressing doubt about Shakespeare's authorship of the plays and poems. In 1769, however, Herbert Lawrence nominated Francis Bacon (1561–1626) in *The Life and Adventures of Common Sense*. Since then, at least two dozen other nominees have been offered, including Christopher Marlowe, Sir Walter Raleigh, Queen Elizabeth I, and Edward de Vere, 17th earl of Oxford. The impulse behind all anti-Stratfordian movements is the scarcely concealed snobbish opinion that "the man from Stratford" simply could not have written the plays because he was a country fellow without a university education and without access to high society. Anyone, the argument goes, who used so many legal terms, medical terms, nautical terms, and so forth, and who showed some familiarity with classical writing, must have attended a university, and anyone who knew so much about courtly elegance and courtly deceit must himself have moved among courtiers. The plays do indeed reveal an author whose interests were exceptionally broad, but specialists in any given field—law, medicine, arms and armor, and so on—soon find that the plays do not reveal deep knowledge in specialized matters; indeed, the playwright often gets technical details wrong.

The claim on behalf of Bacon, forgotten almost as soon as it was put forth in 1769, was independently reasserted by Joseph C. Hart in 1848. In 1856 it was reaffirmed by W. H. Smith in a book, and also by Delia Bacon in an article; in 1857 Delia Bacon published a book, arguing that Francis Bacon had directed a group of intellectuals who wrote the plays.

Francis Bacon's claim has largely faded, perhaps because it was advanced with such evident craziness by Ignatius Donnelly, who in *The Great Cryptogram* (1888) claimed to break a code in the plays that proved Bacon had written not only the plays attributed to Shakespeare but also other Renaissance works, for instance the plays of Christopher Marlowe and the essays of Montaigne.

Consider the last two lines of the Epilogue in *The Tempest*:

> As you from crimes would pardoned be,
> Let your indulgence set me free.

What was Shakespeare—sorry, Francis Bacon, Baron Verulam—*really* saying in these two lines? According to Baconians, the lines are an anagram reading, "Tempest of Francis Bacon, Lord Verulam; do ye ne'er divulge me, ye words." Ingenious, and it is a pity that in the quotation the letter *a* appears only twice in the cryptogram, whereas in the deciphered message it appears three times. Oh, no problem; just alter "Verulam" to "Verul'm" and it works out very nicely.

Most people understand that with sufficient ingenuity one can torture any text and find in it what one wishes. For instance: Did Shakespeare have a hand in the King James Version of the Bible? It was nearing completion in 1610, when Shakespeare was forty-six years old. If you look at the 46th Psalm and count forward for forty-six words, you will find the word *shake*. Now if you go to the end of the psalm and count backward forty-six words, you will find the word *spear*. Clear evidence, according to some, that Shakespeare slyly left his mark in the book.

Bacon's candidacy has largely been replaced in the twentieth century by the candidacy of Edward de Vere (1550–1604), 17th earl of Oxford. The basic ideas behind the Oxford theory, advanced at greatest length by Dorothy and Charlton Ogburn in *This Star of England* (1952, rev. 1955), a book of 1297 pages, and by Charlton Ogburn in *The Mysterious William Shakespeare* (1984), a book of 892 pages, are these: (1) The man from Stratford could not possibly have had the mental equipment and the experience to have written the plays—only a courtier could have written them; (2) Oxford had the requisite background (social position, education, years at Queen Elizabeth's court); (3) Oxford did not wish his authorship to be known for two basic reasons: writing for the public theater was a vulgar pursuit, and the plays show so much courtly and royal disreputable behavior that they would have compromised Oxford's position at court. Oxfordians offer countless details to support the claim. For example, Hamlet's phrase "that ever I was born to set it right" (1.5.89) barely conceals "E. Ver, I was born to set it right," an unambiguous announcement of de Vere's authorship, according to *This Star of England* (p. 654). A second example: Consider Ben

Jonson's poem entitled "To the Memory of My Beloved Master William Shakespeare," prefixed to the first collected edition of Shakespeare's plays in 1623. According to Oxfordians, when Jonson in this poem speaks of the author of the plays as the "swan of Avon," he is alluding not to William Shakespeare, who was born and died in Stratford-on-Avon and who throughout his adult life owned property there; rather, he is alluding to Oxford, who, the Ogburns say, used "William Shakespeare" as his pen name, and whose manor at Bilton was on the Avon River. Oxfordians do not offer any evidence that Oxford took a pen name, and they do not mention that Oxford had sold the manor in 1581, forty-two years before Jonson wrote his poem. Surely a reference to the Shakespeare who was born in Stratford, who had returned to Stratford, and who had died there only seven years before Jonson wrote the poem is more plausible. And exactly why Jonson, who elsewhere also spoke of Shakespeare as a playwright, and why Heminges and Condell, who had acted with Shakespeare for about twenty years, should speak of Shakespeare as the author in their dedication in the 1623 volume of collected plays is never adequately explained by Oxfordians. Either Jonson, Heminges and Condell, and numerous others were in on the conspiracy, or they were all duped—equally unlikely alternatives. Another difficulty in the Oxford theory is that Oxford died in 1604, and some of the plays are clearly indebted to works and events later than 1604. Among the Oxfordian responses are: At his death Oxford left some plays, and in later years these were touched up by hacks, who added the material that points to later dates. *The Tempest*, almost universally regarded as one of Shakespeare's greatest plays and pretty clearly dated to 1611, does indeed date from a period after the death of Oxford, but it is a crude piece of work that should not be included in the canon of works by Oxford.

The anti-Stratfordians, in addition to assuming that the author must have been a man of rank and a university man, usually assume two conspiracies: (1) a conspiracy in Elizabethan and Jacobean times, in which a surprisingly large number of persons connected with the theater knew that the actor Shakespeare did not write the plays attributed to him but for some reason or other pretended that he did; (2) a conspiracy of today's Stratfordians, the professors who teach Shakespeare in the colleges and universities, who are said to have a vested interest in preserving Shakespeare as the author of the plays they teach. In fact, (1) it is inconceivable that the secret of Shakespeare's non-authorship could have been preserved by all of the people who supposedly were in on the conspiracy, and (2) academic fame awaits any scholar today who can disprove Shakespeare's authorship.

The Stratfordian case is convincing not only because hundreds or even thousands of anti-Stratford arguments—of the sort that say "ever I was born" has the secret double meaning "E. Ver, I was born"—add up to nothing at all but also because irrefutable evidence connects the man from Stratford with the London theater and with the authorship of particular plays. The anti-Stratfordians do not seem to understand that it is not enough to dismiss the Stratford case by saying that a fellow from the provinces simply couldn't have written the plays. Nor do they understand that it is not enough to dismiss all of the evidence connecting Shakespeare with the plays by asserting that it is perjured.

The Shakespeare Canon

We return to William Shakespeare. Thirty-seven plays as well as some nondramatic poems are generally held to constitute the Shakespeare canon, the body of authentic works. The exact dates of composition of most of the works are highly uncertain, but evidence of a starting point and/or of a final limiting point often provides a framework for informed guessing. For example, *Richard II* cannot be earlier than 1595, the publication date of some material to which it is indebted; *The Merchant of Venice* cannot be later than 1598, the year Francis Meres mentioned it. Sometimes arguments for a date hang on an alleged topical allusion, such as the lines about the unseasonable weather in *A Midsummer Night's Dream*, 2.1.81–117, but such an allusion, if indeed it is an allusion to an event in the real world, can be variously interpreted, and in any case there is always the possibility that a topical allusion was inserted years later, to bring the play up to date. (The issue of alterations in a text between the time that Shakespeare drafted it and the time that it was printed—alterations due to censorship or playhouse practice or Shakespeare's own second thoughts—will be discussed in "The Play Text as a Collaboration" later in this overview.) Dates are often attributed on the basis of style, and although conjectures about style usually rest on other conjectures (such as Shakespeare's development as a playwright, or the appropriateness of lines to character), sooner or later one must rely on one's literary sense. There is no documentary proof, for example, that *Othello* is not as early as *Romeo and Juliet*, but one feels that *Othello* is a later, more mature work, and because the first record of its performance is 1604, one is glad enough to set its composition at that date and not push it back into Shakespeare's early years. (*Romeo and Juliet* was first published in 1597, but evidence suggests that it was written a little earlier.) The following chronology, then, is indebted not only to facts but also to informed guesswork and sensitivity. The dates, necessarily imprecise for some works, indicate something like a scholarly consensus concerning the time of original composition. Some plays show evidence of later revision.

Plays. The first collected edition of Shakespeare, published in 1623, included thirty-six plays. These are all accepted as Shakespeare's, though for one of them, *Henry VIII*, he is thought to have had a collaborator. A thirty-seventh play, *Pericles*, published in 1609 and attributed to Shakespeare on the title page, is also widely accepted as being partly by Shakespeare even though it is not included in the 1623 volume. Still another play not in the 1623 volume, *The Two Noble Kinsmen*, was first published in 1634, with a title page attributing it to John Fletcher and Shakespeare. Probably most students of the subject now believe that Shakespeare did indeed have a hand in it. Of the remaining plays attributed at one time or another to Shakespeare, only one, *Edward III*, anonymously published in 1596, is now regarded by some scholars as a serious candidate. The prevailing opinion, however, is that this rather simple-minded play is not Shakespeare's; at most he may have revised some passages, chiefly scenes with the Countess of

Salisbury. We include *The Two Noble Kinsmen* but do not include *Edward III* in the following list.

1588–94	*The Comedy of Errors*
1588–94	*Love's Labor's Lost*
1589–91	*2 Henry VI*
1590–91	*3 Henry VI*
1589–92	*1 Henry VI*
1592–93	*Richard III*
1589–94	*Titus Andronicus*
1593–94	*The Taming of the Shrew*
1592–94	*The Two Gentlemen of Verona*
1594–96	*Romeo and Juliet*
1595	*Richard II*
1595–96	*A Midsummer Night's Dream*
1596–97	*King John*
1594–96	*The Merchant of Venice*
1596–97	*1 Henry IV*
1597	*The Merry Wives of Windsor*
1597–98	*2 Henry IV*
1598–99	*Much Ado About Nothing*
1598–99	*Henry V*
1599	*Julius Caesar*
1599–1600	*As You Like It*
1599–1600	*Twelfth Night*
1600–1601	*Hamlet*
1601–1602	*Troilus and Cressida*
1602–1604	*All's Well That Ends Well*
1603–1604	*Othello*
1604	*Measure for Measure*
1605–1606	*King Lear*
1605–1606	*Macbeth*
1606–1607	*Antony and Cleopatra*
1605–1608	*Timon of Athens*
1607–1608	*Coriolanus*
1607–1608	*Pericles*
1609–10	*Cymbeline*
1610–11	*The Winter's Tale*
1611	*The Tempest*

| 1612–13 | *Henry VIII* |
| 1613 | *The Two Noble Kinsmen* |

Poems. In 1989 Donald W. Foster published a book in which he argued that "A Funeral Elegy for Master William Peter," published in 1612, ascribed only to the initials W.S., *may* be by Shakespeare. Foster later published an article in a scholarly journal, *PMLA* 111 (1996), in which he asserted the claim more positively. The evidence begins with the initials, and includes the fact that the publisher and the printer of the elegy had published Shakespeare's *Sonnets* in 1609. But such facts add up to rather little, especially because no one has found any connection between Shakespeare and William Peter (an Oxford graduate about whom little is known, who was murdered at the age of twenty-nine). The argument is based chiefly on statistical examinations of word patterns, which are said to correlate with Shakespeare's known work. Despite such correlations, however, many readers feel that the poem does not sound like Shakespeare. True, Shakespeare has a great range of styles, but his work is consistently imaginative and interesting. Many readers find neither of these qualities in "A Funeral Elegy."

1592–93	*Venus and Adonis*
1593–94	*The Rape of Lucrece*
1593–1600	*Sonnets*
1600–1601	*The Phoenix and the Turtle*

Shakespeare's English

1. Spelling and Pronunciation. From the philologist's point of view, Shakespeare's English is modern English. It requires footnotes, but the inexperienced reader can comprehend substantial passages with very little help, whereas for the same reader Chaucer's Middle English is a foreign language. By the beginning of the fifteenth century the chief grammatical changes in English had taken place, and the final unaccented *-e* of Middle English had been lost (though it survives even today in spelling, as in *name*); during the fifteenth century the dialect of London, the commercial and political center, gradually displaced the provincial dialects, at least in writing; by the end of the century, printing had helped to regularize and stabilize the language, especially spelling. Elizabethan spelling may seem erratic to us (there were dozens of spellings of *Shakespeare*, and a simple word like *been* was also spelled *beene* and *bin*), but it had much in common with our spelling. Elizabethan spelling was conservative in that for the most part it reflected an older pronunciation (Middle English) rather than the sound of the language as it was then spoken, just as our spelling continues to reflect medieval pronunciation—most obviously in the now silent but formerly pronounced letters in a word such as *knight*. Elizabethan pronunciation, though not identical with ours, was much closer to ours than to that of the Middle Ages. Incidentally, though no one can be certain about what Elizabethan English sounded like, specialists tend to believe it was rather like the speech of a modern stage Irishman (*time* apparently was pronounced *toime*, *old* pronounced *awld*, *day* pronounced *die*, and *join* pronounced *jine*) and not at all like the Oxford speech that most of us think it was.

An awareness of the difference between our pronunciation and Shakespeare's is crucial in three areas—in accent, or number of syllables (many metrically regular lines may look irregular to us); in rhymes (which may not look like rhymes); and in puns (which may not look like puns). Examples will be useful. Some words that were at least on occasion stressed differently from today are *aspèct*, *còmplete*, *fòrlorn*, *revènue*, and *sepùlcher*. Words that sometimes had an additional syllable are *emp[e]ress*, *Hen[e]ry*, *mon[e]th*, and *villain* (three syllables, *vil-lay-in*). An additional syllable is often found in possessives, like *moon*'s (pronounced *moones*) and in words ending in *-tion* or *-sion*. Words that had one less syllable than they now have are *needle* (pronounced *neel*) and *violet* (pronounced *vilet*). Among rhymes now lost are *one* with *loan*, *love* with *prove*, *beast* with *jest*, *eat* with *great*. (In reading, trust your sense of metrics and your ear, more than your eye.) An example of a pun that has become obliterated by a change in pronunciation is Falstaff's reply to Prince Hal's "Come, tell us your

reason" in *1 Henry IV*: "Give you a reason on compulsion?
If reasons were as plentiful as blackberries, I would give no
man a reason upon compulsion, I" (2.4.237–40). The *ea* in
reason was pronounced rather like a long *a,* like the *ai* in
raisin, hence the comparison with blackberries.

Puns are not merely attempts to be funny; like metaphors
they often involve bringing into a meaningful relationship
areas of experience normally seen as remote. In *2 Henry IV,*
when Feeble is conscripted, he stoically says, "I care not. A
man can die but once. We owe God a death" (3.2.242–43),
punning on *debt,* which was the way *death* was pronounced.
Here an enormously significant fact of life is put into simple
commercial imagery, suggesting its commonplace quality.
Shakespeare used the same pun earlier in *1 Henry IV,* when
Prince Hal says to Falstaff, "Why, thou owest God a death,"
and Falstaff replies, " 'Tis not due yet: I would be loath
to pay him before his day. What need I be so forward with
him that calls not on me?" (5.1.126–29).

Sometimes the puns reveal a delightful playfulness;
sometimes they reveal aggressiveness, as when, replying to
Claudius's "But now, my cousin Hamlet, and my son,"
Hamlet says, "A little more than kin, and less than kind!"
(1.2.64–65). These are Hamlet's first words in the play, and
we already hear him warring verbally against Claudius.
Hamlet's "less than kind" probably means (1) Hamlet is not
of Claudius's family or nature, *kind* having the sense it still
has in our word *mankind*; (2) Hamlet is not kindly (affec-
tionately) disposed toward Claudius; (3) Claudius is not
naturally (but rather unnaturally, in a legal sense incestu-
ously) Hamlet's father. The puns evidently were not put in
as sops to the groundlings; they are an important way of
communicating a complex meaning.

2. *Vocabulary.* A conspicuous difficulty in reading Shakespeare is rooted in the fact that some of his words are no
longer in common use—for example, words concerned with
armor, astrology, clothing, coinage, hawking, horsemanship, law, medicine, sailing, and war. Shakespeare had a
large vocabulary—something near thirty thousand words—
but it was not so much a vocabulary of big words as a
vocabulary drawn from a wide range of life, and it is partly

his ability to call upon a great body of concrete language that gives his plays the sense of being in close contact with life. When the right word did not already exist, he made it up. Among words thought to be his coinages are *accommodation, all-knowing, amazement, bare-faced, countless, dexterously, dislocate, dwindle, fancy-free, frugal, indistinguishable, lackluster, laughable, overawe, premeditated, sea change, star-crossed.* Among those that have not survived are the verb *convive,* meaning to feast together, and *smilet,* a little smile.

Less overtly troublesome than the technical words but more treacherous are the words that seem readily intelligible to us but whose Elizabethan meanings differ from their modern ones. When Horatio describes the Ghost as an "erring spirit," he is saying not that the ghost has sinned or made an error but that it is wandering. Here is a short list of some of the most common words in Shakespeare's plays that often (but not always) have a meaning other than their most usual modern meaning:

'a	he
abuse	deceive
accident	occurrence
advertise	inform
an, and	if
annoy	harm
appeal	accuse
artificial	skillful
brave	fine, splendid
censure	opinion
cheer	(1) face (2) frame of mind
chorus	a single person who comments on the events
closet	small private room
competitor	partner
conceit	idea, imagination
cousin	kinsman
cunning	skillful
disaster	evil astrological influence
doom	judgment
entertain	receive into service

envy	malice
event	outcome
excrement	outgrowth (of hair)
fact	evil deed
fancy	(1) love (2) imagination
fell	cruel
fellow	(1) companion (2) low person (often an insulting term if addressed to someone of approximately equal rank)
fond	foolish
free	(1) innocent (2) generous
glass	mirror
hap, haply	chance, by chance
head	army
humor	(1) mood (2) bodily fluid thought to control one's psychology
imp	child
intelligence	news
kind	natural, acting according to nature
let	hinder
lewd	base
mere(ly)	utter(ly)
modern	commonplace
natural	a fool, an idiot
naughty	(1) wicked (2) worthless
next	nearest
nice	(1) trivial (2) fussy
noise	music
policy	(1) prudence (2) stratagem
presently	immediately
prevent	anticipate
proper	handsome
prove	test
quick	alive
sad	serious
saw	proverb
secure	without care, incautious
silly	innocent

sensible	capable of being perceived by the senses
shrewd	sharp
so	provided that
starve	die
still	always
success	that which follows
tall	brave
tell	count
tonight	last night
wanton	playful, careless
watch	keep awake
will	lust
wink	close both eyes
wit	mind, intelligence

All glosses, of course, are mere approximations; sometimes one of Shakespeare's words may hover between an older meaning and a modern one, and as we have seen, his words often have multiple meanings.

3. Grammar. A few matters of grammar may be surveyed, though it should be noted at the outset that Shakespeare sometimes made up his own grammar. As E.A. Abbott says in *A Shakespearian Grammar,* "Almost any part of speech can be used as any other part of speech": a noun as a verb ("he childed as I fathered"); a verb as a noun ("She hath made compare"); or an adverb as an adjective ("a seldom pleasure"). There are hundreds, perhaps thousands, of such instances in the plays, many of which at first glance would not seem at all irregular and would trouble only a pedant. Here are a few broad matters.

Nouns: The Elizabethans thought the *-s* genitive ending for nouns (as in *man's*) derived from *his*; thus the line " 'gainst the count his galleys I did some service," for "the count's galleys."

Adjectives: By Shakespeare's time adjectives had lost the endings that once indicated gender, number, and case. About the only difference between Shakespeare's adjectives and ours is the use of the now redundant *more* or *most* with the comparative ("some more fitter place") or superlative

("This was the most unkindest cut of all"). Like double comparatives and double superlatives, double negatives were acceptable; Mercutio "will not budge for no man's pleasure."

Pronouns: The greatest change was in pronouns. In Middle English *thou, thy,* and *thee* were used among familiars and in speaking to children and inferiors; *ye, your,* and *you* were used in speaking to superiors (servants to masters, nobles to the king) or to equals with whom the speaker was not familiar. Increasingly the "polite" forms were used in all direct address, regardless of rank, and the accusative *you* displaced the nominative *ye.* Shakespeare sometimes uses *ye* instead of *you,* but even in Shakespeare's day *ye* was archaic, and it occurs mostly in rhetorical appeals.

Thou, thy, and *thee* were not completely displaced, however, and Shakespeare occasionally makes significant use of them, sometimes to connote familiarity or intimacy and sometimes to connote contempt. In *Twelfth Night* Sir Toby advises Sir Andrew to insult Cesario by addressing him as *thou:* "If thou thou'st him some thrice, it shall not be amiss" (3.2.46–47). In *Othello* when Brabantio is addressing an unidentified voice in the dark he says, "What are you?" (1.1.91), but when the voice identifies itself as the foolish suitor Roderigo, Brabantio uses the contemptuous form, saying, "I have charged thee not to haunt about my doors" (93). He uses this form for a while, but later in the scene, when he comes to regard Roderigo as an ally, he shifts back to the polite *you,* beginning in line 163, "What said she to you?" and on to the end of the scene. For reasons not yet satisfactorily explained, Elizabethans used *thou* in addresses to God—"O God, thy arm was here," the king says in *Henry V* (4.8.108)—and to supernatural characters such as ghosts and witches. A subtle variation occurs in *Hamlet.* When Hamlet first talks with the Ghost in 1.5, he uses *thou,* but when he sees the Ghost in his mother's room, in 3.4, he uses *you,* presumably because he is now convinced that the ghost is not a counterfeit but is his father.

Perhaps the most unusual use of pronouns, from our point of view, is the neuter singular. In place of our *its, his* was often used, as in "How far that little candle throws *his* beams." But the use of a masculine pronoun for a neuter noun came to seem unnatural, and so *it* was used for the possessive as well as the nominative: "The hedge-sparrow fed the cuckoo so long / That it had it head bit off by it young." In the late sixteenth century the possessive form *its* developed, apparently by analogy with the *-s* ending used to indicate a genitive noun, as in *book*'s, but *its* was not yet common usage in Shakespeare's day. He seems to have used *its* only ten times, mostly in his later plays. Other usages, such as "you have seen Cassio and she together" or the substitution of *who* for *whom,* cause little problem even when noticed.

Verbs, Adverbs, and Prepositions: Verbs cause almost no difficulty: The third person singular present form commonly ends in *-s,* as in modern English (e.g., "He blesses"), but sometimes in *-eth* (Portia explains to Shylock that mercy "blesseth him that gives and him that takes"). Broadly speaking, the *-eth* ending was old-fashioned or dignified or "literary" rather than colloquial, except for the words *doth, hath,* and *saith.* The *-eth* ending (regularly used in the King James Bible, 1611) is very rare in Shakespeare's dramatic prose, though not surprisingly it occurs twice in the rather formal prose summary of the narrative poem *Lucrece.* Sometimes a plural subject, especially if it has collective force, takes a verb ending in *-s,* as in "My old bones aches." Some of our strong or irregular preterites (such as *broke*) have a different form in Shakespeare (*brake*); some verbs that now have a weak or regular preterite (such as *helped*) in Shakespeare have a strong or irregular preterite (*holp*). Some adverbs that today end in *-ly* were not inflected: "grievous sick," "wondrous strange." Finally, prepositions often are not the ones we expect: "We are such stuff as dreams are made on," "I have a king here to my flatterer."

Again, none of the differences (except meanings that have substantially changed or been lost) will cause much difficulty. But it must be confessed that for some elliptical passages there is no widespread agreement on meaning. Wise editors resist saying more than they know, and when they are uncertain they add a question mark to their gloss.

Shakespeare's Theater

In Shakespeare's infancy, Elizabethan actors performed wherever they could—in great halls, at court, in the courtyards of inns. These venues implied not only different audiences but also different playing conditions. The innyards must have made rather unsatisfactory theaters: on some days they were unavailable because carters bringing goods to London used them as depots; when available, they had to be rented from the innkeeper. In 1567, presumably to avoid such difficulties, and also to avoid regulation by the Common Council of London, which was not well disposed toward theatricals, one John Brayne, brother-in-law of the carpenter turned actor James Burbage, built the Red Lion in an eastern suburb of London. We know nothing about its shape or its capacity; we can say only that it may have been the first building in Europe constructed for the purpose of giving plays since the end of antiquity, a thousand years earlier. Even after the building of the Red Lion theatrical activity continued in London in makeshift circumstances, in marketplaces and inns, and always uneasily. In 1574 the Common Council required that plays and playing places in London be licensed because

> sundry great disorders and inconveniences have been found to ensue to this city by the inordinate haunting of great multitudes of people, specially youth, to plays, interludes, and shows, namely occasion of frays and quarrels, evil practices of incontinency in great inns having chambers and secret places adjoining to their open stages and galleries.

The Common Council ordered that innkeepers who wished licenses to hold performance put up a bond and make contributions to the poor.

The requirement that plays and innyard theaters be licensed, along with the other drawbacks of playing at inns and presumably along with the success of the Red Lion, led James Burbage to rent a plot of land northeast of the city walls, on property outside the jurisdiction of the city. Here he built England's second playhouse, called simply the Theatre. About all that is known of its construction is that it was wood. It soon had imitators, the most famous being the Globe (1599), essentially an amphitheater built across the Thames (again outside the city's jurisdiction), constructed with timbers of the Theatre, which had been dismantled when Burbage's lease ran out.

Admission to the theater was one penny, which allowed spectators to stand at the sides and front of the stage that jutted into the yard. An additional penny bought a seat in a covered part of the theater, and a third penny bought a more comfortable seat and a better location. It is notoriously difficult to translate prices into today's money, since some things that are inexpensive today would have been expensive in the past and vice versa—a pipeful of tobacco (imported, of course) cost a lot of money, about three pennies, and an orange (also imported) cost two or three times what a chicken cost—but perhaps we can get some idea of the low cost of the penny admission when we realize that a penny could also buy a pot of ale. An unskilled laborer made about five or sixpence a day, an artisan about twelve pence a day, and the hired actors (as opposed to the sharers in the company, such as Shakespeare) made about ten pence a performance. A printed play cost five or sixpence. Of course a visit to the theater (like a visit to a baseball game today) usually cost more than the admission since the spectator probably would also buy food and drink. Still, the low entrance fee meant that the theater was available to all except the very poorest people, rather as movies and most athletic events are today. Evidence indicates that the audience ranged from apprentices who somehow managed to scrape together the minimum entrance fee and to escape from their masters for a few hours, to prosperous members of the middle class and aristocrats who paid the additional fee for admission to the galleries. The exact proportion of men to women cannot be determined, but women of all classes certainly were present. Theaters were open every afternoon but Sundays for much of the year, except in times of plague, when they were closed because of fear of infection. By the way, no evidence suggests the presence of toilet facilities. Presumably the patrons relieved themselves by making a quick trip to the fields surrounding the playhouses.

There are four important sources of information about the

structure of Elizabethan public playhouses—drawings, a contract, recent excavations, and stage directions in the plays. Of drawings, only the so-called de Witt drawing (c. 1596) of the Swan—really his friend Aernout van Buchell's copy of Johannes de Witt's drawing—is of much significance. The drawing, the only extant representation of the interior of an Elizabethan theater, shows an amphitheater of three tiers, with a stage jutting from a wall into the yard or

Johannes de Witt, a Continental visitor to London, made a drawing of the Swan theater in about the year 1596. The original drawing is lost; this is Aernout van Buchell's copy of it.

enter of the building. The tiers are roofed, and part of the
stage is covered by a roof that projects from the rear and is
supported at its front on two posts, but the groundlings, who
paid a penny to stand in front of the stage or at its sides, were
exposed to the sky. (Performances in such a playhouse were
held only in the daytime; artificial illumination was not used.)
At the rear of the stage are two massive doors; above the
stage is a gallery.

The second major source of information, the contract for
the Fortune (built in 1600), specifies that although the Globe
(built in 1599) is to be the model, the Fortune is to be square,
eighty feet outside and fifty-five inside. The stage is to be
forty-three feet broad, and is to extend into the middle of the
yard, i.e., it is twenty-seven and a half feet deep.

The third source of information, the 1989 excavations of
the Rose (built in 1587), indicate that the Rose was fourteen-
sided, about seventy-two feet in diameter with an inner yard
almost fifty feet in diameter. The stage at the Rose was about
sixteen feet deep, thirty-seven feet wide at the rear, and
twenty-seven feet wide downstage. The relatively small
dimensions and the tapering stage, in contrast to the rectan-
gular stage in the Swan drawing, surprised theater historians
and have made them more cautious in generalizing about the
Elizabethan theater. Excavations at the Globe have not
yielded much information, though some historians believe
that the fragmentary evidence suggests a larger theater, perhaps one hundred feet in diameter.

From the fourth chief source, stage directions in the plays,
one learns that entrance to the stage was by the doors at
the rear (*"Enter one citizen at one door, and another at the
other"*). A curtain hanging across the doorway—or a curtain
hanging between the two doorways—could provide a place
where a character could conceal himself, as Polonius does,
when he wishes to overhear the conversation between
Hamlet and Gertrude. Similarly, withdrawing a curtain from
the doorway could "discover" (reveal) a character or two.
Such discovery scenes are very rare in Elizabethan drama,
but a good example occurs in *The Tempest* (5.1.171), where
a stage direction tells us, *"Here Prospero discovers Ferdi-
nand and Miranda playing at chess."* There was also some
sort of playing space "aloft" or "above" to represent, for

instance, the top of a city's walls or a room above the street. Doubtless each theater had its own peculiarities, but perhaps we can talk about a "typical" Elizabethan theater if we realize that no theater need exactly fit the description, just as no mother is the average mother with 2.7 children.

This hypothetical theater is wooden, round, or polygonal (in *Henry V* Shakespeare calls it a "wooden *O*") capable of holding some eight hundred spectators who stood in the yard around the projecting elevated stage—these spectators were the "groundlings"—and some fifteen hundred additional spectators who sat in the three roofed galleries. The stage, protected by a "shadow" or "heavens" or roof, is entered from two doors; behind the doors is the "tiring house" (attiring house, i.e., dressing room), and above the stage is some sort of gallery that may sometimes hold spectators but can be used (for example) as the bedroom from which Romeo—according to a stage direction in one text—"goeth down." Some evidence suggests that a throne can be lowered onto the platform stage, perhaps from the "shadow"; certainly characters can descend from the stage through a trap or traps into the cellar or "hell." Sometimes this space beneath the stage accommodates a sound-effects man or musician (in *Antony and Cleopatra* "*music of the hautboy* [oboes] *is under the stage*") or an actor (in *Hamlet* the "*Ghost cries under the stage*"). Most characters simply walk on and off through the doors, but because there is no curtain in front of the platform, corpses will have to be carried off (Hamlet obligingly clears the stage of Polonius' corpse, when he says, "I'll lug the guts into the neighbor room"). Other characters may have fallen at the rear, where a curtain on a doorway could be drawn to conceal them.

Such may have been the "public theater," so called because its inexpensive admission made it available to a wide range of the populace. Another kind of theater has been called the "private theater" because its much greater admission charge (sixpence versus the penny for general admission at the public theater) limited its audience to the wealthy or the prodigal. The private theater was basically a large room, entirely roofed and therefore artificially illuminated, with a stage at one end. The theaters thus were distinct in two ways: One was essentially an amphitheater that catered to the general public; the other was a hall that catered to the wealthy. In 1576 a hall theater was established in Blackfriars, a Dominican priory in London that had been suppressed in 1538 and confiscated by the Crown and thus was not under the city's jurisdiction. All the actors in this Blackfriars theater were boys about eight to thirteen years old (in the public theaters similar boys played female parts; a boy Lady Macbeth played to a man Macbeth). Near the end of this section on Shakespeare's theater we will talk at some length about possible implications in this convention of using boys to play female roles, but for the moment we should say that it doubtless accounts for the relative lack of female roles in Elizabethan drama. Thus, in *A Midsummer Night's Dream*, out of twenty-one named roles, only four are female; in *Hamlet*, out of twenty-four, only two (Gertrude and Ophelia) are female. Many of Shakespeare's characters have fathers but no mothers—for instance, King Lear's daughters. We need not bring in Freud to explain the disparity; a dramatic company had only a few boys in it.

To return to the private theaters, in some of which all of the performers were children—the "eyrie of . . . little eyases" (nest of unfledged hawks—2.2.347–48) which Rosencrantz mentions when he and Guildenstern talk with Hamlet. The theater in Blackfriars had a precarious existence, and ceased operations in 1584. In 1596 James Burbage, who had already made theatrical history by building the Theatre, began to construct a second Blackfriars theater. He died in 1597, and for several years this second Blackfriars theater was used by a troupe of boys, but in 1608 two of Burbage's sons and five other actors (including Shakespeare) became joint operators of the theater, using it in the winter when the open-air Globe was unsuitable. Perhaps such a smaller theater, roofed, artificially illuminated, and with a tradition of a wealthy audience, exerted an influence in Shakespeare's late plays.

Performances in the private theaters may well have had intermissions during which music was played, but in the public theaters the action was probably uninterrupted, flowing from scene to scene almost without a break. Actors would enter, speak, exit, and others would immediately enter and establish (if necessary) the new locale by a few properties and by words and gestures. To indicate that the

scene took place at night, a player or two would carry a
torch. Here are some samples of Shakespeare establishing
the scene:

This is Illyria, lady.   (*Twelfth Night*, 1.2.2)

Well, this is the Forest of Arden.   (*As You Like It*, 2.4.14)

This castle has a pleasant seat; the air
Nimbly and sweetly recommends itself
Unto our gentle senses.   (*Macbeth*, 1.6.1–3)

The west yet glimmers with some streaks of day.
                                                            (*Macbeth*, 3.3.5)

Sometimes a speech will go far beyond evoking the minimal
setting of place and time, and will, so to speak, evoke the
social world in which the characters move. For instance,
early in the first scene of *The Merchant of Venice* Salerio
suggests an explanation for Antonio's melancholy. (In the
following passage, *pageants* are decorated wagons, floats,
and *cursy* is the verb "to curtsy," or "to bow.")

Your mind is tossing on the ocean,
There where your argosies with portly sail—
Like signiors and rich burghers on the flood,
Or as it were the pageants of the sea—
Do overpeer the petty traffickers
That cursy to them, do them reverence,
As they fly by them with their woven wings.   (1.1.8–14)

Late in the nineteenth century, when Henry Irving produced the play with elaborate illusionistic sets, the first
scene showed a ship moored in the harbor, with fruit vendors
and dock laborers, in an effort to evoke the bustling and
exotic life of Venice. But Shakespeare's words give us this
exotic, rich world of commerce in his highly descriptive language when Salerio speaks of "argosies with portly sail" that
fly with "woven wings"; equally important, through Salerio
Shakespeare conveys a sense of the orderly, hierarchical

society in which the lesser ships, "the petty traffickers," curtsy and thereby "do . . . reverence" to their superiors, the merchant prince's ships, which are "Like signiors and rich burghers."

On the other hand, it is a mistake to think that except for verbal pictures the Elizabethan stage was bare. Although Shakespeare's Chorus in *Henry V* calls the stage an "unworthy scaffold" (Prologue 1.10) and urges the spectators to "eke out our performance with your mind" (Prologue 3.35), there was considerable spectacle. The last act of *Macbeth*, for instance, has five stage directions calling for *"drum and colors,"* and another sort of appeal to the eye is indicated by the stage direction *"Enter Macduff, with Macbeth's head."* Some scenery and properties may have been substantial; doubtless a throne was used, but the pillars supporting the roof would have served for the trees on which Orlando pins his poems in *As You Like It*.

Having talked about the public theater—"this wooden *O*"—at some length, we should mention again that Shakespeare's plays were performed also in other locales. Alvin Kernan, in *Shakespeare, the King's Playwright: Theater in the Stuart Court 1603–1613* (1995) points out that "several of [Shakespeare's] plays contain brief theatrical performances, set always in a court or some noble house. When Shakespeare portrayed a theater, he did not, except for the choruses in *Henry V*, imagine a public theater" (p. 195). (Examples include episodes in *The Taming of the Shrew*, *A Midsummer Night's Dream*, *Hamlet*, and *The Tempest*.)

A Note on the Use of Boy Actors in Female Roles

Until fairly recently, scholars were content to mention that the convention existed; they sometimes also mentioned that it continued the medieval practice of using males in female roles, and that other theaters, notably in ancient Greece and in China and Japan, also used males in female roles. (In classical Noh drama in Japan, males still play the female roles.) Prudery may have been at the root of the academic failure to talk much about the use of boy actors, or maybe there really is not much more to say than that it was a convention of a male-centered culture (Stephen Greenblatt's view, in *Shakespearean Negotiations* [1988]). Further, the very nature of a convention is that it is not thought about: Hamlet is a Dane and Julius Caesar is a Roman, but in Shakespeare's plays they speak English, and we in the audience never give this odd fact a thought. Similarly, a character may speak in the presence of others and we understand, again without thinking about it, that he or she is not heard by the figures on the stage (the aside); a character alone on the stage may speak (the soliloquy), and we do not take the character to be unhinged; in a realistic (box) set, the fourth wall, which allows the us to see what is going on, is miraculously missing. The no-nonsense view, then, is that the boy actor was an accepted convention, accepted unthinkingly—just as today we know that Kenneth Branagh is not Hamlet, Al Pacino is not Richard III, and Denzel Washington is not the Prince of Aragon. In this view, the audience takes the performer for the role, and that is that; such is the argument we now make for race-free casting, in which African-Americans and Asians can play roles of persons who lived in medieval Denmark and ancient Rome. But gender perhaps is different, at least today. It is a matter of abundant academic study: The Elizabethan theater is now sometimes called a transvestite theater, and we hear much about cross-dressing.

Shakespeare himself in a very few passages calls attention to the use of boys in female roles. At the end of *As You Like It* the boy who played Rosalind addresses the audience, and says, "O men, . . . if I were a woman, I would kiss as many of you as had beards that pleased me." But this is in the Epilogue; the plot is over, and the actor is stepping out of the play and into the audience's everyday world. A second reference to the practice of boys playing female roles occurs in *Antony and Cleopatra*, when Cleopatra imagines that she and Antony will be the subject of crude plays, her role being performed by a boy:

> The quick comedians
> Extemporally will stage us, and present
> Our Alexandrian revels: Antony
> Shall be brought drunken forth, and I shall see
> Some squeaking Cleopatra boy my greatness.   (5.2.216–20)

In a few other passages, Shakespeare is more indirect. For instance, in *Twelfth Night* Viola, played of course by a boy, disguises herself as a young man and seeks service in the house of a lord. She enlists the help of a Captain, and (by way of explaining away her voice and her beardlessness) says,

> I'll serve this duke
> Thou shalt present me as an eunuch to him.   (1.2.55–56)

In *Hamlet*, when the players arrive in 2.2, Hamlet jokes with the boy who plays a female role. The boy has grown since Hamlet last saw him: "By'r Lady, your ladyship is nearer to heaven than when I saw you last by the altitude of a chopine" (a lady's thick-soled shoe). He goes on: "Pray God your voice . . . be not cracked" (434–38).

Exactly how sexual, how erotic, this material was and is, is now much disputed. Again, the use of boys may have been unnoticed, or rather not thought about—an unexamined convention—by most or all spectators most of the time, perhaps *all* of the time, except when Shakespeare calls the convention to the attention of the audience, as in the passages just quoted. Still, an occasional bit seems to invite erotic thoughts. The clearest example is the name that Rosalind takes in *As You Like It*, Ganymede—the beautiful youth whom Zeus abducted. Did boys dressed to play female roles carry homoerotic appeal for straight men (Lisa Jardine's view, in *Still Harping on Daughters* [1983]), or for gay men, or for some or all women in the audience? Further, when the boy actor played a woman who (for the purposes of the plot) disguised herself as a male, as Rosalind, Viola, and Portia do—so we get a boy playing a woman playing a man—what sort of appeal was generated, and for what sort of spectator?

Some scholars have argued that the convention empowered women by letting female characters display a freedom unavailable in Renaissance patriarchal society; the convention, it is said, undermined rigid gender distinctions. In this view, the convention (along with plots in which female characters for a while disguised themselves as young men) allowed Shakespeare to say what some modern gender

critics say: Gender is a constructed role rather than a bio
logical given, something we make, rather than a fixed binary
opposition of male and female (see Juliet Dusinberre, in
Shakespeare and the Nature of Women [1975]). On the other
hand, some scholars have maintained that the male disguise
assumed by some female characters serves only to reaffirm
traditional social distinctions since female characters who
don male garb (notably Portia in *The Merchant of Venice*
and Rosalind in *As You Like It*) return to their female garb
and at least implicitly (these critics say) reaffirm the status
quo. (For this last view, see Clara Claiborne Park, in an
essay in *The Woman's Part*, ed. Carolyn Ruth Swift Lenz et
al. [1980].) Perhaps no one answer is right for all plays; in
As You Like It cross-dressing empowers Rosalind, but in
Twelfth Night cross-dressing comically traps Viola.

Shakespeare's Dramatic Language: Costumes, Gestures and Silences; Prose and Poetry

Because Shakespeare was a dramatist, not merely a poet,
he worked not only with language but also with costumes,
sound effects, gestures, and even silences. We have already
discussed some kinds of spectacle in the preceding section,
and now we will begin with other aspects of visual language;
a theater, after all, is literally a "place for seeing." Consider
the opening stage direction in *The Tempest*, the first play in
the first published collection of Shakespeare's plays: *"A
tempestuous noise of thunder and Lightning heard: Enter a
Ship-master, and a Boteswain."*

Costumes: What did that shipmaster and that boatswain
wear? Doubtless they wore something that identified them
as men of the sea. Not much is known about the costumes
that Elizabethan actors wore, but at least three points are
clear: (1) many of the costumes were splendid versions of
contemporary Elizabethan dress; (2) some attempts were
made to approximate the dress of certain occupations and of
antique or exotic characters such as Romans, Turks, and
Jews; (3) some costumes indicated that the wearer was

supernatural. Evidence for elaborate Elizabethan clothing can be found in the plays themselves and in contemporary comments about the "sumptuous" players who wore the discarded clothing of noblemen, as well as in account books that itemize such things as "a scarlet cloak with two broad gold laces, with gold buttons down the sides."

The attempts at approximation of the dress of certain occupations and nationalities also can be documented from the plays themselves, and it derives additional confirmation from a drawing of the first scene of Shakespeare's *Titus Andronicus*—the only extant Elizabethan picture of an identifiable episode in a play. (See pp. xxxviii–xxxix.) The drawing, probably done in 1594 or 1595, shows Queen Tamora pleading for mercy. She wears a somewhat medieval-looking robe and a crown; Titus wears a toga and a wreath, but two soldiers behind him wear costumes fairly close to Elizabethan dress. We do not know, however, if the drawing represents an actual stage production in the public theater, or perhaps a private production, or maybe only a reader's visualization of an episode. Further, there is some conflicting evidence: In *Julius Caesar* a reference is made to Caesar's doublet (a close-fitting jacket), which, if taken literally, suggests that even the protagonist did not wear Roman clothing; and certainly the lesser characters, who are said to wear hats, did not wear Roman garb.

It should be mentioned, too, that even ordinary clothing can be symbolic: Hamlet's "inky cloak," for example, sets him apart from the brightly dressed members of Claudius's court and symbolizes his mourning; the fresh clothes that are put on King Lear partly symbolize his return to sanity. Consider, too, the removal of disguises near the end of some plays. For instance, Rosalind in *As You Like It* and Portia and Nerissa in *The Merchant of Venice* remove their male attire, thus again becoming fully themselves.

Gestures and Silences: Gestures are an important part of a dramatist's language. King Lear kneels before his daughter Cordelia for a benediction (4.7.57–59), an act of humility that contrasts with his earlier speeches banishing her and that contrasts also with a comparable gesture, his ironic

kneeling before Regan (2.4.153–55). Northumberland's failure to kneel before King Richard II (3.3.71–72) speaks volumes. As for silences, consider a moment in *Coriolanus*: Before the protagonist yields to his mother's entreaties (5.3.182), there is this stage direction: *"Holds her by the hand, silent."* Another example of "speech in dumbness" occurs in *Macbeth*, when Macduff learns that his wife and children have been murdered. He is silent at first, as Malcolm's speech indicates: "What, man! Ne'er pull your hat upon your brows. Give sorrow words" (4.3.208–09). (For a discussion of such moments, see Philip C. McGuire's *Speechless Dialect: Shakespeare's Open Silences* [1985].)

Of course when we think of Shakespeare's work, we think primarily of his language, both the poetry and the prose.

Prose: Although two of his plays (*Richard II* and *King John*) have no prose at all, about half the others have at least one quarter of the dialogue in prose, and some have notably more: *1 Henry IV* and *2 Henry IV*, about half; *As You Like It*

and *Twelfth Night*, a little more than half; *Much Ado About Nothing*, more than three quarters; and *The Merry Wives of Windsor*, a little more than five sixths. We should remember that despite Molière's joke about M. Jourdain, who was amazed to learn that he spoke prose, most of us do not speak prose. Rather, we normally utter repetitive, shapeless, and often ungrammatical torrents; prose is something very different—a sort of literary imitation of speech at its most coherent.

Today we may think of prose as "natural" for drama; or even if we think that poetry is appropriate for high tragedy we may still think that prose is the right medium for comedy. Greek, Roman, and early English comedies, however, were written in verse. In fact, prose was not generally considered a literary medium in England until the late fifteenth century; Chaucer tells even his bawdy stories in verse. By the end of the 1580s, however, prose had established itself on the English comic stage. In tragedy, Marlowe made some use of prose, not simply in the speeches of clownish servants but even in the speech of a tragic hero, Doctor Faustus. Still, before Shakespeare, prose normally was used in the theater only for special circumstances: (1) letters and proclamations, to set them off from the poetic dialogue; (2) mad characters, to indicate that normal thinking has become disordered; and (3) low comedy, or speeches uttered by clowns even when they are not being comic. Shakespeare made use of these conventions, but he also went far beyond them. Sometimes he begins a scene in prose and then shifts into verse as the emotion is heightened; or conversely, he may shift from verse to prose when a speaker is lowering the emotional level, as when Brutus speaks in the Forum.

Shakespeare's prose usually is not prosaic. Hamlet's prose includes not only small talk with Rosencrantz and Guildenstern but also princely reflections on "What a piece of work is a man" (2.2.312). In conversation with Ophelia, he shifts from light talk in verse to a passionate prose denunciation of women (3.1.103), though the shift to prose here is perhaps also intended to suggest the possibility of madness. (Consult Brian Vickers, *The Artistry of Shakespeare's Prose* [1968].)

Poetry: Drama in rhyme in England goes back to the Middle Ages, but by Shakespeare's day rhyme no longer dominated poetic drama; a finer medium, blank verse (strictly speaking, unrhymed lines of ten syllables, with the stress on every second syllable) had been adopted. But before looking at unrhymed poetry, a few things should be said about the chief uses of rhyme in Shakespeare's plays. (1) A couplet (a pair of rhyming lines) is sometimes used to convey emotional heightening at the end of a blank verse speech; (2) characters sometimes speak a couplet as they leave the stage, suggesting closure; (3) except in the latest plays, scenes fairly often conclude with a couplet, and sometimes, as in *Richard II*, 2.1.145–46, the entrance of a new character within a scene is preceded by a couplet, which wraps up the earlier portion of that scene; (4) speeches of two characters occasionally are linked by rhyme, most notably in *Romeo and Juliet*, 1.5.95–108, where the lovers speak a sonnet between them; elsewhere a taunting reply occasionally rhymes with the previous speaker's last line; (5) speeches with sententious or gnomic remarks are sometimes in rhyme, as in the duke's speech in *Othello* (1.3.199–206); (6) speeches of sardonic mockery are sometimes in rhyme—for example, Iago's speech on women in *Othello* (2.1.146–58)—and they sometimes conclude with an emphatic couplet, as in Bolingbroke's speech on comforting words in *Richard II* (1.3.301–2); (7) some characters are associated with rhyme, such as the fairies in *A Midsummer Night's Dream*; (8) in the early plays, especially *The Comedy of Errors* and *The Taming of the Shrew*, comic scenes that in later plays would be in prose are in jingling rhymes; (9) prologues, choruses, plays-within-the-play, inscriptions, vows, epilogues, and so on are often in rhyme, and the songs in the plays are rhymed.

Neither prose nor rhyme immediately comes to mind when we first think of Shakespeare's medium: It is blank verse, unrhymed iambic pentameter. (In a mechanically exact line there are five iambic feet. An iambic foot consists of two syllables, the second accented, as in *away*; five feet make a pentameter line. Thus, a strict line of iambic pentameter contains ten syllables, the even syllables being stressed more heavily than the odd syllables. Fortunately, Shakespeare usually varies the line somewhat.) The first speech in *A Midsummer Night's Dream*, spoken by Duke Theseus to his betrothed, is an example of blank verse:

> Now, fair Hippolyta, our nuptial hour
> Draws on apace. Four happy days bring in
> Another moon; but, O, methinks, how slow
> This old moon wanes! She lingers my desires,
> Like to a stepdame, or a dowager,
> Long withering out a young man's revenue.   (1.1.1–6)

As this passage shows, Shakespeare's blank verse is not mechanically unvarying. Though the predominant foot is the iamb (as in *apace* or *desires*), there are numerous variations. In the first line the stress can be placed on "fair," as the regular metrical pattern suggests, but it is likely that "Now" gets almost as much emphasis; probably in the second line "Draws" is more heavily emphasized than "on," giving us a trochee (a stressed syllable followed by an unstressed one); and in the fourth line each word in the phrase "This old moon wanes" is probably stressed fairly heavily, conveying by two spondees (two feet, each of two stresses) the oppressive tedium that Theseus feels.

In Shakespeare's early plays much of the blank verse is end-stopped (that is, it has a heavy pause at the end of each line), but he later developed the ability to write iambic pentameter verse paragraphs (rather than lines) that give the illusion of speech. His chief techniques are (1) enjambing, i.e., running the thought beyond the single line, as in the first three lines of the speech just quoted; (2) occasionally replacing an iamb with another foot; (3) varying the position of the chief pause (the caesura) within a line; (4) adding an occasional unstressed syllable at the end of a line, traditionally called a feminine ending; (5) and beginning or ending a speech with a half line.

Shakespeare's mature blank verse has much of the rhythmic flexibility of his prose; both the language, though richly figurative and sometimes dense, and the syntax seem natural. It is also often highly appropriate to a particular character. Consider, for instance, this speech from *Hamlet*, in which Claudius, King of Denmark ("the Dane"), speaks to Laertes:

> And now, Laertes, what's the news with you?
> You told us of some suit. What is't, Laertes?
> You cannot speak of reason to the Dane
> And lose your voice. What wouldst thou beg, Laertes,
> That shall not be my offer, not thy asking?   (1.2.42–46)

Notice the short sentences and the repetition of the name "Laertes," to whom the speech is addressed. Notice, too, the shift from the royal "us" in the second line to the more intimate "my" in the last line, and from "you" in the first three lines to the more intimate "thou" and "thy" in the last two lines. Claudius knows how to ingratiate himself with Laertes.

For a second example of the flexibility of Shakespeare's blank verse, consider a passage from *Macbeth*. Distressed by the doctor's inability to cure Lady Macbeth and by the imminent battle, Macbeth addresses some of his remarks to the doctor and others to the servant who is arming him. The entire speech, with its pauses, interruptions, and irresolution (in "Pull't off, I say," Macbeth orders the servant to remove the armor that the servant has been putting on him), catches Macbeth's disintegration. (In the first line, *physic* means "medicine," and in the fourth and fifth lines, *cast the water* means "analyze the urine.")

> Throw physic to the dogs, I'll none of it.
> Come, put mine armor on. Give me my staff.
> Seyton, send out.—Doctor, the thanes fly from me.—
> Come, sir, dispatch. If thou couldst, doctor, cast
> The water of my land, find her disease
> And purge it to a sound and pristine health,
> I would applaud thee to the very echo,
> That should applaud again.—Pull't off, I say.—
> What rhubarb, senna, or what purgative drug,
> Would scour these English hence? Hear'st thou of them?
>
> (5.3.47–56)

Blank verse, then, can be much more than unrhymed iambic pentameter, and even within a single play Shakespeare's blank verse often consists of several styles, depending on the speaker and on the speaker's emotion at the moment.

The Play Text as a Collaboration

Shakespeare's fellow dramatist Ben Jonson reported that the actors said of Shakespeare, "In his writing, whatsoever he penned, he never blotted out line," i.e., never crossed out material and revised his work while composing. None of Shakespeare's plays survives in manuscript (with the possible exception of a scene in *Sir Thomas More*), so we cannot fully evaluate the comment, but in a few instances the published work clearly shows that he revised his manuscript. Consider the following passage (shown here in facsimile) from the best early text of *Romeo and Juliet*, the Second Quarto (1599):

Ro. Would I were sleepe and peace so sweet to rest
The grey eyde morne smiles on the frowning night,
Checkring the Easterne Clouds with streaks of light,
And darknesse fleckted like a drunkard reeles,
From forth daies pathway, made by *Tytans* wheeles.
Hence will I to my ghostly Friers close cell,
His helpe to craue, and my deare hap to tell.

Exit.

Enter Frier alone with a basket. (night,
Fri. The grey-eyed morne smiles on the frowning
Checking the Easterne clowdes with streaks of light:
And fleckeld darknesse like a drunkard reeles,
From forth daies path, and *Titans* burning wheeles:
Now ere the sun aduance his burning eie,

Romeo rather elaborately tells us that the sun at dawn is
dispelling the night (morning is smiling, the eastern clouds
are checked with light, and the sun's chariot—Titan's
wheels—advances), and he will seek out his spiritual father,
the friar. He exits and, oddly, the Friar enters and says pretty
much the same thing about the sun. Both speakers say that
"the gray-eyed morn smiles on the frowning night," but there
are small differences, perhaps having more to do with the
business of printing the book than with the author's
composition: For Romeo's "checkring," "fleckted," and
"pathway," we get the Friar's "checking," "fleckeld," and
"path." (Notice, by the way, the inconsistency in Elizabethan
spelling: Romeo's "clouds" become the Friar's "clowdes.")

Both versions must have been in the printer's copy, and it
seems safe to assume that both were in Shakespeare's manuscript. He must have written one version—let's say he first
wrote Romeo's closing lines for this scene—and then he
decided, no, it's better to give this lyrical passage to the
Friar, as the opening of a new scene, but he neglected to
delete the first version. Editors must make a choice, and they
may feel that the reasonable thing to do is to print the text as
Shakespeare intended it. But how can we know what he
intended? Almost all modern editors delete the lines from

Romeo's speech, and retain the Friar's lines. They don't do this because they know Shakespeare's intention, however. They give the lines to the Friar because the first published version (1597) of *Romeo and Juliet* gives only the Friar's version, and this text (though in many ways inferior to the 1599 text) is thought to derive from the memory of some actors, that is, it is thought to represent a performance, not just a script. Maybe during the course of rehearsals Shakespeare—an actor as well as an author—unilaterally decided that the Friar should speak the lines; if so (remember that we don't know this to be a fact) his final intention was to give the speech to the Friar. Maybe, however, the actors talked it over and settled on the Friar, with or without Shakespeare's approval. On the other hand, despite the 1597 version, one might argue (if only weakly) on behalf of giving the lines to Romeo rather than to the Friar, thus: (1) Romeo's comment on the coming of the daylight emphasizes his separation from Juliet, and (2) the figurative language seems more appropriate to Romeo than to the Friar. Having said this, in the Signet edition we have decided in this instance to draw on the evidence provided by earlier text and to give the lines to the Friar, on the grounds that since Q1 reflects a production, in the theater (at least on one occasion) the lines were spoken by the Friar.

A playwright sold a script to a theatrical company. The script thus belonged to the company, not the author, and author and company alike must have regarded this script not as a literary work but as the basis for a play that the actors would create on the stage. We speak of Shakespeare as the author of the plays, but readers should bear in mind that the texts they read, even when derived from a single text, such as the First Folio (1623), are inevitably the collaborative work not simply of Shakespeare with his company—doubtless during rehearsals the actors would suggest alterations—but also with other forces of the age. One force was governmental censorship. In 1606 parliament passed "an Act to restrain abuses of players," prohibiting the utterance of oaths and the name of God. So where the earliest text of *Othello* gives us "By heaven" (3.3.106), the first Folio gives "Alas," presumably reflecting the compliance of stage practice with the law. Similarly, the 1623 version of *King Lear* omits the oath "Fut" (probably from "By God's foot") at 1.2.142, again presumably reflecting the line as it was spoken on the stage. Editors who seek to give the reader the play that Shakespeare initially conceived—the "authentic" play conceived by the solitary Shakespeare— probably will restore the missing oaths and references to God. Other editors, who see the play as a collaborative work, a construction made not only by Shakespeare but also by actors and compositors and even government censors, may claim that what counts is the play as it was actually performed. Such editors regard the censored text as legitimate, since it is the play that was (presumably) finally put on. A performed text, they argue, has more historical reality than a text produced by an editor who has sought to get at what Shakespeare initially wrote. In this view, the text of a play is rather like the script of a film; the script is not the film, and the play text is not the performed play. Even if we want to talk about the play that Shakespeare "intended," we will find ourselves talking about a script that he handed over to a company with the intention that it be implemented by actors. The "intended" play is the one that the actors—we might almost say "society"—would help to construct.

Further, it is now widely held that a play is also the work of readers and spectators, who do not simply receive meaning, but who create it when they respond to the play. This idea is fully in accord with contemporary post-structuralist critical thinking, notably Roland Barthes's "The Death of the Author," in *Image-Music-Text* (1977) and Michel Foucault's "What Is an Author?," in *The Foucault Reader* (1984). The gist of the idea is that an author is not an isolated genius; rather, authors are subject to the politics and other social structures of their age. A dramatist especially is a worker in a collaborative project, working most obviously with actors—parts may be written for particular actors—but working also with the audience. Consider the words of Samuel Johnson, written to be spoken by the actor David Garrick at the opening of a theater in 1747:

> The stage but echoes back the public voice;
> The drama's laws, the drama's patrons give,
> For we that live to please, must please to live.

The audience—the public taste as understood by the playwright—helps to determine what the play is. Moreover, even members of the public who are not part of the playwright's immediate audience may exert an influence through censorship. We have already glanced at governmental censorship, but there are also other kinds. Take one of Shakespeare's most beloved characters, Falstaff, who appears in three of Shakespeare's plays, the two parts of *Henry IV* and *The Merry Wives of Windsor*. He appears with this name in the earliest printed version of the first of these plays, *1 Henry IV*, but we know that Shakespeare originally called him (after an historical figure) Sir John Oldcastle. Oldcastle appears in Shakespeare's source (partly reprinted in the Signet edition of *1 Henry IV*), and a trace of the name survives in Shakespeare's play, 1.2.43–44, where Prince Hal punningly addresses Falstaff as "my old lad of the castle." But for some reason—perhaps because the family of the historical Oldcastle complained—Shakespeare had to change the name. In short, the play as we have it was (at least in this detail) subject to some sort of censorship. If we think that a text should present what we take to be the author's intention, we probably will want to replace *Falstaff* with *Oldcastle*. But if we recognize that a play is a collaboration, we may welcome the change, even if it was forced on Shakespeare. Somehow *Falstaff*, with its hint of *false-staff*, i.e., inadequate prop, seems just right for this fat knight who, to our delight, entertains the young prince with untruths. We can go as far as saying that, at least so far as a play is concerned, an insistence on the author's original intention (even if we could know it) can sometimes impoverish the text.

The tiny example of Falstaff's name illustrates the point that the text we read is inevitably only a version—something in effect produced by the collaboration of the playwright with his actors, audiences, compositors, and editors—of a fluid text that Shakespeare once wrote, just as the *Hamlet* that we see on the screen starring Kenneth Branagh is not the *Hamlet* that Shakespeare saw in an open-air playhouse starring Richard Burbage. *Hamlet* itself, as we shall note in a moment, also exists in several versions. It is not surprising that there is now much talk about the *instability* of Shakespeare's texts.

Because he was not only a playwright but was also an actor and a shareholder in a theatrical company, Shakespeare probably was much involved with the translation of the play from a manuscript to a stage production. He may or may not have done some rewriting during rehearsals, and he may or may not have been happy with cuts that were made. Some plays, notably *Hamlet* and *King Lear*, are so long that it is most unlikely that the texts we read were acted in their entirety. Further, for both of these plays we have more than one early text that demands consideration. In *Hamlet*, the Second Quarto (1604) includes some two hundred lines not found in the Folio (1623). Among the passages missing from the Folio are two of Hamlet's reflective speeches, the "dram of evil" speech (1.4.13–38) and "How all occasions do inform against me" (4.4.32–66). Since the Folio has more numerous and often fuller stage directions, it certainly looks as though in the Folio we get a theatrical version of the play, a text whose cuts were probably made—this is only a hunch, of course—not because Shakespeare was changing his conception of Hamlet but because the playhouse demanded a modified play. (The problem is complicated, since the Folio not only cuts some of the Quarto but adds some material. Various explanations have been offered.)

Or take an example from *King Lear*. In the First and Second Quarto (1608, 1619), the final speech of the play is given to Albany, Lear's surviving son-in-law, but in the First Folio version (1623), the speech is given to Edgar. The Quarto version is in accord with tradition—usually the highest-ranking character in a tragedy speaks the final words. Why does the Folio give the speech to Edgar? One possible answer is this: The Folio version omits some of Albany's speeches in earlier scenes, so perhaps it was decided (by Shakespeare? by the players?) not to give the final lines to so pale a character. In fact, the discrepancies are so many between the two texts, that some scholars argue we do not simply have texts showing different theatrical productions. Rather, these scholars say, Shakespeare substantially revised the play, and we really have two versions of *King Lear* (and of *Othello* also, say some)—two different plays—not simply two texts, each of which is in some ways imperfect.

In this view, the 1608 version of *Lear* may derive from Shakespeare's manuscript, and the 1623 version may derive from his later revision. The Quartos have almost three hundred lines not in the Folio, and the Folio has about a hundred lines not in the Quartos. It used to be held that all the texts were imperfect in various ways and from various causes— some passages in the Quartos were thought to have been set from a manuscript that was not entirely legible, other passages were thought to have been set by a compositor who was new to setting plays, and still other passages were thought to have been provided by an actor who misremembered some of the lines. This traditional view held that an editor must draw on the Quartos and the Folio in order to get Shakespeare's "real" play. The new argument holds (although not without considerable strain) that we have two authentic plays, Shakespeare's early version (in the Quarto) and Shakespeare's—or his theatrical company's—revised version (in the Folio). Not only theatrical demands but also Shakespeare's own artistic sense, it is argued, called for extensive revisions. Even the titles vary: Q1 is called *True Chronicle Historie of the life and death of King Lear and his three Daughters*, whereas the Folio text is called *The Tragedie of King Lear*. To combine the two texts in order to produce what the editor thinks is the play that Shakespeare intended to write is, according to this view, to produce a text that is false to the history of the play. If the new view is correct, and we do have texts of two distinct versions of *Lear* rather than two imperfect versions of one play, it supports in a textual way the poststructuralist view that we cannot possibly have an unmediated vision of (in this case) a play by Shakespeare; we can only recognize a plurality of visions.

Editing Texts

Though eighteen of his plays were published during his lifetime, Shakespeare seems never to have supervised their publication. There is nothing unusual here; when a playwright sold a play to a theatrical company he surrendered his ownership to it. Normally a company would not publish the play, because to publish it meant to allow competitors to

acquire the piece. Some plays did get published: Apparently
hard up actors sometimes pieced together a play for a publisher; sometimes a company in need of money sold a play;
and sometimes a company allowed publication of a play that
no longer drew audiences. That Shakespeare did not concern
himself with publication is not remarkable; of his contemporaries, only Ben Jonson carefully supervised the publication of his own plays.

In 1623, seven years after Shakespeare's death, John
Heminges and Henry Condell (two senior members of
Shakespeare's company, who had worked with him for
about twenty years) collected his plays—published and
unpublished—into a large volume, of a kind called a folio.
(A folio is a volume consisting of large sheets that have been
folded once, each sheet thus making two leaves, or four
pages. The size of the page of course depends on the size of
the sheet—a folio can range in height from twelve to sixteen
inches, and in width from eight to eleven; the pages in the
1623 edition of Shakespeare, commonly called the First
Folio, are approximately thirteen inches tall and eight inches
wide.) The eighteen plays published during Shakespeare's
lifetime had been issued one play per volume in small for-
mats called quartos. (Each sheet in a quarto has been folded
twice, making four leaves, or eight pages, each page being
about nine inches tall and seven inches wide, roughly the
size of a large paperback.)

Heminges and Condell suggest in an address "To the great
variety of readers" that the republished plays are presented
in better form than in the quartos:

> Before you were abused with diverse stolen and surreptitious
> copies, maimed and deformed by the frauds and stealths of inju-
> rious impostors that exposed them; even those, are now offered to
> your view cured and perfect of their limbs, and all the rest
> absolute in their numbers, as he [i.e., Shakespeare] conceived
> them.

There is a good deal of truth to this statement, but some of
the quarto versions are better than others; some are in fact
preferable to the Folio text.

Whoever was assigned to prepare the texts for publication

in the first Folio seems to have taken the job seriously and yet not to have performed it with uniform care. The sources of the texts seem to have been, in general, good unpublished copies or the best published copies. The first play in the collection, *The Tempest*, is divided into acts and scenes, has unusually full stage directions and descriptions of spectacle, and concludes with a list of the characters, but the editor was not able (or willing) to present all of the succeeding texts so fully dressed. Later texts occasionally show signs of carelessness: in one scene of *Much Ado About Nothing* the names of actors, instead of characters, appear as speech prefixes, as they had in the Quarto, which the Folio reprints; proofreading throughout the Folio is spotty and apparently was done without reference to the printer's copy; the pagination of *Hamlet* jumps from 156 to 257. Further, the proofreading was done while the presses continued to print, so that each play in each volume contains a mix of corrected and uncorrected pages.

Modern editors of Shakespeare must first select their copy; no problem if the play exists only in the Folio, but a considerable problem if the relationship between a Quarto and the Folio—or an early Quarto and a later one—is unclear. In the case of *Romeo and Juliet*, the First Quarto (Q1), published in 1597, is vastly inferior to the Second (Q2), published in 1599. The basis of Q1 apparently is a version put together from memory by some actors. Not surprisingly, it garbles many passages and is much shorter than Q2. On the other hand, occasionally Q1 makes better sense than Q2. For instance, near the end of the play, when the parents have assembled and learned of the deaths of Romeo and Juliet, in Q2 the Prince says (5.3.208–9),

> Come, *Montague;* for thou art early vp
> To see thy sonne and heire, now earling downe.

The last three words of this speech surely do not make sense, and many editors turn to Q1, which instead of "now earling downe" has "more early downe." Some modern editors take only "early" from Q1, and print "now early down"; others take "more early," and print "more early down." Further, Q1 (though, again, quite clearly a garbled and abbreviated text) includes some stage directions that are not found in Q2, and today many editors who base their text on Q2 are glad to add these stage directions, because the directions help to give us a sense of what the play looked like on Shakespeare's stage. Thus, in 4.3.58, after Juliet drinks the potion, Q1 gives us this stage direction, not in Q2: *"She falls upon her bed within the curtains."*

In short, an editor's decisions do not end with the choice of a single copy text. First of all, editors must reckon with Elizabethan spelling. If they are not producing a facsimile, they probably modernize the spelling, but ought they to preserve the old forms of words that apparently were pronounced quite unlike their modern forms—*lanthorn, alablaster*? If they preserve these forms are they really preserving Shakespeare's forms or perhaps those of a compositor in the printing house? What is one to do when one finds *lanthorn* and *lantern* in adjacent lines? (The editors of this series in general, but not invariably, assume that words should be spelled in their modern form, unless, for instance, a rhyme is involved.) Elizabethan punctuation, too, presents problems. For example, in the First Folio, the only text for the play, Macbeth rejects his wife's idea that he can wash the blood from his hand (2.2.60–62):

> No: this my Hand will rather
> The multitudinous Seas incarnardine,
> Making the Greene one, Red.

Obviously an editor will remove the superfluous capitals, and will probably alter the spelling to "incarnadine," but what about the comma before "Red"? If we retain the comma, Macbeth is calling the sea "the green one." If we drop the comma, Macbeth is saying that his bloody hand will make the sea ("the Green") *uniformly* red.

An editor will sometimes have to change more than spelling and punctuation. Macbeth says to his wife (1.7.46–47):

> I dare do all that may become a man,
> Who dares no more, is none.

For two centuries editors have agreed that the second line is unsatisfactory, and have emended "no" to "do": "Who dares do more is none." But when in the same play (4.2.21–22) Ross says that fearful persons

> Floate vpon a wilde and violent Sea
> Each way, and moue,

need we emend the passage? On the assumption that the compositor misread the manuscript, some editors emend "each way, and move" to "and move each way"; others emend "move" to "none" (i.e., "Each way and none"). Other editors, however, let the passage stand as in the original. The editors of the Signet Classic Shakespeare have restrained themselves from making abundant emendations. In their minds they hear Samuel Johnson on the dangers of emendation: "I have adopted the Roman sentiment, that it is more honorable to save a citizen than to kill an enemy." Some departures (in addition to spelling, punctuation, and lineation) from the copy text have of course been made, but the original readings are listed in a note following the play, so that readers can evaluate the changes for themselves.

Following tradition, the editors of the Signet Classic Shakespeare have prefaced each play with a list of characters, and throughout the play have regularized the names of the speakers. Thus, in our text of *Romeo and Juliet*, all speeches by Juliet's mother are prefixed "Lady Capulet," although the 1599 Quarto of the play, which provides our copy text, uses at various points seven speech tags for this one character: *Capu. Wi.* (i.e., Capulet's wife), *Ca. Wi., Wi., Wife, Old La.* (i.e., Old Lady), *La.,* and *Mo.* (i.e., Mother). Similarly, in *All's Well That Ends Well*, the character whom we regularly call "Countess" is in the Folio (the copy text) variously identified as *Mother, Countess, Old Countess, Lady,* and *Old Lady*. Admittedly there is some loss in regularizing, since the various prefixes may give us a hint of the way Shakespeare (or a scribe who copied Shakespeare's manuscript) was thinking of the character in a particular scene—for instance, as a mother, or as an old lady. But too much can be made of these differing prefixes, since the social relationships implied are *not* always relevant to the given scene.

We have also added line numbers and in many cases act and scene divisions as well as indications of locale at the beginning of scenes. The Folio divided most of the plays into acts and some into scenes. Early eighteenth-century editors increased the divisions. These divisions, which provide a convenient way of referring to passages in the plays, have been retained, but when not in the text chosen as the basis for the Signet Classic text they are enclosed within square brackets, [ ], to indicate that they are editorial additions. Similarly, though no play of Shakespeare's was equipped with indications of the locale at the heads of scene divisions, locales have here been added in square brackets for the convenience of readers, who lack the information that costumes, properties, gestures, and scenery afford to spectators. Spectators can tell at a glance they are in the throne room, but without an editorial indication the reader may be puzzled for a while. It should be mentioned, incidentally, that there are a few authentic stage directions—perhaps Shakespeare's, perhaps a prompter's—that suggest locales, such as *"Enter Brutus in his orchard,"* and *"They go up into the Senate house."* It is hoped that the bracketed additions in the Signet text will provide readers with the sort of help provided by these two authentic directions, but it is equally hoped that the reader will remember that the stage was not loaded with scenery.

Shakespeare on the Stage

Each volume in the Signet Classic Shakespeare includes a brief stage (and sometimes film) history of the play. When we read about earlier productions, we are likely to find them eccentric, obviously wrongheaded—for instance, Nahum Tate's version of *King Lear*, with a happy ending, which held the stage for about a century and half, from the late seventeenth century until the end of the first quarter of the nineteenth. We see engravings of David Garrick, the greatest actor of the eighteenth century, in eighteenth-century garb as King Lear, and we smile, thinking how absurd the production must have been. If we are more thoughtful, we say, with the English novelist L. P. Hartley, "The past is a foreign country: they do things differently there." But if the eighteenth-century staging is a foreign country, what of the plays of the late sixteenth and seventeenth centuries? A foreign language, a foreign theater, a foreign audience.

Probably all viewers of Shakespeare's plays, beginning with Shakespeare himself, at times have been unhappy with the plays on the stage. Consider three comments about production that we find in the plays themselves, which suggest Shakespeare's concerns. The Chorus in *Henry V* complains that the heroic story cannot possibly be adequately staged:

> But pardon, gentles all,
> The flat unraisèd spirits that hath dared
> On this unworthy scaffold to bring forth
> So great an object. Can this cockpit hold
> The vasty fields of France? Or may we cram
> Within this wooden *O* the very casques
> That did affright the air at Agincourt?
>
> . . . .
>
> Piece out our imperfections with your thoughts.
>
> (Prologue 1.8–14,23)

Second, here are a few sentences (which may or may not represent Shakespeare's own views) from Hamlet's longish lecture to the players:

> Speak the speech, I pray you, as I pronounced it to you, trippingly on the tongue. But if you mouth it, as many of our players do, I had as lief the town crier spoke my lines. . . . O, it offends me to the soul to hear a robustious periwig-pated fellow tear a passion to tatters, to very rags, to split the ears of the groundlings. . . . And let those that play your clowns speak no more than is set down for them, for there be of them that will themselves laugh, to set on some quantity of barren spectators to laugh too, though in the meantime some necessary question of the play be then to be considered. That's villainous and shows a most pitiful ambition in the fool that uses it. (3.2.1–47)

Finally, we can quote again from the passage cited earlier in this introduction, concerning the boy actors who played the female roles. Cleopatra imagines with horror a theatrical version of her activities with Antony:

> The quick comedians
> Extemporally will stage us, and present
> Our Alexandrian revels: Antony
> Shall be brought drunken forth, and I shall see
> Some squeaking Cleopatra boy my greatness
> I' th' posture of a whore.   (5.2.216–21)

It is impossible to know how much weight to put on such passages—perhaps Shakespeare was just being modest about his theater's abilities—but it is easy enough to think that he was unhappy with some aspects of Elizabethan production. Probably no production can fully satisfy a playwright, and for that matter, few productions can fully satisfy *us;* we regret this or that cut, this or that way of costuming the play, this or that bit of business.

One's first thought may be this: Why don't they just do "authentic" Shakespeare, "straight" Shakespeare, the play as Shakespeare wrote it? But as we read the plays—words written to be performed—it sometimes becomes clear that we do not know *how* to perform them. For instance, in *Antony and Cleopatra* Antony, the Roman general who has succumbed to Cleopatra and to Egyptian ways, says, "The nobleness of life / Is to do thus" (1.1.36–37). But what is "thus"? Does Antony at this point embrace Cleopatra? Does he embrace and kiss her? (There are, by the way, very few scenes of kissing on Shakespeare's stage, possibly because boys played the female roles.) Or does he make a sweeping gesture, indicating the Egyptian way of life?

This is not an isolated example; the plays are filled with lines that call for gestures, but we are not sure what the gestures should be. *Interpretation* is inevitable. Consider a passage in *Hamlet*. In 3.1, Polonius persuades his daughter, Ophelia, to talk to Hamlet while Polonius and Claudius eavesdrop. The two men conceal themselves, and Hamlet encounters Ophelia. At 3.1.131 Hamlet suddenly says to her, "Where's your father?" Why does Hamlet, apparently out of nowhere—they have not been talking about Polonius—ask this question? Is this an example of the "antic disposition" (fantastic behavior) that Hamlet earlier (1.5.172) had told Horatio and others—including us—he would display? That is, is the question about the whereabouts of her father a seemingly irrational one, like his earlier question (3.1.103) to Ophelia, "Ha, ha! Are you honest?" Or, on the other hand, has Hamlet (as in many productions) suddenly glimpsed Polonius's foot protruding from beneath a drapery at the rear? That is, does Hamlet ask the question because he has suddenly seen something suspicious and now is testing Ophelia? (By the way, in productions that do give Hamlet a physical cue, it is almost always Polonius rather than Claudius who provides the clue. This itself is an act of interpretation on the part of the director.) Or (a third possibility) does Hamlet get a clue from Ophelia, who inadvertently betrays the spies by nervously glancing at their place of hiding? This is the interpretation used in the BBC television version, where Ophelia glances in fear toward the hiding place just after Hamlet says "Why wouldst thou be a breeder of sinners?" (121–22). Hamlet, realizing that he is being observed, glances here and there *before* he asks "Where's your father?" The question thus is a climax to what he has been doing while speaking the preceding lines. Or (a fourth interpretation) does Hamlet suddenly, without the aid of any clue whatsoever, intuitively (insightfully, mysteriously, wonderfully) sense that someone is spying? Directors must decide, of course—and so must readers.

Recall, too, the preceding discussion of the texts of the plays, which argued that the texts—though they seem to be before us in permanent black on white—are unstable. The Signet text of *Hamlet*, which draws on the Second Quarto (1604) and the First Folio (1623) is considerably longer than any version staged in Shakespeare's time. Our version, even if spoken very briskly and played without any intermission, would take close to four hours, far beyond "the two hours' traffic of our stage" mentioned in the Prologue to *Romeo and Juliet*. (There are a few contemporary references to the duration of a play, but none mentions more than three hours.) Of Shakespeare's plays, only *The Comedy of Errors*, *Macbeth*, and *The Tempest* can be done in less than three hours without cutting. And even if we take a play that exists only in a short text, *Macbeth*, we cannot claim that we are experiencing the very play that Shakespeare conceived, partly because some of the Witches' songs almost surely are non-Shakespearean additions, and partly because we are not willing to watch the play performed without an intermission and with boys in the female roles.

Further, as the earlier discussion of costumes mentioned, the plays apparently were given chiefly in contemporary, that is, in Elizabethan dress. If today we give them in the costumes that Shakespeare probably saw, the plays seem not contemporary but curiously dated. Yet if we use our own dress, we find lines of dialogue that are at odds with what we see; we may feel that the language, so clearly not our own, is inappropriate coming out of people in today's dress. A common solution, incidentally, has been to set the plays in the nineteenth century, on the grounds that this attractively distances the play (gives them a degree of foreignness, allowing for interesting costumes) and yet doesn't put them into a museum world of Elizabethan England.

Inevitably our productions are adaptations, *our* adaptations, and inevitably they will look dated, not in a century but in twenty years, or perhaps even in a decade. Still, we cannot escape from our own conceptions. As the director Peter Brook has said, in *The Empty Space* (1968):

> It is not only the hair-styles, costumes and make-ups that look dated. All the different elements of staging—the shorthands of behavior that stand for emotions; gestures, gesticulations and tones of voice—are all fluctuating on an invisible stock exchange all the time. . . . A living theatre that thinks it can stand aloof from anything as trivial as fashion will wilt. (p. 16)

As Brook indicates, it is through today's hairstyles, costumes, makeup, gestures, gesticulations, tones of voice—this includes our *conception* of earlier hairstyles, costumes, and so forth if we stage the play in a period other than our own—that we inevitably stage the plays.

It is a truism that every age invents its own Shakespeare, just as, for instance, every age has invented its own classical world. Our view of ancient Greece, a slave-holding society in which even free Athenian women were severely circumscribed, does not much resemble the Victorians' view of ancient Greece as a glorious democracy, just as, perhaps, our view of Victorianism itself does not much resemble theirs. We cannot claim that the Shakespeare on our stage is the true Shakespeare, but in our stage productions we find a Shakespeare that speaks to us, a Shakespeare that our ancestors doubtless did not know but one that seems to us to be the true Shakespeare—at least for a while.

Our age is remarkable for the wide variety of kinds of staging that it uses for Shakespeare, but one development deserves special mention. This is the now common practice of race-blind or color-blind or nontraditional casting, which allows persons who are not white to play in Shakespeare. Previously blacks performing in Shakespeare were limited to a mere three roles, Othello, Aaron (in *Titus Andronicus*), and the Prince of Morocco (in *The Merchant of Venice*), and there were no roles at all for Asians. Indeed, African-Americans rarely could play even one of these three roles, since they were not welcome in white companies. Ira Aldridge (c.1806–1867), a black actor of undoubted talent, was forced to make his living by performing Shakespeare in England and in Europe, where he could play not only Othello but also—in whiteface—other tragic roles such as King Lear. Paul Robeson (1898–1976) made theatrical history when he played Othello in London in 1930, and there was some talk about bringing the production to the United States, but there was more talk about whether American audiences would tolerate the sight of a black man—a real black man, not a white man in blackface—kissing and then killing a white woman. The idea was tried out in summer stock in 1942, the reviews were enthusiastic, and in the following year Robeson opened on Broadway in a production that ran an astounding 296 performances. An occasional all-black company sometimes performed Shakespeare's plays, but otherwise blacks (and other minority members) were in effect shut out from performing Shakespeare. Only since about 1970 has it been common for nonwhites to play major roles along with whites. Thus, in a 1996–97 production of *Antony and Cleopatra*, a white Cleopatra, Vanessa Redgrave, played opposite a black Antony, David Harewood.

Multiracial casting is now especially common at the New York Shakespeare Festival, founded in 1954 by Joseph Papp, and in England, where even siblings such as Claudio and Isabella in *Measure for Measure* or Lear's three daughters may be of different races. Probably most viewers today soon stop worrying about the lack of realism, and move beyond the color of the performers' skin to the quality of the performance.

Nontraditional casting is not only a matter of color or race; it includes sex. In the past, occasionally a distinguished woman of the theater has taken on a male role—Sarah Bernhardt (1844–1923) as Hamlet is perhaps the most famous example—but such performances were widely regarded as eccentric. Although today there have been some performances involving cross-dressing (a drag *As You Like It* staged by the National Theatre in England in 1966 and in the United States in 1974 has achieved considerable fame in the annals of stage history), what is more interesting is the casting of women in roles that traditionally are male but that need not be. Thus, a 1993–94 English production of *Henry V* used a woman—*not* cross-dressed—in the role of the governor of Harfleur. According to Peter Holland, who reviewed the production in *Shakespeare Survey* 48 (1995), "having a female Governor of Harfleur feminized the city and provided a direct response to the horrendous threat of rape and murder that Henry had offered, his language and her body in direct connection and opposition" (p. 210). Ten years from now the device may not play so effectively, but today it speaks to us. Shakespeare, born in the Elizabethan Age, has been dead nearly four hundred years, yet he is, as Ben Jonson said, "not of an age but for all time." We must understand, however, that he is "for all time" precisely because each age finds in his abundance something for itself and something of itself.

And here we come back to two issues discussed earlier in this introduction—the instability of the text and, curiously, the Bacon/Oxford heresy concerning the authorship of the plays. *Of course* Shakespeare wrote the plays, and we should daily fall on our knees to thank him for them—and yet there is something to the idea that he is not their only author. Every editor, every director and actor, and every reader to some degree shapes them, too, for when we edit, direct, act, or read, we inevitably become Shakespeare's collaborator and re-create the plays. The plays, one might say, are so cunningly contrived that they guide our responses, tell us how we ought to feel, and make a mark on us, but (for better or for worse) we also make a mark on them.

—SYLVAN BARNET
Tufts University

Introduction

A study of Shakespeare's development as a dramatic artist shows that one of his supreme achievements during his "middle period" consists in combining heterogeneous elements in a single play. The dramas of Shakespeare's predecessors all exist on a smaller scale, mostly adhering to one particular type and keeping within more limited resources of style and subject matter. However, even in his very first comedies, *The Two Gentlemen of Verona*, *The Comedy of Errors*, and *Love's Labor's Lost,* we see Shakespeare widening the scope of the dramatic genre to which these plays belong and introducing new elements taken over from other sections of the literary tradition of the past. *A Midsummer Night's Dream*, then, which must have been written about 1595, combines for the first time totally disparate worlds into one unified whole; the sharp contrasts brought together there would have destroyed the play's balance in the hands of any lesser playwright. For, indeed, it required Shakespeare's genius to bring together Bottom and Puck, the crude realism of the artisans and the exquisite delicacy of the fairy world, the stylized and pointed repartee of the Athenian lovers and the dignified manner of Theseus and Hippolyta. What we find are contrasts on many levels, exemplified by diversified means. Yet Shakespeare strikes an equilibrium between these contrasts, reconciling and fusing the discordant factors within the organic body of his comedy. *A Midsummer Night's Dream*, therefore, not only exhibits bold contrasts and divergent elements of plot, atmosphere, and character; it also illustrates the unifying power of the spirit of comedy and the poetic imagination. We further find that the play's unity is reinforced by a subtle technique of counterpoint and juxtaposition, a skillful contrasting of different strands of plot, and the creation of an atmosphere full of illusion, wonder, and strangeness, all of which facilitate the many transitions occurring during the course of the play.

Some facts about its origin and title may help us better to understand the particular nature of the play. *A Midsummer Night's Dream* is clearly related to the practices of midsummer night, the night before June 24, which was the date of St. John the Baptist's festival and hence connected with merrymaking, various superstitions and folk customs, dances, pageants, and revels. More than any other night in the year, midsummer night suggested enchantment and witchcraft, something which Shakespeare has superbly embodied in his fairy world. To an Elizabethan audience, moreover, the play's title would have immediately called to mind the so-called "midsummer madness," which was a state of mind marked by a heightened readiness to believe in the delusions of the imagination that were thought to befall the minds of men after days of great summer heat. Thus, by means of his highly suggestive title, Shakespeare has firmly planted the dreamlike action of his drama in the popular beliefs and customs of his time. Furthermore the title gives theatergoers and readers a clue as to how the work should be understood—namely, as an unrealistic creation of the imagination, a series of dream images containing all the contradictions and inconsistencies that dreams normally possess, but containing too their symbolic content. Indeed, the dreamlike character of what takes place is repeatedly alluded to. In Puck's epilogue, for instance, the audience themselves are explicitly addressed:

> And this weak and idle theme,
> No more yielding but a dream,
> Gentles, do not reprehend.

> (5.1.429–31)

In short, the play's title makes significant allusion to the nature and meaning of the work, though it makes no reference to the period of time during which the events of the drama occur. In fact, the action takes place between April 29 and May 1, the latter date, being that of May Day, demanding of course particular celebrations, and for that reason it is perhaps a suitable day for the marriage of Theseus and Hippolyta.

Now the wedding of the princely pair is not only the destination of the action; it is also the occasion for which the play itself was written. *A Midsummer Night's Dream* was undoubtedly intended as a dramatic epithalamium to celebrate the marriage of some aristocratic couple. (The attempts made to fix on a definite historical marriage, however, must remain conjectural.) Plays written for such festive occasions addressed themselves to an aristocratic audience. They were mostly performed on private stages rather than in public theaters and revealed an entirely different style of performance from the popular dramas. The relationship of *A Midsummer Night's Dream* to the court masque—something which Act 5, Scene 1, line 40 draws attention to—also comes in here. The masques formed a central part of the entertainments that were always given at court celebrations, and several noticeable features in *A Midsummer Night's Dream* clearly relate to the genre of the court masque. The music and dances, the appearance of fairylike creatures possessed of supernatural qualities, the employment of motifs involving magic and metamorphosis, and the vigorous stylization and symmetrical structure of some parts do indeed remind one of the court masque. Finally, the scenes with Bottom, Quince, and company may be compared to the antimasque, which formed the burlesque and realistic counterpart performed together with the masque itself.

In referring to the masque, one is only pointing out a single aspect of *A Midsummer Night's Dream*. We must also remember that Shakespeare has similarly taken over stylistic and formal elements from his own early comedies, popular drama, the romantic play, and the mythological dream plays of John Lyly. Shakespeare has tapped many sources, but he has nevertheless been able to create an original and independent form of drama that includes skillful organization of plot—involving the manipulation of three subplots that run parallel to one another—as well as a rich suffusion of the whole by both the atmosphere of nature and that of magic. Between a descriptive and retrospective kind of dramatic method and one that makes us see the process of things in action Shakespeare has struck a perfect sense of balance.

A study of the interrelation of the four plots reveals how their contrasts, juxtapositions, and dovetailing help to disclose the meaning of the drama. The play begins with a scene between Theseus and Hippolyta, who do not appear again until Act 4. In Act 5 their wedding is celebrated. The plot involving Theseus and Hippolyta can therefore be styled an "enveloping action" that provides the play with a definite framework and a firmly established temporal scaffolding; it stands outside the world of dream, enchantment, and love entanglements, suggesting the sphere of everyday reality out of which the events of the drama first develop and to which they then ultimately return. The section in Scene 1 with Egeus, Hermia, Lysander, and Demetrius relates the Theseus-Hippolyta plot to that of the lovers, for Theseus himself appears as arbitrator in the love dispute and it will be on his wedding day that the harsh verdict he passes on Hermia is to take effect, should she not have changed her mind by that date. This verdict is the cause of Hermia and Lysander's decision to flee into the wood near Athens, so that with this the events of the second and third acts have already been determined. The comic subplot, moreover, beginning in Scene 2 with the gathering of the artisans to prepare themselves for rehearsal, is also announced in Scene 1, insofar as we learn of the entertainments to be presented on Theseus' wedding day. Theseus' promise to woo Hippolyta "With pomp, with triumph, and with reveling" (1.1.19) can also be understood as an allusion to the dramatic entertainments that are to come later. From the very beginning, then, our expectations are raised in connection with the wedding day, which is to bring with it the artisans' play, the decision regarding the love dispute between the Athenian couples, and the festive marriage of Theseus and Hippolyta.

If this were all that Shakespeare had given us, we would have had a comedy little different from his early ones. The plot connected with the fairies, however, with Oberon and Titania at its center, not only brings considerable complications into the course of the above-mentioned matters, but also adds to the whole drama a new feature that Shakespeare had never employed before. For the supernatural, which intervenes in the activities of the characters, turns their intentions upside down, and directs their actions. It is the fairies who are responsible for the confusion, and also for the final reconciliation, thus substituting enchantment and arbitrariness for the lovers' own responsibility and power of will. Yet these influences also have repercussions on the fairies themselves, because Titania thereby falls in love with the ass-headed Bottom. Thus the world of the fairies is linked with that of the artisans, and we get those incomparably comic situations that are themselves the outcome of the fairies' intervention. Finally, a link between the plots dealing with the fairies and Theseus emerges in the conversation between Oberon and Titania in which the fairy rulers' earlier connections with Theseus and Hippolyta are recalled; and this is a moment that accelerates the pair's mutual jealousy and estrangement.

Since the fairies remain always invisible to the other members of the *dramatis personae* (only Bottom is ironically allowed the privilege of seeing Titania), and their deeds are accomplished without the knowledge of the other characters, Shakespeare has been able to achieve a highly dramatic effect of "double awareness." We as audience are aware of Puck's magic juice and therefore look forward with pleasure to what might develop. We know even more than the usually omniscient Oberon, who does not realize till some time later the confusion that Puck has caused by mistake. This error on Puck's part bears deeper significance, for it shows that even the fairies can err and that the influences they exert as supernatural agents in the play do not in the least answer to anything providential, but rather contain filaments of arbitrariness, self-deception, and folly.

An insight into the peculiar nature of the fairy world in *A Midsummer Night's Dream* helps us to understand the entire play, for although the fairies certainly possess supernatural qualities, they are nevertheless closely linked to the world of mankind and have their share of human frailties. Their origin in the realm of the elemental and their partly instinctive, partly playful nature, together with their capriciousness and irrationality, indicate which forces and qualities Shakespeare wanted us to see as conditioning and influencing human love relationships; for the haphazard and arbitrary game that love plays with the two Athenian couples appears as a projection of the irrationality, irresponsibility, and playfulness characterizing the nature of the fairies themselves. However, the fairies not only make other people behave in a way that corresponds, as it were, to their own fairy natures; they also strengthen and reinforce people's latent tendencies. Previous to the fairies' intervention, we learn from Demetrius that he has loved Helena before bestowing his affections on Hermia (1.1.106–07, 242–43); it is not for nothing that he is termed "spotted and inconstant man" (110).

Shakespeare has interspersed his text with numerous illuminating hints referring to the fairies' peculiar traits of character and sphere of existence, so that we are able to get a vivid picture of the type of creatures they are. Although the world of the fairies exhibits several characteristics common to popular belief and folklore tradition, it is to a considerable extent a new creation of Shakespeare's own. This is particularly true when we think of Puck, whose descent from Robin Goodfellow or Hobgoblin, as he is called by one of the fairies when he first appears (2.1.34,40), only accounts for one aspect of his being. If one examines the numerous statements that Puck utters about himself and that the other characters utter about him, one immediately realizes that Shakespeare has created a complex dramatic figure to whom is assigned a key position within the fabric of the play. Not only is Puck the comically rough and earth-bound goblin with his mischievous pranks, blunt speech, and intervention in day-to-day affairs; he is also a spirit closely linked with the elements, having command over supernatural powers and capable of moving at incredible speed. As "Oberon's jester" he is close to the fools of Shakespeare's later comedies, enjoying his own jests and possessing the gift of sharp, critical observation. Keeping this last point in mind, we see that Shakespeare has assigned him the role of spectator several times during the course of the play, and as such he comments on the action and aptly characterizes the people taking part. Hence it is he who, in view of the confusion he has caused among the lovers, cries out:

> Shall we their fond pageant see?
> Lord, what fools these mortals be!
>
> (3.2.114–15)

Thus Puck becomes the interpreter of the play's dramatic situations and intermediary between stage and audience as he places himself at a distance from events that have depended on and been influenced by him, and to which in the epilogue, significantly spoken by him, he is able to look back, as from a higher vantage point. Indeed, it is remarkable how many motives determining the play's action derive from Puck, how many invisible wires he holds in his hand. Yet his interventions in the development of the plot are as much the result of a casual mood or mischievous whim as they are the result of premeditated instructions from his master, Oberon. This is shown, for instance, in the case of Bottom's transformation in the first scene of Act 3. It is a paradox of the dramatic action that Oberon's well-meaning intention is turned into its opposite through Puck's mistake (Lysander, instead of Demetrius, is anointed with the magic herb), so that the activity of the supernatural forces seems to be largely conditioned by error and coincidence. Still, it is precisely this fickleness and inconstancy of fate that Puck acknowledges in his laconic answer to Oberon when the latter reproves him for the mistake: "Then fate o'errules . . ." (3.2.92) With these words Puck gives utterance to a basic motif in the drama.

It has often been stressed that in *A Midsummer Night's Dream* Shakespeare wanted to portray the irrational nature of love, the shifting and unstable "fancy" that continually falls prey to illusion, regards itself as being playful and short-lived, and is accompanied by a certain irresponsibility; whereas in *Romeo and Juliet,* written during the same period, love appears in quite a different shape, as a fateful and all-consuming force making claims to absolute authority and demanding that the whole of the self be yielded up to it.

But Shakespeare makes clear to us in several ways that the love between the Athenian couples is not rooted in actuality. Puck's magic juice, operating as a supernatural medium, is of course only one of the means by which Shakespeare places the relationships of the four Athenian lovers outside of reality. The love entanglements occur during a night full of dreams and enchantment, of which only an imprecise picture afterward remains in the memory of those concerned.

Furthermore, it is undoubtedly the poet's deliberate intention (contrary to his practice in other plays of the same period) that the lovers should be so weakly characterized that it is impossible for us to retain them in our memory as real and differentiated human beings. We may likewise take it for granted that their symmetrical grouping and their appearance in pairs is the result of conscious stylization on Shakespeare's part. And if the style of their dialogues, together with the handling of the verse, often seems to be flat, trite, and frankly silly, this neither signifies Shakespeare's lack of skill nor justifies the contention that passages have been left in from an earlier version of the same play. Rather it gives evidence that Shakespeare intended the four lovers to be just what they are, puppets and not fully realized characters. Even the spectator to those scenes of confusion in the wood soon has no idea where he is or who precisely is in love with whom.

Above all, however, the dreamlike atmosphere of such scenes accentuates our feeling that the four lovers appear to be quite removed from any criteria applicable to reality. "The willing suspension of disbelief" that Coleridge designated as one of the poet's chief aims Shakespeare achieves by creating a world of illusion that manifests itself from the first scene onward. Dream world and reality merge imperceptibly, so that the persons concerned are not sure themselves in which sphere they move, nor whether what they have experienced has been imagination or truth. The idea that what has happened has been a dream, illusion, or "vision" is often expressed from various standpoints by the characters themselves. "Dream" is a key word in the drama, and the idea that everything is based on imagination is given frequent and subtle variation. The art with which Shakespeare shifts from the dream world to reality is unique. This is evident in the first scene of Act 4, where both the lovers and Bottom are depicted as awaking out of their dreams—a scene in which all four plots are brought together for the first time, whereby the mind of the spectator is made to see the boundaries separating them as being simultaneously nonexistent and yet firmly fixed. Finally, as if in a series of flashbacks, the incidents that have occurred during the night of dreams are lit up once again from a distance by means of

Theseus' famous speech describing "the lunatic, the lover, and the poet" as being "of imagination all compact" (5.1.7–8). These words refer once more to that faculty which lies behind not only dreams, but the poet's own creations as well and under whose spell we, as spectators, have been kept during the whole course of the play; for we too have been enchanted, responding eagerly to the call of the poetry and accepting the play as an organism that conforms to its own rules, a world where strange and real things mingle in a curious way.

The illusion of a dream sequence scurrying past is also enhanced by a sense of the forward surge of time. Not only is the passing of night into morning given expression through the shifting movement of light and dark within a series of superb images and subtle allusions: the impatience and longing with which the different characters look forward to the future are perceptible from the very start, thus making time flow in an anticipatory way. Again, the language of the play is rich in images and expressions indicating quick movement, lightness, and transitoriness, thereby contributing to the over-all atmospheric impression. How delicately and accurately the play's particular atmosphere, together with its theme and leitmotifs, is rendered from the very beginning, an examination of the first scene of the play alone would show, although we can permit ourselves only a few observations here.

The very first exchange between Theseus and Hippolyta conveys to us a twofold awareness of time, from the standpoint of which we contemplate a time span that culminates in the wedding day, the date of which is fixed immediately at the outset. This emerges when Hippolyta's "Four days will quickly steep themselves in night, / Four nights will quickly dream away the time" (1.1.7–8) is contrasted with Theseus' ". . . but, O, methinks, how slow / This old moon wanes" (3–4). During this initial dialogue Shakespeare skillfully puts us in tune with the moonlit scenes that follow by means of Theseus' comparison of the "old moon" with "a stepdame, or a dowager / Long withering out a young man's revenue" (5–6). In this scene alone "moon" and "night" each occur five times, "dream" three times. The lines just quoted also suggest the aristocratic world of the court, where a part of the action is to take place. A further element is introduced when, immediately following, we read these instructions to Philostrate:

> Stir up the Athenian youth to merriments,
> Awake the pert and nimble spirit of mirth. . . .
>
> (12–13)

Yet the entry of Egeus immediately afterward, leading in his daughter Hermia and, "full of vexation," bringing accusations against Lysander because the latter "hath bewitched the bosom of [his] child" (22, 27), ushers in the radically contrasting note of discord, deception, and trickery, something that is never missing in any Shakespearean comedy and is always present as an undercurrent in *A Midsummer Night's Dream*; for the final state of harmony reached at the end of the play both in the world of the fairies and that of the court turns out to be a resolution of previously opposed forces, a reconciliation attained after former estrangement, and "the concord of this discord" (5.1.60).

The main theme of the drama—namely, the transitoriness and inconstancy of love—is also anticipated in this first scene when Lysander describes love as

> . . . momentany as a sound,
> Swift as a shadow, short as any dream,
> Brief as the lightning in the collied night,
> That, in a spleen, unfolds both heaven and earth,
> And ere a man hath power to say "Behold!"
> The jaws of darkness do devour it up:
> So quick bright things come to confusion.
>
> (1.1.143–49)

This passage is illuminating because it shows how Shakespeare not only bodies forth the themes and motifs of his drama in terms of action, but also gives them expression through imagery. In no other play of Shakespeare's middle period do we find so much poetry and verse melody, or indeed nature imagery, with its references to plants, animals, and other natural phenomena; nature itself even enters the drama as a participating agent alongside the characters. *A*

Midsummer Night's Dream should therefore be apprehended as poetry and music, and not only be absorbed and endorsed by the eye and intellect as a connected series of actions. For the play's language, by means of its images, its subtle allusions and suggestions, its verbal repetitions and rhythmic patterns, has built up a complex and finely varied tissue of ideas, impressions, and associations that constantly act on our powers of imagination and stimulate them to participate. The great range and delicacy of impact that poetic drama possesses, as opposed to prose drama, can be perfectly witnessed in *A Midsummer Night's Dream*.

The degree to which the language, with its proliferation of allusions, ironies, and ambiguities, creates the over-all dramatic effect is made clear by those prose scenes with the artisans, where the lyrical and poetic are completely lacking. Apart from suggesting a wealth of gestures, the language used by Bottom and company is rich in implications and evokes delightful misunderstandings; it gives expression to the artisans' ludicrous ambition for higher things as well as to their rustic limitations. All this gives rise to that constant incongruity which is the prerequisite for great comedy—the incongruity existing between the basic natures of the characters and their pretensions. The scenes with Bottom, Quince, and company provide a comic and realistic contrast to the poetry of the fairies and the artificial and stylized love scenes of the Athenians. Thus the delicacy, polished bearing, and lightness inherent in all other sections of the play are counterbalanced by the uncouthness, the heavy solidity of everyday life, and a naïve roughness that the artisans bring into the magical fairy world of the moonlit scenes. Puck, the shrewd onlooker, at one stage justly calls them "hempen homespuns." But Shakespeare has made far more out of this antimasque than a merely amusing subplot filled with clownlike figures; during the course of the play one of them has come to be the most unforgettable character in the entire drama. For the lack of vitality and pronounced individuality noticeable in the other personages we are fully recompensed in Bottom, who has justly been described as the greatest comic creation in the dramatist's early work. Abundantly endowed with remarkable qualities, Bottom is continually putting himself in a comic light. There are no features of his character that at one point or another do not lead to some ridiculous situation, some unforgettable moment of contrast or unintentionally provoked comparison. Bottom's supreme satisfaction with himself and his sense of ease remain with him even in his transformed state, while his stage ambitions (he wants to play the part of the lion as well as that of Pyramus, Thisby and the tyrant) parody the profession of acting and yet at the same time form a characteristic trait that fits him remarkably well. That his ambitions are fulfilled even before the Pyramus and Thisby drama takes place, insofar as Bottom has to play the parts of both ass and lover, is significant, just as is the marked irony that Bottom alone, out of all the persons in the play, is permitted to come into contact with the fairies—though this encounter does not impress him in the least or signify for him any unusual experience. In Titania's presence he discards nothing at all of his own personality; the ass's head, which with other people would have resulted in monstrous caricature, in his case is something that illuminates for us his real nature.

If the story of the craftsmen forms a satirical counterbalance to the plot of the lovers, then it is also true to say that the drama of Pyramus and Thisby initiates a twofold, even threefold kind of awareness. For what we get in this parody of the love tragedy is an exaggerated depiction of the four lovers' sentimentality, their high-flown protestations of love, and their pseudo-solemnity—a depiction in the form of a flashback that they themselves are now able to contemplate as spectators, serenely calm and reconciled with one another. The lovers' own relationships have likewise been a play that the fairies have found highly amusing, and these entanglements parallel the quarrel between Oberon and Titania, the quarrel from which the confusion among the lovers originated.

"The play within the play," superbly worked out by Shakespeare, makes us particularly aware that the entire drama has indeed been a "play," summoned into life by the dramatist's magic wand and just as easily made to vanish. When Puck refers in the first line of his epilogue ("If we shadows have offended") not merely to the fairies, previously termed "shadows," but also to all the actors who have taken part, we realize that Shakespeare is once more making it clear to us that we have been watching a "magic-lantern show," something where appearance, not reality, is the operative factor.

It is peculiarly ironic that Bottom, Quince, and company perform the tragedy of Pyramus and Thisby as an auspicious offering on behalf of the newly established love union, thereby, one might say, presenting the material of *Romeo and Juliet* in a comic and grotesque manner. Thus an exaggerated form of tragedy is employed so that the preceding scenes may be parodied as comedy. The play of Pyramus and Thisby parodies not only the torments of love, which the Athenian lovers can now look back on with serene calmness, but also the Senecan style of Elizabethan tragedy with its melodrama and ponderous conventions. Shakespeare parodies these conventions here by means of exaggeration or clumsy and grotesque usage—the too explicit prologue, for instance; the verbose self-explanation and commentaries; the stereotyped phrases for expressing grief; and the excessive use of such rhetorical devices as apostrophe, alliteration, hyperbole, and rhetorical question.

Even the elements of comedy and parody in the Pyramus and Thisby performance appear in a twofold light. Though they themselves are being mocked, the lovers smile at these awkward efforts on the part of the craftsmen, and Theseus even adds a highly suggestive commentary.

In the craftsmen's play, Shakespeare is also parodying the whole life of the theater. He calmly takes the shortcomings of all theatrical production and acting, drives them to absurd lengths, and holds them up for inspection. The lantern, which is supposed to represent the moon, makes us conscious of how equally inadequate Pyramus and Thisby are in their roles and suggests that such inadequacy may time and again have made its appearance on the Elizabethan stage. For those Elizabethan playgoers who viewed a play superficially, without using their own powers of imagination, much in Shakespearean drama must have remained completely unintelligible. It is at such narrow-minded theatergoers as these that Shakespeare is indirectly poking fun. And he enables us to see the limitations of his own stage, which had to portray a large world and create atmosphere without the elaborate scenery and technical equipment that we have today.

But the very inadequacy of the artisans' production gives emphasis to the true art of dramatic illusion and magic, as we have witnessed it in the preceding scenes, in which the evocative power of Shakespeare's language, assisted by our imagination, enables us to experience moonlight and night-time in the woods. Theseus himself makes this point when, in answer to Hippolyta's remark, "This is the silliest stuff that ever I heard," he says: "The best in this kind are but shadows; and the worst are no worse, if imagination amend them" (5.1.211, 212–13).

—WOLFGANG CLEMEN
University of Munich

The editor wishes to express his thanks to Dr. Dieter Mehl for assistance in the compilation of the notes.

A Midsummer Night's Dream

[Dramatis Personae

Theseus, Duke of Athens
Egeus, father to Hermia
Lysander ⎱
Demetrius ⎰ in love with Hermia
Philostrate, Master of the Revels to Theseus
Peter Quince, a carpenter; Prologue in the play
Snug, a joiner; Lion in the play
Nick Bottom, a weaver; Pyramus in the play
Francis Flute, a bellows mender; Thisby in the play
Tom Snout, a tinker; Wall in the play
Robin Starveling, a tailor; Moonshine in the play
Hippolyta, Queen of the Amazons, betrothed to These
Hermia, daughter to Egeus, in love with Lysander
Helena, in love with Demetrius
Oberon, King of the Fairies
Titania, Queen of the Fairies
Puck, or Robin Goodfellow
Peaseblossom ⎤
Cobweb ⎟
Moth ⎬ fairies
Mustardseed ⎦
Other Fairies attending their King and Queen
Attendants on Theseus and Hippolyta

Scene: Athens, and a wood near it]

A Midsummer Night's Dream

[ACT 1

Scene 1. *The palace of Theseus.*]

Enter Theseus, Hippolyta, [Philostrate,] with others.

Theseus. Now, fair Hippolyta, our nuptial hour
    Draws on apace. Four happy days bring in
    Another moon; but, O, methinks, how slow
    This old moon wanes! She lingers°1 my desires,
    Like to a stepdame, or a dowager,   5
    Long withering out a young man's revenue.°

Hippolyta. Four days will quickly steep themselves in
        night,
    Four nights will quickly dream away the time;
    And then the moon, like to a silver bow
    New-bent in heaven, shall behold the night   10
    Of our solemnities.

Theseus.   Go, Philostrate,
    Stir up the Athenian youth to merriments,
    Awake the pert° and nimble spirit of mirth,
    Turn melancholy forth to funerals;

---

¹The degree sign (°) indicates a footnote, which is keyed to the
ext by line number. Text references are printed in **boldface** type; the
annotation follows in roman type.
.1.4 **lingers** makes to linger, delays   6 **Long withering out a young
man's revenue** diminishing the young man's money (because she
must be supported by him)   13 **pert** lively

15   The pale companion° is not for our pomp.°

                                 [Exit Philostrate.

    Hippolyta, I wooed thee with my sword,°
    And won thy love, doing thee injuries;
    But I will wed thee in another key,
    With pomp, with triumph, and with reveling.

*Enter Egeus and his daughter Hermia, and Lysander,
and Demetrius.*

20   *Egeus.* Happy be Theseus, our renownèd Duke!

    Theseus. Thanks, good Egeus.° What's the news with
      thee?

    Egeus. Full of vexation come I, with complaint
    Against my child, my daughter Hermia.
    Stand forth, Demetrius. My noble lord,
25   This man hath my consent to marry her.
    Stand forth, Lysander. And, my gracious Duke
    This man hath bewitched the bosom of my child.
    Thou, thou, Lysander, thou hast given her rhymes,
    And interchanged love tokens with my child.
30   Thou hast by moonlight at her window sung,
    With feigning voice, verses of feigning love,
    And stol'n the impression of her fantasy°
    With bracelets of thy hair, rings, gauds, conceits,
    Knacks,° trifles, nosegays, sweetmeats, messengers
35   Of strong prevailment in unhardened youth.
    With cunning hast thou filched my daughter's heart,
    Turned her obedience, which is due to me,
    To stubborn harshness. And, my gracious Duke,
    Be it so she will not here before your Grace
40   Consent to marry with Demetrius,
    I beg the ancient privilege of Athens:

---

15 **companion** fellow (contemptuous)   15 **pomp** festive procession
16 **I wooed thee with my sword** (Theseus had captured Hippolyta
when he conquered the Amazons)   21 **Egeus** (pronounced "E-gé-us")
32 **stol'n the impression of her fantasy** fraudulently impressed your
image upon her imagination   33–34 **gauds, conceits, Knacks** trinkets,
cleverly devised tokens, knickknacks

As she is mine, I may dispose of her,
Which shall be either to this gentleman
Or to her death, according to our law
Immediately° provided in that case.   45

Theseus. What say you, Hermia? Be advised, fair
    maid.
To you your father should be as a god,
One that composed your beauties; yea, and one
To whom you are but as a form in wax
By him imprinted and within his power   50
To leave the figure or disfigure it.
Demetrius is a worthy gentleman.

Hermia. So is Lysander.

Theseus.   In himself he is;
But in this kind, wanting your father's voice,°
The other must be held the worthier.   55

Hermia. I would my father looked but with my eyes.

Theseus. Rather your eyes must with his judgment
    look.

Hermia. I do entreat your Grace to pardon me.
I know not by what power I am made bold,
Nor how it may concern my modesty,   60
In such a presence here to plead my thoughts;
But I beseech your Grace that I may know
The worst that may befall me in this case,
If I refuse to wed Demetrius.

Theseus. Either to die the death, or to abjure   65
Forever the society of men.
Therefore, fair Hermia, question your desires;
Know of° your youth, examine well your blood,°
Whether, if you yield not to your father's choice,
You can endure the livery of a nun,   70
For aye to be in shady cloister mewed,°
To live a barren sister all your life,

45 **Immediately** expressly   54 **But in ... father's voice** but in this
particular respect, lacking your father's approval   68 **Know of** ascer-
tain from   68 **blood** passions   71 **mewed** caged

Chanting faint hymns to the cold fruitless moon.°
Thrice-blessèd they that master so their blood,
75 To undergo such maiden pilgrimage;
But earthlier happy is the rose distilled,°
Than that which, withering on the virgin thorn,
Grows, lives, and dies in single blessedness.

Hermia. So will I grow, so live, so die, my lord,
80 Ere I will yield my virgin patent° up
Unto his lordship, whose unwished yoke
My soul consents not to give sovereignty.

Theseus. Take time to pause; and, by the next new
moon—
The sealing day betwixt my love and me,
85 For everlasting bond of fellowship—
Upon that day either prepare to die
For disobedience to your father's will,
Or else to wed Demetrius, as he would,
Or on Diana's altar to protest
90 For aye austerity and single life.

Demetrius. Relent, sweet Hermia: and, Lysander,
yield
Thy crazèd title° to my certain right.

Lysander. You have her father's love, Demetrius;
Let me have Hermia's: do you marry him.

95 *Egeus.* Scornful Lysander! True, he hath my love,
And what is mine my love shall render him.
And she is mine, and all my right of her
I do estate unto° Demetrius.

Lysander. I am, my lord, as well derived as he,
100 As well possessed;° my love is more than his;
My fortunes every way as fairly ranked
(If not with vantage°) as Demetrius';
And, which is more than all these boasts can be,

I am beloved of beauteous Hermia.
Why should not I then prosecute my right?   105
Demetrius, I'll avouch it to his head,°
Made love to Nedar's daughter, Helena,
And won her soul; and she, sweet lady, dotes,
Devoutly dotes, dotes in idolatry,
Upon this spotted° and inconstant man.   110

Theseus. I must confess that I have heard so much,
And with Demetrius thought to have spoke thereof;
But, being overfull of self-affairs,
My mind did lose it. But, Demetrius, come;
And come, Egeus. You shall go with me;   115
I have some private schooling for you both.
For you, fair Hermia, look you arm yourself
To fit your fancies to your father's will;
Or else the law of Athens yields you up—
Which by no means we may extenuate—   120
To death, or to a vow of single life.
Come, my Hippolyta. What cheer, my love?
Demetrius and Egeus, go along.
I must employ you in some business
Against° our nuptial, and confer with you   125
Of something nearly° that concerns yourselves.

Egeus. With duty and desire we follow you.
                    Exeunt [all but Lysander and Hermia].

Lysander. How now, my love! Why is your cheek so
        pale?
How chance° the roses there do fade so fast?

Hermia. Belike° for want of rain, which I could well   130
        Beteem° them from the tempest of my eyes.

Lysander. Ay me! For aught that I could ever read,
        Could ever hear by tale or history,

---

106 **to his head** in his teeth   110 **spotted** i.e., morally stained
125 **Against** in preparation for   126 **nearly** closely   129 **How
chance** how does it come that   130 **Belike** perhaps   131 **Beteem**
bring forth

The course of true love never did run smooth;
135 But, either it was different in blood—

Hermia. O cross! Too high to be enthralled to low!

Lysander. Or else misgraffèd° in respect of years—

Hermia. O spite! Too old to be engaged to young!

Lysander. Or else it stood upon the choice of friends—

140 *Hermia.* O hell! To choose love by another's eyes!

Lysander. Or, if there were a sympathy in choice,
      War, death, or sickness did lay siege to it,
      Making it momentany° as a sound,
      Swift as a shadow, short as any dream,
145   Brief as the lightning in the collied° night,
      That, in a spleen,° unfolds both heaven and earth,
      And ere a man hath power to say "Behold!"
      The jaws of darkness do devour it up:
      So quick bright things come to confusion.

150 *Hermia.* If then true lovers have been ever crossed,
      It stands as an edict in destiny:
      Then let us teach our trial patience,°
      Because it is a customary cross,
      As due to love as thoughts and dreams and sighs,
155   Wishes and tears, poor Fancy's° followers.

Lysander. A good persuasion.° Therefore, hear me
      Hermia.
      I have a widow aunt, a dowager
      Of great revenue, and she hath no child.
      From Athens is her house remote seven leagues,
160   And she respects me as her only son.
      There, gentle Hermia, may I marry thee,
      And to that place the sharp Athenian law
      Cannot pursue us. If thou lovest me, then,

---

137 **misgraffèd** ill matched, misgrafted   143 **momentany** momentary
passing   145 **collied** blackened   146 **spleen** flash   152 **teach ou
trial patience** i.e., teach ourselves to be patient   155 **Fancy's** Love'
156 **persuasion** principle

Steal forth thy father's house tomorrow night;
And in the wood, a league without the town,   165
Where I did meet thee once with Helena,
To do observance to a morn of May,
There will I stay for thee.

Hermia.   My good Lysander!
I swear to thee, by Cupid's strongest bow,
By his best arrow with the golden head,°   170
By the simplicity of Venus' doves,
By that which knitteth souls and prospers loves,
And by that fire which burned the Carthage
    queen,°
When the false Troyan under sail was seen,
By all the vows that ever men have broke,   175
In number more than ever women spoke,
In that same place thou hast appointed me,
Tomorrow truly will I meet with thee.

Lysander. Keep promise, love. Look, here comes
    Helena.

Enter Helena.

Hermia. God speed fair Helena! Whither away?   180

Helena. Call you me fair? That fair again unsay.
Demetrius loves your fair.° O happy fair!
Your eyes are lodestars,° and your tongue's sweet
    air°
More tunable than lark to shepherd's ear,
When wheat is green, when hawthorn buds appear.   185
Sickness is catching. O, were favor° so,
Yours would I catch, fair Hermia, ere I go;
My ear should catch your voice, my eye your eye,

---

170 **arrow with the golden head** (Cupid's gold-headed arrows caused
love, the leaden ones dislike) 173 **Carthage queen** Dido (who
burned herself on a funeral pyre when the Trojan Aeneas left her)
182 **fair** beauty 183 **lodestars** guiding stars 183 **air** music
186 **favor** looks

My tongue should catch your tongue's sweet mel-
ody.
190   Were the world mine, Demetrius being bated,°
The rest I'd give to be to you translated.°
O, teach me how you look, and with what art
You sway the motion of Demetrius' heart!

Hermia. I frown upon him, yet he loves me still.

Helena. O that your frowns would teach my smiles
195   such skill!

Hermia. I give him curses, yet he gives me love.

Helena. O that my prayers could such affection move!

Hermia. The more I hate, the more he follows me.

Helena. The more I love, the more he hateth me.

200 *Hermia.* His folly, Helena, is no fault of mine.

Helena. None, but your beauty: would that fault were
mine!

Hermia. Take comfort. He no more shall see my face;
Lysander and myself will fly this place.
Before the time I did Lysander see,
205   Seemed Athens as a paradise to me.
O, then, what graces in my love do dwell,
That he hath turned a heaven unto a hell!

Lysander. Helen, to you our minds we will unfold.
Tomorrow night, when Phoebe° doth behold
210   Her silver visage in the wat'ry glass,
Decking with liquid pearl the bladed grass,
A time that lovers' flights doth still° conceal,
Through Athens' gates have we devised to steal.

Hermia. And in the wood, where often you and I
215   Upon faint primrose beds were wont to lie,
Emptying our bosoms of their counsel sweet,
There my Lysander and myself shall meet,

190 **bated** excepted 191 **translated** transformed 209 **Phoebe** the
moon 212 **still** always

And thence from Athens turn away our eyes,
To seek new friends and stranger companies.°
Farewell, sweet playfellow. Pray thou for us;   220
And good luck grant thee thy Demetrius!
Keep word, Lysander. We must starve our sight
From lovers' food till tomorrow deep midnight.

Lysander. I will, my Hermia.   *Exit Hermia.*
                    Helena, adieu.
As you on him, Demetrius dote on you!   225
                    Exit Lysander.

Helena. How happy some o'er other some° can be!
Through Athens I am thought as fair as she.
But what of that? Demetrius thinks not so;
He will not know what all but he do know.
And as he errs, doting on Hermia's eyes,   230
So I, admiring of his qualities.
Things base and vile, holding no quantity,°
Love can transpose to form and dignity.
Love looks not with the eyes, but with the mind,
And therefore is winged Cupid painted blind.   235
Nor hath Love's mind of any judgment taste;
Wings, and no eyes, figure° unheedy haste:
And therefore is Love said to be a child,
Because in choice he is so oft beguiled.
As waggish boys in game themselves forswear,   240
So the boy Love is perjured everywhere.
For ere Demetrius looked on Hermia's eyne,°
He hailed down oaths that he was only mine;
And when this hail some heat from Hermia felt,
So he dissolved, and show'rs of oaths did melt.   245
I will go tell him of fair Hermia's flight.
Then to the wood will he tomorrow night
Pursue her; and for this intelligence°

---

219 **stranger companies** the company of strangers   226 **some o'er
other some** some in comparison with others   232 **holding no quantity** having no proportion (therefore unattractive)   237 **figure** symbolize   242 **eyne** eyes   248 **intelligence** piece of news

If I have thanks, it is a dear expense:°
250   But herein mean I to enrich my pain,
      To have his sight thither and back again.   *Exit.*

[Scene 2.   *Quince's house.*]

*Enter Quince the Carpenter, and Snug the Joiner,
and Bottom the Weaver, and Flute the Bellows
Mender, and Snout the Tinker, and Starveling the
Tailor.°*

Quince. Is all our company here?

Bottom. You were best to call them generally,° man by
man, according to the scrip.

Quince. Here is the scroll of every man's name,
5   which is thought fit, through all Athens, to play in
      our interlude° before the Duke and the Duchess,
      on his wedding day at night.

Bottom. First, good Peter Quince, say what the play
      treats on; then read the names of the actors; and
10   so grow to a point.

Quince. Marry,° our play is, "The most lamentable
      comedy, and most cruel death of Pyramus and
      Thisby."

Bottom. A very good piece of work, I assure you,

249 **dear expense** (1) expense gladly incurred (2) heavy cost (in
Demetrius' opinion) 1.2.s.d. (the names of the clowns suggest their
trades. **Bottom** skein on which the yarn is wound; **Quince** quines,
blocks of wood used for building; **Snug** close-fitting; **Flute** suggesting
fluted bellows [for church organs]; **Snout** spout of a kettle;
Starveling an allusion to the proverbial thinness of tailors) 2 **generally** (Bottom means "individually") 6 **interlude** dramatic entertainment 11 **Marry** (an interjection, originally an oath, "By the
Virgin Mary")

and a merry. Now, good Peter Quince, call forth   *15*
your actors by the scroll. Masters, spread yourselves.

Quince. Answer as I call you. Nick Bottom, the
weaver.

Bottom. Ready. Name what part I am for, and pro-   *20*
ceed.

Quince. You, Nick Bottom, are set down for Pyramus.

Bottom. What is Pyramus? A lover, or a tyrant?

Quince. A lover that kills himself, most gallant, for
love.   *25*

Bottom. That will ask some tears in the true performing of it: if I do it, let the audience look to
their eyes. I will move storms, I will condole° in
some measure. To the rest: yet my chief humor°
is for a tyrant. I could play Ercles° rarely, or a   *30*
part to tear a cat in, to make all split.

> The raging rocks
> And shivering shocks
> Shall break the locks
>   Of prison gates;   *35*
> And Phibbus' car°
> Shall shine from far,
> And make and mar
>   The foolish Fates.

This was lofty! Now name the rest of the players.   *40*
This is Ercles' vein, a tyrant's vein. A lover is
more condoling.

Quince. Francis Flute, the bellows mender.

Flute. Here, Peter Quince.

---

28 **condole** lament   29 **humor** disposition   30 **Ercles** Hercules (a
part notorious for ranting)   36 **Phibbus' car** (mispronunciation for
"Phoebus' car," or chariot, i.e., the sun)

45 *Quince.* Flute, you must take Thisby on you.

Flute. What is Thisby? A wand'ring knight?

Quince. It is the lady that Pyramus must love.

Flute. Nay, faith, let not me play a woman. I have
a beard coming.

50 *Quince.* That's all one.° You shall play it in a mask,
and you may speak as small° as you will.

Bottom. An° I may hide my face, let me play Thisby
too, I'll speak in a monstrous little voice, "Thisne,
Thisne!" "Ah Pyramus, my lover dear! Thy Thisby
55 dear, and lady dear!"

Quince. No, no; you must play Pyramus: and, Flute,
you Thisby.

Bottom. Well, proceed.

Quince. Robin Starveling, the tailor.

60 *Starveling.* Here, Peter Quince.

Quince. Robin Starveling, you must play Thisby's
mother. Tom Snout, the tinker.

Snout. Here, Peter Quince.

Quince. You, Pyramus' father: myself, Thisby's
65 father: Snug, the joiner; you, the lion's part. And
I hope here is a play fitted.

Snug. Have you the lion's part written? Pray you, if
it be, give it me, for I am slow of study.

Quince. You may do it extempore, for it is nothing
70 but roaring.

Bottom. Let me play the lion too. I will roar that° I
will do any man's heart good to hear me. I will
roar, that I will make the Duke say, "Let him roar
again, let him roar again."

50 **That's all one** it makes no difference   51 **small** softly   52 **An** if
71 **that** so that

Quince. An you should do it too terribly, you would   75
fright the Duchess and the ladies, that they would
shriek; and that were enough to hang us all.

All. That would hang us, every mother's son.

Bottom. I grant you, friends, if you should fright the
ladies out of their wits, they would have no more   80
discretion but to hang us: but I will aggravate°
my voice so that I will roar you as gently as any
sucking dove; I will roar you an 'twere° any nightingale.

Quince. You can play no part but Pyramus; for   85
Pyramus is a sweet-faced man; a proper° man as
one shall see in a summer's day; a most lovely,
gentlemanlike man: therefore you must needs play
Pyramus.

Bottom. Well, I will undertake it. What beard were   90
I best to play it in?

Quince. Why, what you will.

Bottom. I will discharge it in either your straw-color
beard, your orange-tawny beard, your purple-in-
grain° beard, or your French-crown-color° beard,   95
your perfit° yellow.

Quince. Some of your French crowns° have no hair
at all, and then you will play barefaced.° But, masters, here are your parts; and I am to entreat you,
request you, and desire you, to con° them by to-   100
morrow night; and meet me in the palace wood, a
mile without the town, by moonlight. There will
we rehearse, for if we meet in the city, we shall be
dogged with company, and our devices° known.

---

81 **aggravate** (Bottom means "moderate")   83 **an 'twere** as if it were
86 **proper** handsome   94–95 **purple-in-grain** dyed with a fast purple
95 **French-crown-color** color of French gold coin   96 **perfit** perfect
97 **crowns** (1) gold coins (2) heads bald from the French disease
(syphilis)   98 **barefaced** (1) bald (2) brazen   100 **con** study   104
devices plans

105   In the meantime I will draw a bill of properties,°
      such as our play wants. I pray you, fail me not.

   Bottom. We will meet; and there we may rehearse
      most obscenely° and courageously. Take pains; be
      perfit: adieu.

110 *Quince.* At the Duke's Oak we meet.

   Bottom. Enough; hold or cut bowstrings.°   *Exeunt.*

---

105 bill of properties list of stage furnishings   **108 obscenely** (Bottom means "seemly")   **111 hold or cut bowstrings** i.e., keep your word or give it up (?)

[ACT 2

Scene 1. *A wood near Athens.*]

*Enter a Fairy at one door, and Robin Goodfellow
[Puck] at another.*

Puck. How now, spirit! Whither wander you?

Fairy.   Over hill, over dale,
       Thorough bush, thorough brier,
    Over park, over pale,°
       Thorough flood, thorough fire,   5
    I do wander everywhere,
    Swifter than the moon's sphere;°
    And I serve the Fairy Queen,
    To dew her orbs° upon the green.
    The cowslips tall her pensioners° be: 10
    In their gold coats spots you see;
    Those be rubies, fairy favors,°
    In those freckles live their savors.°
I must go seek some dewdrops here,
And hang a pearl in every cowslip's ear.   15

2.1.4 **pale** enclosed land, park   7 **moon's sphere** (according to the
Ptolemaic system the moon was fixed in a hollow sphere that surrounded
and revolved about the earth)   9 **orbs** fairy rings, i.e., circles of darker
grass   10 **pensioners** bodyguards (referring to Elizabeth I's bodyguard
of fifty splendid young noblemen)   12 **favors** gifts   13 **savors** per-
fumes

Farewell, thou lob° of spirits; I'll be gone.
Our Queen and all her elves come here anon.

Puck. The King doth keep his revels here tonight.
Take heed the Queen come not within his sight.
20 For Oberon is passing fell and wrath,°
Because that she as her attendant hath
A lovely boy, stolen from an Indian king;
She never had so sweet a changeling.°
And jealous Oberon would have the child
25 Knight of his train, to trace° the forests wild.
But she perforce withholds the lovèd boy,
Crowns him with flowers, and makes him all her
    joy.
And now they never meet in grove or green,
By fountain clear, or spangled starlight sheen,°
30 But they do square,° that all their elves for fear
Creep into acorn cups and hide them there.

Fairy. Either I mistake your shape and making quite,
Or else you are that shrewd and knavish sprite
Called Robin Goodfellow. Are not you he
35 That frights the maidens of the villagery,°
Skim milk, and sometimes labor in the quern,°
And bootless° make the breathless housewife
    churn,
And sometime make the drink to bear no barm,°
Mislead night wanderers, laughing at their harm?
40 Those that Hobgoblin call you, and sweet Puck,
You do their work, and they shall have good luck.
· Are not you he?

Puck.   Thou speakest aright;
I am that merry wanderer of the night.
I jest to Oberon, and make him smile,

---

16 **lob** lubber, clumsy fellow   20 **passing fell and wrath** very fierce
and angry   23 **changeling** (usually a child left behind by fairies in
exchange for one stolen, but here applied to the stolen child)   25
trace traverse   29 **starlight sheen** brightly shining starlight   30
square clash, quarrel   35 **villagery** villagers   36 **quern** hand mill for
grinding grain   37 **bootless** in vain   38 **barm** yeast, froth

When I a fat and bean-fed horse beguile,   45
Neighing in likeness of a filly foal:
And sometime lurk I in a gossip's° bowl,
In very likeness of a roasted crab;°
And when she drinks, against her lips I bob
And on her withered dewlap° pour the ale.   50
The wisest aunt, telling the saddest° tale,
Sometime for three-foot stool mistaketh me;
Then slip I from her bum, down topples she,
And "tailor"° cries, and falls into a cough;
And then the whole quire° hold their hips and
    laugh,   55
And waxen° in their mirth, and neeze,° and swear
A merrier hour was never wasted° there.
But, room, fairy! Here comes Oberon.

Fairy. And here my mistress. Would that he were
    gone!

*Enter [Oberon,] the King of Fairies, at one door,
with his train; and [Titania,] the Queen, at another,
with hers.*

Oberon. Ill met by moonlight, proud Titania.   60

Titania. What, jealous Oberon! Fairy, skip hence.
I have forsworn his bed and company.

Oberon. Tarry, rash wanton;° am not I thy lord?

Titania. Then I must be thy lady: but I know
When thou hast stolen away from fairy land   65
And in the shape of Corin° sat all day,
Playing on pipes of corn,° and versing love

---

47 **gossip's** old woman's   48 **crab** crab apple   50 **dewlap** fold of
skin on the throat   51 **saddest** most serious   54 **tailor** (suggesting
the posture of a tailor squatting; or a term of abuse: Middle English
taillard, "thief")   55 **quire** company, choir   56 **waxen** increase
56 **neeze** sneeze   57 **wasted** passed   63 **rash wanton** hasty willful creature   66 **Corin** (like **Phillida,** line 68, a traditional name for
a lover in pastoral poetry)   67 **pipes of corn** musical instruments
made of grain stalks

To amorous Phillida. Why art thou here,
Come from the farthest steep of India?
70 But that, forsooth, the bouncing° Amazon,
Your buskined° mistress and your warrior love,
To Theseus must be wedded, and you come
To give their bed joy and prosperity.

Oberon. How canst thou thus for shame, Titania,
75 Glance at my credit with Hippolyta,
Knowing I know thy love to Theseus?
Didst not thou lead him through the glimmering
    night
From Perigenia, whom he ravishèd?
And make him with fair Aegles break his faith,
80 With Ariadne and Antiopa?°

Titania. These are the forgeries of jealousy:
And never, since the middle summer's spring,°
Met we on hill, in dale, forest, or mead,
By pavèd° fountain or by rushy brook,
85 Or in the beachèd margent° of the sea,
To dance our ringlets to the whistling wind,
But with thy brawls thou hast disturbed our sport.
Therefore the winds, piping to us in vain,
As in revenge, have sucked up from the sea
90 Contagious° fogs; which, falling in the land,
Hath every pelting° river made so proud,
That they have overborne their continents.°
The ox hath therefore stretched his yoke in vain,
The plowman lost his sweat, and the green corn°
95 Hath rotted ere his youth attained a beard;
The fold stands empty in the drownèd field,
And crows are fatted with the murrion flock;°

---

70 **bouncing** swaggering 71 **buskined** wearing a hunter's boot
(buskin) 78–80 **Perigenia, Aegles, Ariadne, Antiopa** (girls Theseus
loved and deserted) 82 **middle summer's spring** beginning of midsummer 84 **pavèd** i.e., with pebbly bottom 85 **margent** margin,
shore 90 **contagious** generating pestilence 91 **pelting** petty 92
continents containers (i.e., banks) 94 **corn** grain 97 **murrion
flock** flock dead of cattle disease (murrain)

The nine men's morris° is filled up with mud;
And the quaint mazes° in the wanton green,°
For lack of tread, are undistinguishable.   *100*
The human mortals want their winter here;°
No night is now with hymn or carol blest.
Therefore the moon, the governess of floods,
Pale in her anger, washes all the air,
That rheumatic diseases do abound.   *105*
And thorough this distemperature° we see
The seasons alter: hoary-headed frosts
Fall in the fresh lap of the crimson rose,
And on old Hiems'° thin and icy crown
An odorous chaplet° of sweet summer buds   *110*
Is, as in mockery, set. The spring, the summer,
The childing° autumn, angry winter, change
Their wonted liveries;° and the mazèd° world,
By their increase, now knows not which is which.
And this same progeny of evils comes   *115*
From our debate,° from our dissension;
We are their parents and original.

Oberon. Do you amend it, then; it lies in you:
Why should Titania cross her Oberon?
I do but beg a little changeling boy,   *120*
To be my henchman.°

Titania.   Set your heart at rest.
The fairy land buys not° the child of me.
His mother was a vot'ress° of my order,
And, in the spicèd Indian air, by night,
Full often hath she gossiped by my side,   *125*
And sat with me on Neptune's yellow sands,

---

98 **nine men's morris** square cut in the turf (for a game in which
each player has nine counters or "men") 99 **quaint mazes** intricate
meandering paths on the grass (kept fresh by running along them)
99 **wanton green** grass growing without check 101 **want their
winter here** lack their usual winter festivities (?; some editors emend
"here" to "cheer"). 106 **distemperature** disturbance in nature 109
old Hiems' the winter's 110 **chaplet** wreath 112 **childing** breed-
ing, fruitful 113 **wonted liveries** accustomed apparel 113 **mazèd**
bewildered 116 **debate** quarrel 121 **henchman** page 122 **The
fairy land buys not** i.e., even your whole domain could not buy
123 **vot'ress** woman who has taken a vow

Marking th' embarkèd traders on the flood;
When we have laughed to see the sails conceive
And grow big-bellied with the wanton wind;
130   Which she, with pretty and with swimming gait
Following—her womb then rich with my young
    squire—
Would imitate, and sail upon the land,
To fetch me trifles, and return again,
As from a voyage, rich with merchandise.
135   But she, being mortal, of that boy did die;
And for her sake do I rear up her boy,
And for her sake I will not part with him.

Oberon. How long within this wood intend you stay?

Titania. Perchance till after Theseus' wedding day.
140   If you will patiently dance in our round,°
And see our moonlight revels, go with us.
If not, shun me, and I will spare° your haunts.

Oberon. Give me that boy, and I will go with thee.

Titania. Not for thy fairy kingdom. Fairies, away!
145   We shall chide downright, if I longer stay.
                    Exeunt [*Titania with her train*].

Oberon. Well, go thy way. Thou shalt not from this
    grove
Till I torment thee for this injury.
My gentle Puck, come hither. Thou rememb'rest
Since° once I sat upon a promontory,
150   And heard a mermaid, on a dolphin's back,
Uttering such dulcet and harmonious breath,
That the rude sea grew civil° at her song,
And certain stars shot madly from their spheres,
To hear the sea maid's music.

Puck.   I remember.

155 *Oberon.* That very time I saw, but thou couldst not,
Flying between the cold moon and the earth,

140 **round** circular dance 142 **spare** keep away from 149 **Since**
when 152 **civil** well behaved

Cupid all armed. A certain aim he took
At a fair vestal° thronèd by the west,
And loosed his love shaft smartly from his bow,
As it should° pierce a hundred thousand hearts.   160
But I might° see young Cupid's fiery shaft
Quenched in the chaste beams of the wat'ry moon,
And the imperial vot'ress passèd on,
In maiden meditation, fancy-free.°
Yet marked I where the bolt of Cupid fell.   165
It fell upon a little western flower,
Before milk-white, now purple with love's wound,
And maidens call it love-in-idleness.°
Fetch me that flow'r; the herb I showed thee once:
The juice of it on sleeping eyelids laid   170
Will make or man or woman° madly dote
Upon the next live creature that it sees.
Fetch me this herb, and be thou here again
Ere the leviathan° can swim a league.

Puck. I'll put a girdle round about the earth   175
In forty minutes.   [*Exit.*]

Oberon.   Having once this juice,
I'll watch Titania when she is asleep,
And drop the liquor of it in her eyes.
The next thing then she waking looks upon,
Be it on lion, bear, or wolf, or bull,   180
On meddling monkey, or on busy° ape,
She shall pursue it with the soul of love.
And ere I take this charm from off her sight,
As I can take it with another herb,
I'll make her render up her page to me.   185
But who comes here? I am invisible,
And I will overhear their conference.

Enter Demetrius, Helena following him.

158 **vestal** virgin (possibly an allusion to Elizabeth, the Virgin Queen)
160 **As it should** as if it would   161 **might** could   164 **fancy-free**
free from the power of love   168 **love-in-idleness** pansy   171 **or man
or woman** either man or woman   174 **leviathan** sea monster, whale
181 **busy** meddlesome

Demetrius. I love thee not, therefore pursue me not.
Where is Lysander and fair Hermia?
190 The one I'll slay, the other slayeth me.
Thou told'st me they were stol'n unto this wood;
And here am I, and wood° within this wood,
Because I cannot meet my Hermia.
Hence, get thee gone, and follow me no more!

195 *Helena.* You draw me, you hardhearted adamant;°
But yet you draw not iron, for my heart
Is true as steel. Leave you your power to draw,
And I shall have no power to follow you.

Demetrius. Do I entice you? Do I speak you fair?°
200 Or, rather, do I not in plainest truth
Tell you, I do not nor I cannot love you?

Helena. And even for that do I love you the more.
I am your spaniel; and, Demetrius,
The more you beat me, I will fawn on you.
205 Use me but as your spaniel, spurn me, strike me,
Neglect me, lose me; only give me leave,
Unworthy as I am, to follow you.
What worser place can I beg in your love—
And yet a place of high respect with me—
210 Than to be usèd as you use your dog?

Demetrius. Tempt not too much the hatred of my
spirit,
For I am sick when I do look on thee.

Helena. And I am sick when I look not on you.

Demetrius. You do impeach° your modesty too much,
215 To leave the city, and commit yourself
Into the hands of one that loves you not,
To trust the opportunity of night
And the ill counsel of a desert° place
With the rich worth of your virginity.

192 **wood** out of my mind (with perhaps an additional pun on "wooed")
195 **adamant** (1) very hard gem (2) loadstone, magnet   199 **speak you
fair** speak kindly to you   214 **impeach** expose to reproach   218
desert deserted, uninhabited

Helena. Your virtue is my privilege.° For that   220
  It is not night when I do see your face,
  Therefore I think I am not in the night;
  Nor doth this wood lack worlds of company,
  For you in my respect° are all the world.
  Then how can it be said I am alone,   225
  When all the world is here to look on me?

Demetrius. I'll run from thee and hide me in the
    brakes,°
  And leave thee to the mercy of wild beasts.

Helena. The wildest hath not such a heart as you.
  Run when you will, the story shall be changed: 230
  Apollo flies, and Daphne° holds the chase;
  The dove pursues the griffin;° the mild hind°
  Makes speed to catch the tiger; bootless speed,
  When cowardice pursues, and valor flies.

Demetrius. I will not stay° thy questions. Let me go!   235
  Or, if thou follow me, do not believe
  But I shall do thee mischief in the wood.

Helena. Ay, in the temple, in the town, the field,
  You do me mischief. Fie, Demetrius!
  Your wrongs do set a scandal on my sex.   240
  We cannot fight for love, as men may do;
  We should be wooed, and were not made to woo.
                              [*Exit Demetrius.*]
  I'll follow thee, and make a heaven of hell,
  To die upon° the hand I love so well.   [*Exit.*]

Oberon. Fare thee well, nymph: ere he do leave this
    grove,   245
  Thou shalt fly him, and he shall seek thy love.

---

220 **Your virtue is my privilege** your inherent power is my warrant
224 **in my respect** in my opinion   227 **brakes** thickets   231 **Daphne**
a nymph who fled from Apollo (at her prayer she was changed into
a laurel tree)   232 **griffin** fabulous monster with an eagle's head
and a lion's body   232 **hind** doe   235 **stay** wait for   244 **To die
upon** dying by

Enter Puck.
Hast thou the flower there? Welcome, wanderer.

Puck. Ay, there it is.

Oberon.   I pray thee, give it me.
I know a bank where the wild thyme blows,
250 Where oxlips and the nodding violet grows,
Quite overcanopied with luscious woodbine,
With sweet musk roses, and with eglantine.
There sleeps Titania sometime of the night,
Lulled in these flowers with dances and delight;
255 And there the snake throws° her enameled skin,
Weed° wide enough to wrap a fairy in.
And with the juice of this I'll streak her eyes,
And make her full of hateful fantasies.
Take thou some of it, and seek through this grove.
260 A sweet Athenian lady is in love
With a disdainful youth. Anoint his eyes;
But do it when the next thing he espies
May be the lady. Thou shalt know the man
By the Athenian garments he hath on.
265 Effect it with some care that he may prove
More fond on her° than she upon her love:
And look thou meet me ere the first cock crow.

Puck. Fear not, my lord, your servant shall do so.
                                        Exeunt.

[Scene 2.   *Another part of the wood.*]

Enter Titania, Queen of Fairies, with her train.

Titania. Come, now a roundel° and a fairy song;
Then, for the third part of a minute, hence;

255 **throws** casts off   256 **Weed** garment   266 **fond on her** foolishly
in love with her   2.2.1 **roundel** dance in a ring

Some to kill cankers in the musk-rose buds,
Some war with reremice° for their leathern wings
To make my small elves coats, and some keep back   5
The clamorous owl, that nightly hoots and wonders
At our quaint° spirits. Sing me now asleep.
Then to your offices, and let me rest.

Fairies sing.

1st   You spotted snakes with double tongue,
Fairy.   Thorny hedgehogs, be not seen;   10
              Newts and blindworms,° do no wrong,
                  Come not near our Fairy Queen.

Chorus.   Philomele,° with melody
                  Sing in our sweet lullaby;
              Lulla, lulla, lullaby, lulla, lulla, lullaby: 15
                      Never harm
                      Nor spell nor charm,
                  Come our lovely lady nigh;
                  So, good night, with lullaby.

1st   Weaving spiders, come not here;   20
Fairy.   Hence, you long-legged spinners, hence!
              Beetles black, approach not near;
                  Worm nor snail, do no offense.

Chorus.   Philomele, with melody, &c.

2nd   Hence, away! Now all is well.   25
Fairy.   One aloof stand sentinel.
                          [*Exeunt Fairies. Titania sleeps.*]

          Enter Oberon [and squeezes the flower on
                      Titania's eyelids].

Oberon.   What thou seest when thou dost wake,
                  Do it for thy truelove take;
                  Love and languish for his sake.
                  Be it ounce,° or cat, or bear,   30

4 **reremice** bats   7 **quaint** dainty   11 **blindworms** small snakes   13
Philomele nightingale   30 **ounce** lynx

Pard,° or boar with bristled hair,
In thy eye that shall appear
When thou wak'st, it is thy dear.
Wake when some vile thing is near.   [*Exit.*]

Enter Lysander and Hermia.

Lysander. Fair love, you faint with wand'ring in the
35   wood;
And to speak troth,° I have forgot our way.
We'll rest us, Hermia, if you think it good,
And tarry for the comfort of the day.

Hermia. Be't so, Lysander. Find you out a bed;
40   For I upon this bank will rest my head.

Lysander. One turf shall serve as pillow for us both,
One heart, one bed, two bosoms, and one troth.

Hermia. Nay, good Lysander. For my sake, my dear,
Lie further off yet, do not lie so near.

45 *Lysander.* O, take the sense,° sweet, of my innocence!
Love takes the meaning° in love's conference.
I mean, that my heart unto yours is knit,
So that but one heart we can make of it:
Two bosoms interchainèd with an oath;
50   So then two bosoms and a single troth.°
Then by your side no bed-room me deny,
For lying so, Hermia, I do not lie.°

Hermia. Lysander riddles very prettily.
Now much beshrew° my manners and my pride,
55   If Hermia meant to say Lysander lied.
But, gentle friend, for love and courtesy
Lie further off, in human modesty.
Such separation as may well be said

31 **Pard** leopard   36 **troth** truth   45 **take the sense** understand the
true meaning   46 **Love takes the meaning** lovers understand the
true meaning of what they say to each other   50 **troth** faithful love
52 **lie** be untrue   54 **beshrew** curse (but commonly, as here, in a
light sense)

Becomes a virtuous bachelor and a maid,
So far be distant; and, good night, sweet friend.   60
Thy love ne'er alter till thy sweet life end!

Lysander. Amen, amen, to that fair prayer, say I,
And then end life when I end loyalty!
Here is my bed. Sleep give thee all his rest!

Hermia. With half that wish the wisher's eyes be
      pressed!   [*They sleep.*]   65

Enter Puck.

Puck.   Through the forest have I gone,
      But Athenian found I none,
      On whose eyes I might approve°
      This flower's force in stirring love.
      Night and silence.—Who is here?   70
      Weeds° of Athens he doth wear:
      This is he, my master said,
      Despisèd the Athenian maid;
      And here the maiden, sleeping sound,
      On the dank and dirty ground.   75
      Pretty soul! She durst not lie
      Near this lack-love, this kill-courtesy.
      Churl,° upon thy eyes I throw
      All the power this charm doth owe.°
      When thou wak'st, let love forbid   80
      Sleep his seat on thy eyelid.
      So awake when I am gone,
      For I must now to Oberon.   *Exit.*

Enter Demetrius and Helena, running.

Helena. Stay, though thou kill me, sweet Demetrius.

Demetrius. I charge thee, hence, and do not haunt me
      thus.   85

68 **approve** try   71 **Weeds** garments   78 **Churl** boorish fellow   79 **owe**
possess

Helena. O, wilt thou darkling° leave me? Do not so.

Demetrius. Stay, on thy peril! I alone will go.   [*Exit.*]

Helena. O, I am out of breath in this fond° chase!
    The more my prayer, the lesser is my grace.
90   Happy is Hermia, wheresoe'er she lies,
    For she hath blessèd and attractive eyes.
    How came her eyes so bright? Not with salt tears.
    If so, my eyes are oft'ner washed than hers.
    No, no, I am as ugly as a bear,
95   For beasts that meet me run away for fear.
    Therefore no marvel though Demetrius
    Do, as a monster, fly my presence thus.
    What wicked and dissembling glass of mine
    Made me compare with Hermia's sphery eyne?°
100   But who is here? Lysander! On the ground!
    Dead? Or asleep? I see no blood, no wound.
    Lysander, if you live, good sir, awake.

Lysander. [*Awaking*] And run through fire I will for
    thy sweet sake.
    Transparent° Helena! Nature shows art,
105   That through thy bosom makes me see thy heart.
    Where is Demetrius? O, how fit a word
    Is that vile name to perish on my sword!

Helena. Do not say so, Lysander, say not so.
    What though he love your Hermia? Lord, what
    though?
110   Yet Hermia still loves you. Then be content.

Lysander. Content with Hermia! No; I do repent
    The tedious minutes I with her have spent.
    Not Hermia but Helena I love:
    Who will not change a raven for a dove?
115   The will° of man is by his reason swayed
    And reason says you are the worthier maid.
    Things growing are not ripe until their season:
    So I, being young, till now ripe not° to reason.

86 **darkling** in the dark   88 **fond** (1) doting (2) foolish   99 **sphery
eyne** starry eyes   104 **Transparent** bright   115 **will** desire   118
ripe not have not ripened

    And touching now the point of human skill,°
    Reason becomes the marshal to my will,   *120*
    And leads me to your eyes, where I o'erlook
    Love's stories, written in love's richest book.

Helena. Wherefore was I to this keen mockery born?
    When at your hands did I deserve this scorn?
    Is't not enough, is't not enough, young man,   *125*
    That I did never, no, nor never can,
    Deserve a sweet look from Demetrius' eye,
    But you must flout° my insufficiency?
    Good troth,° you do me wrong, good sooth, you do,
    In such disdainful manner me to woo.   *130*
    But fare you well. Perforce I must confess
    I thought you lord of more true gentleness.°
    O, that a lady, of one man refused,
    Should of another therefore be abused!   *Exit.*

Lysander. She sees not Hermia. Hermia, sleep thou
    there,   *135*
    And never mayst thou come Lysander near!
    For as a surfeit of the sweetest things
    The deepest loathing to the stomach brings,
    Or as the heresies that men do leave
    Are hated most of those they did deceive,   *140*
    So thou, my surfeit and my heresy,
    Of all be hated, but the most of me!
    And, all my powers, address° your love and might
    To honor Helen and to be her knight!   *Exit.*

Hermia. [*Awaking*] Help me, Lysander, help me! Do
    thy best   *145*
    To pluck this crawling serpent from my breast!
    Ay me, for pity! What a dream was here!
    Lysander, look how I do quake with fear.
    Methought a serpent eat° my heart away,

---

119 **touching now ... human skill** now reaching the fulness of human
reason   128 **flout** jeer at   129 **Good troth** indeed (an expletive, like
"good sooth")   132 **gentleness** noble character   143 **address** apply
149 **eat** ate (pronounced "et")

150 And you sat smiling at his cruel prey.°
Lysander! What, removed? Lysander! Lord!
What, out of hearing? Gone? No sound, no word?
Alack, where are you? Speak, an if° you hear;
Speak, of° all loves! I swoon almost with fear.
155 No? Then I well perceive you are not nigh.
Either death or you I'll find immediately.   *Exit.*

150 **prey** act of preying   153 **an if** if   154 **of** for the sake of

[ACT 3

Scene 1.   *The wood. Titania lying asleep.*]

Enter the clowns: [*Quince, Snug, Bottom, Flute,
Snout, and Starveling*].

Bottom. Are we all met?

Quince. Pat,° pat; and here's a marvail's° convenient
place for our rehearsal. This green plot shall be
our stage, this hawthorn brake° our tiring house,°
and we will do it in action as we will do it before   5
the Duke.

Bottom. Peter Quince?

Quince. What sayest thou, bully° Bottom?

Bottom. There are things in this comedy of Pyramus
and Thisby that will never please. First, Pyramus   10
must draw a sword to kill himself; which the ladies
cannot abide. How answer you that?

Snout. By'r lakin,° a parlous° fear.

Starveling. I believe we must leave the killing out,
when all is done.   15

3.1.2 **Pat** exactly, on the dot   2 **marvail's** (Quince means "marvelous")   4 **brake** thicket   4 **tiring house** attiring house, dressing
room   8 **bully** good fellow   13 **By'r lakin** by our lady (ladykin =
little lady)   13 **parlous** perilous, terrible

33

Bottom. Not a whit. I have a device to make all well.
Write me a prologue, and let the prologue seem to
say, we will do no harm with our swords, and that
Pyramus is not killed indeed; and, for the more
20   better assurance, tell them that I Pyramus am not
Pyramus, but Bottom the weaver. This will put
them out of fear.

Quince. Well, we will have such a prologue, and it
shall be written in eight and six.°

25   *Bottom.* No, make it two more; let it be written in
eight and eight.

Snout. Will not the ladies be afeared of the lion?

Starveling. I fear it, I promise you.

Bottom. Masters, you ought to consider with your-
30   selves. To bring in—God shield us!—a lion among
ladies, is a most dreadful thing. For there is not a
more fearful wild fowl than your lion living; and
we ought to look to't.

Snout. Therefore another prologue must tell he is not
35   a lion.

Bottom. Nay, you must name his name, and half his
face must be seen through the lion's neck, and he
himself must speak through, saying thus, or to the
same defect—"Ladies"—or, "Fair ladies—I would
40   wish you"—or, "I would request you"—or, "I
would entreat you—not to fear, not to tremble: my
life for yours. If you think I come hither as a lion,
it were pity of my life.° No, I am no such thing.
I am a man as other men are." And there indeed
45   let him name his name, and tell them plainly, he is
Snug the joiner.

Quince. Well, it shall be so. But there is two hard
things; that is, to bring the moonlight into a

24 **in eight and six** in alternate lines of eight and six syllables (ballad
stanza)   43 **pity of my life** a bad thing for me

chamber; for, you know, Pyramus and Thisby
meet by moonlight.   50

Snout. Doth the moon shine that night we play our
play?

Bottom. A calendar, a calendar! Look in the almanac;
find out moonshine, find out moonshine.

Quince. Yes, it doth shine that night.   55

Bottom. Why, then may you leave a casement of the
great chamber window, where we play, open, and the
moon may shine in at the casement.

Quince. Ay; or else one must come in with a bush of
thorns° and a lantern, and say he comes to dis-   60
figure,° or to present, the person of Moonshine.
Then, there is another thing: we must have a wall
in the great chamber; for Pyramus and Thisby,
says the story, did talk through the chink of a
wall.   65

Snout. You can never bring in a wall. What say you,
Bottom?

Bottom. Some man or other must present Wall: and
let him have some plaster, or some loam, or some
roughcast° about him, to signify Wall; and let him   70
hold his fingers thus, and through that cranny shall
Pyramus and Thisby whisper.

Quince. If that may be, then all is well. Come, sit
down, every mother's son, and rehearse your parts.
Pyramus, you begin. When you have spoken your   75
speech, enter into that brake; and so everyone according to his cue.

Enter Robin [Puck].

59–60 **bush of thorns** (legend held that the man in the moon had
been placed there for gathering firewood on Sunday) 60–61 **disfigure** (Bottom means "figure," "represent") 70 **roughcast** lime
mixed with gravel to plaster outside walls

Puck. What hempen homespuns° have we swagg'ring
here,
So near the cradle of the Fairy Queen?
80   What, a play toward!° I'll be an auditor;
An actor too perhaps, if I see cause.

Quince. Speak, Pyramus. Thisby, stand forth.

Pyramus [*Bottom*]. Thisby, the flowers of odious
savors sweet—

Quince. Odors, odors.

85   *Pyramus.*—odors savors sweet:
So hath thy breath, my dearest Thisby dear.
But hark, a voice! Stay thou but here awhile,
And by and by° I will to thee appear.   *Exit.*

Puck. A stranger Pyramus than e'er played here!
[*Exit.*]

90   *Thisby* [*Flute*]. Must I speak now?

Quince. Ay, marry, must you. For you must understand he goes but to see a noise that he heard, and
is to come again.

Thisby. Most radiant Pyramus, most lily-white of hue,
95   Of color like the red rose on triumphant brier,
Most brisky juvenal,° and eke° most lovely Jew,
As true as truest horse, that yet would never tire,
I'll meet thee, Pyramus, at Ninny's° tomb.

Quince. "Ninus' tomb," man. Why, you must not
100   speak that yet. That you answer to Pyramus. You
speak all your part at once, cues and all. Pyramus
enter. Your cue is past; it is "never tire."

Thisby. O—as true as truest horse, that yet would
never tire.

78 **hempen homespuns** coarse fellows (clad in homespun cloth of
hemp) 80 **toward** in preparation 88 **by and by** shortly 96 **juvenal** youth 96 **eke** also 98 **Ninny's** (blunder for "Ninus' ";
Ninus was the legendary founder of Nineveh)

[*Re-enter Puck, and Bottom with an ass's head.*]

Pyramus. If I were fair, Thisby, I were only thine.

Quince. O monstrous! O strange! We are haunted.   *105*
   Pray, masters! Fly, masters! Help!
                    [*Exeunt all the clowns but Bottom.*]

Puck. I'll follow you, I'll lead you about a round,°
      Through bog, through bush, through brake,
         through brier.
   Sometime a horse I'll be, sometime a hound,
      A hog, a headless bear, sometime a fire;   *110*
   And neigh, and bark, and grunt, and roar, and
      burn,
   Like horse, hound, hog, bear, fire, at every turn.
                                               Exit.

Bottom. Why do they run away? This is a knavery of
   them to make me afeard.

                    Enter Snout.

Snout. O Bottom, thou art changed! What do I see   *115*
   on thee?

Bottom. What do you see? You see an ass head of
   your own, do you?   [*Exit Snout.*]

                    Enter Quince.

Quince. Bless thee, Bottom! Bless thee! Thou art
   translated.°   *Exit.*   *120*

Bottom. I see their knavery. This is to make an ass
   of me; to fright me, if they could. But I will not
   stir from this place, do what they can. I will walk
   up and down here, and will sing, that they shall
   hear I am not afraid.   [*Sings.*]   *125*

107 **about a round** roundabout   120 **translated** transformed

      The woosel° cock so black of hue,
        With orange-tawny bill,
      The throstle with his note so true,
        The wren with little quill°—

Titania. [*Awaking*] What angel wakes me from my
130   flow'ry bed?

Bottom. [*Sings*] The finch, the sparrow, and the lark,
        The plain-song cuckoo° gray,
          Whose note full many a man doth
            mark,
        And dares not answer nay—
135   for, indeed, who would set his wit° to so foolish
    a bird? Who would give a bird the lie,° though he
    cry "cuckoo" never so?°

Titania. I pray thee, gentle mortal, sing again:
    Mine ear is much enamored of thy note;
140   So is mine eye enthrallèd to thy shape;
    And thy fair virtue's force perforce doth move me
    On the first view to say, to swear, I love thee.

Bottom. Methinks, mistress, you should have little
    reason for that. And yet, to say the truth, reason
145   and love keep little company together nowadays;
    the more the pity, that some honest neighbors will
    not make them friends. Nay, I can gleek° upon
    occasion.

Titania. Thou art as wise as thou art beautiful.

150 *Bottom.* Not so, neither; but if I had wit enough to
    get out of this wood, I have enough to serve mine
    own turn.

Titania. Out of this wood do not desire to go.

---

126 **woosel** ouzel, blackbird   129 **quill** (literally, "reed pipe"; here,
"piping voice")   132 **the plain-song cuckoo** the cuckoo, who sings
a simple song   135 **set his wit** use his intelligence to answer
136 **give a bird the lie** contradict a bird (the cuckoo's song supposedly tells a man he is a cuckold)   137 **never so** ever so often
147 **gleek** make a satirical jest

Thou shalt remain here, whether thou wilt or no.
I am a spirit of no common rate.°   *155*
The summer still doth tend° upon my state;
And I do love thee. Therefore, go with me.
I'll give thee fairies to attend on thee,
And they shall fetch thee jewels from the deep,
And sing, while thou on pressèd flowers dost sleep: *160*
And I will purge thy mortal grossness so,
That thou shalt like an airy spirit go.
Peaseblossom! Cobweb! Moth!° And Mustardseed!

Enter four Fairies
[*Peaseblossom, Cobweb, Moth, and Mustardseed*].

Peaseblossom. Ready.

Cobweb.   And I.

Moth.   And I.

Mustardseed.   And I.

All.   Where shall we go.

Titania. Be kind and courteous to this gentleman;   *165*
Hop in his walks, and gambol in his eyes;
Feed him with apricocks and dewberries,°
With purple grapes, green figs, and mulberries;
The honey bags steal from the humblebees,°
And for night tapers crop their waxen thighs,   *170*
And light them at the fiery glowworm's eyes,
To have my love to bed and to arise;
And pluck the wings from painted butterflies,
To fan the moonbeams from his sleeping eyes.
Nod to him, elves, and do him courtesies.   *175*

Peaseblossom. Hail, mortal!

Cobweb.   Hail!

155 **rate** rank   156 **still doth tend** always waits upon   163 **Moth**
(pronounced "mote," and probably a speck rather than an insect is
denoted)   167 **apricocks and dewberries** apricots and blackberries
169 **humblebees** bumblebees

Moth.   Hail!

Mustardseed.   Hail!

Bottom. I cry your worships mercy,° heartily: I beseech your worship's name.

Cobweb. Cobweb.

180 *Bottom.* I shall desire you of more acquaintance,° good Master Cobweb: if I cut my finger,° I shall make bold with you. Your name, honest gentleman?

Peaseblossom. Peaseblossom.

185 *Bottom.* I pray you, commend me to Mistress Squash,° your mother, and to Master Peascod, your father. Good Master Peaseblossom. I shall desire you of more acquaintance too. Your name, I beseech you, sir?

190 *Mustardseed.* Mustardseed.

Bottom. Good Master Mustardseed, I know your patience well. That same cowardly, giantlike ox-beef hath devoured° many a gentleman of your house. I promise you your kindred hath made my eyes
195 water ere now. I desire you of more acquaintance, good Master Mustardseed.

Titania. Come, wait upon him; lead him to my bower.
    The moon methinks looks with a wat'ry eye;
    And when she weeps, weeps every little flower,
200   Lamenting some enforcèd° chastity.
    Tie up my lover's tongue, bring him silently.
                    Exit [Titania with Bottom and Fairies].

---

177 **I cry your worships mercy** I beg pardon of your honors   180 **I shall desire you of more acquaintance** I shall want to be better acquainted with you   181 **if I cut my finger** (cobweb was used for stanching blood)   185 **Squash** unripe pea pod   193 **devoured** (because beef is often eaten with mustard)   200 **enforcèd** violated

[Scene 2.   *Another part of the wood.*]

Enter [Oberon,] King of Fairies, and Robin
Goodfellow [Puck].

Oberon. I wonder if Titania be awaked;
  Then, what it was that next came in her eye,
  Which she must dote on in extremity.°
  Here comes my messenger. How now, mad spirit!
  What night-rule° now about this haunted grove?   5

Puck. My mistress with a monster is in love.
  Near to her close° and consecrated bower,
  While she was in her dull and sleeping hour,
  A crew of patches,° rude mechanicals,°
  That work for bread upon Athenian stalls,   10
  Were met together to rehearse a play,
  Intended for great Theseus' nuptial day.
  The shallowest thickskin of that barren sort,°
  Who Pyramus presented in their sport,
  Forsook his scene, and entered in a brake.   15
  When I did him at this advantage take,
  An ass's nole° I fixèd on his head.
  Anon° his Thisby must be answerèd,
  And forth my mimic comes. When they him spy,
  As wild geese that the creeping fowler eye,   20
  Or russet-pated choughs, many in sort,°
  Rising and cawing at the gun's report,
  Sever themselves and madly sweep the sky,
  So, at his sight, away his fellows fly;

3.2.3 **in extremity** to the extreme 5 **night-rule** happenings during the night 7 **close** private, secret 9 **patches** fools, clowns 9 **rude mechanicals** uneducated workingmen 13 **barren sort** stupid group 17 **nole** "noodle," head 18 **Anon** presently 21 **russet-pated ... in sort** gray-headed jackdaws, many in a flock

25   And, at our stamp, here o'er and o'er one falls;
      He murder cries, and help from Athens calls.
      Their sense thus weak, lost with their fears thus
          strong,
      Made senseless things begin to do them wrong;
      For briers and thorns at their apparel snatch;
      Some sleeves, some hats, from yielders all things
30   catch.
      I led them on in this distracted fear,
      And left sweet Pyramus translated there:
      When in that moment, so it came to pass,
      Titania waked, and straightway loved an ass.

35 *Oberon.* This falls out better than I could devise.
      But hast thou yet latched° the Athenian's eyes
      With the love juice, as I did bid thee do?

    Puck. I took him sleeping—that is finished too—
      And the Athenian woman by his side;
40   That, when he waked, of force° she must be eyed.

                Enter Demetrius and Hermia.

    Oberon. Stand close:° this is the same Athenian.

    Puck. This is the woman, but not this the man.

    Demetrius. O, why rebuke you him that loves you so?
      Lay breath so bitter on your bitter foe.

45 *Hermia.* Now I but chide; but I should use thee worse,
      For thou, I fear, hast given me cause to curse.
      If thou hast slain Lysander in his sleep,
      Being o'er shoes in blood, plunge in the deep,
      And kill me too.
50   The sun was not so true unto the day
      As he to me. Would he have stolen away
      From sleeping Hermia? I'll believe as soon
      This whole° earth may be bored, and that the moon
      May through the center creep, and so displease

36 **latched** fastened (or possibly "moistened")   40 **of force** by necessity   41 **close** concealed   53 **whole** solid

Her brother's° noontide with th' Antipodes.   *55*
It cannot be but thou hast murd'red him.
So should a murderer look, so dead,° so grim.

Demetrius. So should the murdered look; and so
    should I,
Pierced through the heart with your stern cruelty.
Yet you, the murderer, look as bright, as clear,   *60*
As yonder Venus in her glimmering sphere.

Hermia. What's this to my Lysander? Where is he?
   Ah, good Demetrius, wilt thou give him me?

Demetrius. I had rather give his carcass to my hounds.

Hermia. Out, dog! Out, cur! Thou driv'st me past the
    bounds   *65*
Of maiden's patience. Hast thou slain him, then?
Henceforth be never numb'red among men!
O, once tell true! Tell true, even for my sake!
Durst thou have looked upon him being awake?
And hast thou killed him sleeping? O brave touch!°   *70*
Could not a worm, an adder, do so much?
An adder did it; for with doubler tongue
Than thine, thou serpent, never adder stung.

Demetrius. You spend your passion on a misprised
    mood:°
I am not guilty of Lysander's blood;   *75*
Nor is he dead, for aught that I can tell.

Hermia. I pray thee, tell me then that he is well.

Demetrius. An if I could, what should I get there-
    fore?°

Hermia. A privilege, never to see me more.
And from thy hated presence part I so.   *80*
See me no more, whether he be dead or no.   *Exit.*

Demetrius. There is no following her in this fierce vein.

---

55 **Her brother's** i.e., the sun's   57 **dead** deadly pale   70 **brave touch** splendid exploit (ironic)   74 **misprised mood** mistaken anger 78 **therefore** in return

Here therefore for a while I will remain.
So sorrow's heaviness doth heavier grow
85   For debt that bankrout sleep doth sorrow owe;°
Which now in some slight measure it will pay,
If for his tender° here I make some stay.

> *Lies down [and sleeps].*

Oberon. What hast thou done? Thou hast mistaken quite,
And laid the love juice on some truelove's sight.
90   Of thy misprision° must perforce ensue
Some true love turned, and not a false turned true.

Puck. Then fate o'errules, that, one man holding troth,
A million fail, confounding oath on oath.°

Oberon. About the wood go swifter than the wind,
95   And Helena of Athens look thou find.
All fancy-sick° she is and pale of cheer,°
With sighs of love, that costs the fresh blood dear:
By some illusion see thou bring her here.
I'll charm his eyes against she do appear.°

100 *Puck.* I go, I go; look how I go,
Swifter than arrow from the Tartar's bow.   [*Exit.*]

Oberon. Flower of this purple dye,
Hit with Cupid's archery,
Sink in apple of his eye,
105 When his love he doth espy,
Let her shine as gloriously
As the Venus of the sky.
When thou wak'st, if she be by,
Beg of her for remedy.

> *Enter Puck.*

---

85 **For debt ... sorrow owe** because of the debt that bankrupt sleep owes to sorrow   87 **tender** offer   90 **misprision** mistake   93 **confounding oath on oath** breaking oath after oath   96 **fancy-sick** love-sick   96 **cheer** face   99 **against she do appear** in preparation for her appearance

uck. Captain of our fairy band,   *110*
  Helena is here at hand;
  And the youth, mistook by me,
  Pleading for a lover's fee.
  Shall we their fond pageant° see?
  Lord, what fools these mortals be!   *115*

beron. Stand aside. The noise they make
  Will cause Demetrius to awake.

uck. Then will two at once woo one;
  That must needs be sport alone;°
  And those things do best please me   *120*
  That befall prepost'rously.

Enter Lysander and Helena.

ysander. Why should you think that I should woo in
      scorn?
    Scorn and derision never come in tears:
  Look, when I vow, I weep; and vows so born,
    In their nativity all truth appears.   *125*
  How can these things in me seem scorn to you,
  Bearing the badge of faith,° to prove them true?

elena. You do advance° your cunning more and
      more.
    When truth kills truth, O devilish-holy fray!
  These vows are Hermia's: will you give her o'er?   *130*
    Weigh oath with oath, and you will nothing
      weigh.
  Your vows to her and me, put in two scales,
  Will even weigh; and both as light as tales.

ysander. I had no judgment when to her I swore.

elena. Nor none, in my mind, now you give her o'er.   *135*

ysander. Demetrius loves her, and he loves not you.

4 **fond pageant** foolish exhibition 119 **alone** unique, supreme
7 **badge of faith** (Lysander means his tears) 128 **advance** ex-
bit, display

Demetrius. [*Awaking*] O Helen, goddess, nymph, pe
    fect, divine!
    To what, my love, shall I compare thine eyne?
    Crystal is muddy. O, how ripe in show°
140   Thy lips, those kissing cherries, tempting grow!
    That pure congealèd white, high Taurus'° snow,
    Fanned with the eastern wind, turns to a crow
    When thou hold'st up thy hand: O, let me kiss
    This princess of pure white, this seal of bliss!

145 Helena. O spite! O hell! I see you all are bent
    To set against me for your merriment:
    If you were civil° and knew courtesy,
    You would not do me thus much injury.
    Can you not hate me, as I know you do,
150   But you must join in souls to mock me too?
    If you were men, as men you are in show,
    You would not use a gentle° lady so;
    To vow, and swear, and superpraise my parts,°
    When I am sure you hate me with your hearts.
155   You both are rivals, and love Hermia;
    And now both rivals to mock Helena:
    A trim° exploit, a manly enterprise,
    To conjure tears up in a poor maid's eyes
    With your derision! None of noble sort
160   Would so offend a virgin, and extort°
    A poor soul's patience, all to make you sport.

Lysander. You are unkind, Demetrius. Be not so;
    For you love Hermia; this you know I know.
    And here, with all good will, with all my heart,
165   In Hermia's love I yield you up my part;
    And yours of Helena to me bequeath,
    Whom I do love, and will do till my death.

Helena. Never did mockers waste more idle° breath.

Demetrius. Lysander, keep thy Hermia; I will none.

139 **show** appearance   141 **Taurus'** of the Taurus Mountains (
Turkey)   147 **civil** civilized   152 **gentle** well-born   153 **parts** qu.
ities   157 **trim** splendid (ironical)   160 **extort** wear out by torturi
168 **idle** vain, futile

If e'er I loved her, all that love is gone.   *170*
My heart to her but as guestwise sojourned,
And now to Helen is it home returned,
There to remain.

Lysander.   Helen, it is not so.

Demetrius. Disparage not the faith thou dost not
   know,
Lest, to thy peril, thou aby it dear.°   *175*
Look, where thy love comes; yonder is thy dear.

Enter Hermia.

Hermia. Dark night, that from the eye his° function
   takes,
The ear more quick of apprehension makes;
Wherein it doth impair the seeing sense,
It pays the hearing double recompense.   *180*
Thou art not by mine eye, Lysander, found;
Mine ear, I thank it, brought me to thy sound.
But why unkindly didst thou leave me so?

Lysander. Why should he stay, whom love doth press
   to go?

Hermia. What love could press Lysander from my
   side?   *185*

Lysander. Lysander's love, that would not let him
   bide,
Fair Helena, who more engilds the night
Than all yon fiery oes° and eyes of light.
Why seek'st thou me? Could not this make thee
   know,
The hate I bare thee made me leave thee so?   *190*

Hermia. You speak not as you think: it cannot be.

Helena. Lo, she is one of this confederacy!
Now I perceive they have conjoined all three

175 **aby it dear** pay dearly for it   177 **his** its (the eye's)   188 **oes**
orbs

To fashion this false sport, in spite of me.
195 Injurious° Hermia! Most ungrateful maid!
Have you conspired, have you with these contrived
To bait° me with this foul derision?
Is all the counsel that we two have shared,
The sister's vows, the hours that we have spent,
200 When we have chid the hasty-footed time
For parting us—O, is all forgot?
All school days friendship, childhood innocence?
We, Hermia, like two artificial° gods,
Have with our needles created both one flower,
205 Both on one sampler,° sitting on one cushion,
Both warbling of one song, both in one key;
As if our hands, our sides, voices, and minds,
Had been incorporate.° So we grew together,
Like to a double cherry, seeming parted,
210 But yet an union in partition;
Two lovely berries molded on one stem;
So, with two seeming bodies, but one heart;
Two of the first, like coats in heraldry,
Due but to one, and crownèd with one crest.°
215 And will you rent° our ancient love asunder,
To join with men in scorning your poor friend?
It is not friendly, 'tis not maidenly.
Our sex, as well as I, may chide you for it,
Though I alone do feel the injury.

220 *Hermia.* I am amazèd at your passionate words.
I scorn you not. It seems that you scorn me.

Helena. Have you not set Lysander, as in scorn,
To follow me and praise my eyes and face?
And made your other love, Demetrius
225 (Who even but now did spurn me with his foot),
To call me goddess, nymph, divine and rare,

---

195 **Injurious** insulting   196–97 **contrived To bait** plotted to assail
203 **artificial** skilled in art   205 **sampler** work of embroidery
208 **incorporate** one body   213–14 **Two of ... one crest** (Helena
apparently envisages a shield on which the coat of arms appears
twice but which has a single crest; Helena and Hermia have two
bodies but a single heart)   215 **rent** rend, tear

Precious, celestial? Wherefore speaks he this
To her he hates? And wherefore doth Lysander
Deny your love,° so rich within his soul,
And tender me (forsooth) affection,   *230*
But by your setting on, by your consent?
What though I be not so in grace° as you,
So hung upon with love, so fortunate,
But miserable most, to love unloved?
This you should pity rather than despise.   *235*

Hermia. I understand not what you mean by this.

Helena. Ay, do! Persever,° counterfeit sad° looks,
Make mouths° upon me when I turn my back;
Wink each at other; hold the sweet jest up.
This sport, well carried, shall be chronicled.   *240*
If you have any pity, grace, or manners,
You would not make me such an argument.°
But fare ye well. 'Tis partly my own fault,
Which death or absence soon shall remedy.

Lysander. Stay, gentle Helena; hear my excuse: *245*
My love, my life, my soul, fair Helena!

Helena. O excellent!

Hermia.   Sweet, do not scorn her so.

Demetrius. If she cannot entreat,° I can compel.

Lysander. Thou canst compel no more than she en-
    treat.
Thy threats have no more strength than her weak
    prayers.   *250*
Helen, I love thee; by my life, I do!
I swear by that which I will lose for thee,
To prove him false that says I love thee not.

Demetrius. I say I love thee more than he can do.

229 **your love** his love for you   232 **in grace** in favor   237 **persever**
persevere (but accented on second syllable)   237 **sad** grave   238
Make mouths make mocking faces   242 **argument** subject (of scorn)
248 **entreat** prevail by entreating

255 *Lysander.* If thou say so, withdraw and prove it too.

Demetrius. Quick, come!

Hermia.   Lysander, whereto tends all this?

Lysander. Away, you Ethiope!°

Demetrius.   No, no; he'll
Seem to break loose; take on as° you would follow,
But yet come not: you are a tame man, go!

Lysander. Hang off, thou cat, thou burr! Vile thing,
260   let loose,
Or I will shake thee from me like a serpent!

Hermia. Why are you grown so rude! What change is
this,
Sweet love?

Lysander.   Thy love! Out, tawny Tartar, out!
Out, loathèd med'cine! O hated potion, hence!

Hermia. Do you not jest?

265 *Helena.*   Yes, sooth;° and so do you.

Lysander. Demetrius, I will keep my word° with thee.

Demetrius. I would I had your bond, for I perceive
A weak bond holds you. I'll not trust your word.

Lysander. What, should I hurt her, strike her, kill
her dead?
270   Although I hate her, I'll not harm her so.

Hermia. What, can you do me greater harm than
hate?
Hate me! Wherefore? O me! What news, my love!
Am not I Hermia? Are not you Lysander?
I am as fair now as I was erewhile.°

---

257 **Ethiope** blackamoor (brunette) 258 **take on as** make a fuss
as if 265 **sooth** truly 266 **my word** my promise to fight with you
274 **erewhile** a little while ago

Since night° you loved me; yet since night you left
   me.   275
Why, then you left me—O, the gods forbid!—
In earnest, shall I say?

sander.   Ay, by my life!
And never did desire to see thee more.
Therefore be out of hope, of question, of doubt;
Be certain, nothing truer. 'Tis no jest   280
That I do hate thee, and love Helena.

ermia. O me! You juggler! You canker blossom!°
You thief of love! What, have you come by night
And stol'n my love's heart from him?

elena.   Fine, i' faith!
Have you no modesty, no maiden shame,   285
No touch of bashfulness? What, will you tear
Impatient answers from my gentle tongue?
Fie, fie! You counterfeit, you puppet, you!

ermia. Puppet? Why so? Ay, that way goes the
   game.
Now I perceive that she hath made compare°   290
Between our statures; she hath urged her height,
And with her personage, her tall personage,
Her height, forsooth, she hath prevailed with him.
And are you grown so high in his esteem,
Because I am so dwarfish and so low?   295
How low am I, thou painted maypole? Speak!
How low am I? I am not yet so low
But that my nails can reach unto thine eyes.

elena. I pray you, though you mock me, gentlemen,
Let her not hurt me. I was never curst;°   300
I have no gift at all in shrewishness;
I am a right maid° for my cowardice.
Let her not strike me. You perhaps may think,

*5 **Since night** since the beginning of this night   282 **canker blos-
**om dog rose (or possibly worm that cankers the blossom)   290 **com-
are comparison   300 **curst quarrelsome   302 **right maid** true young
oman

Because she is something lower than myself,
That I can match her.

305 *Hermia.*   Lower! Hark, again!

Helena. Good Hermia, do not be so bitter with me.
I evermore did love you, Hermia,
Did ever keep your counsels, never wronged you;
Save that, in love unto Demetrius,
310 I told him of your stealth unto this wood.
He followed you; for love I followed him.
But he hath chid me hence, and threatened me
To strike me, spurn me, nay, to kill me too.
And now, so you will let me quiet go,
315 To Athens will I bear my folly back,
And follow you no further. Let me go.
You see how simple and how fond° I am.

Hermia. Why, get you gone. Who is't that hinders you

Helena. A foolish heart, that I leave here behind.

Hermia. What, with Lysander?

320 *Helena.*   With Demetrius.

Lysander. Be not afraid. She shall not harm the
Helena.

Demetrius. No, sir, she shall not, though you take he
part.

Helena. O, when she's angry, she is keen and shrewd
She was a vixen when she went to school;
325 And though she be but little, she is fierce.

Hermia. "Little" again! Nothing but "low" and "little"
Why will you suffer her to flout me thus?
Let me come to her.

Lysander.   Get you gone, you dwarf;
You minimus,° of hind'ring knotgrass° made;
You bead, you acorn!

317 **fond** foolish   323 **keen and shrewd** sharp-tongued and shrewi
329 **minimus** smallest thing   329 **knotgrass** (a weed that alleged
stunted one's growth)

Demetrius.   You are too officious   *330*
In her behalf that scorns your services.
Let her alone. Speak not of Helena;
Take not her part; for, if thou dost intend°
Never so little show of love to her,
Thou shalt aby° it.

Lysander.   Now she holds me not.   *335*
Now follow, if thou dar'st, to try whose right,
Of thine or mine, is most in Helena.

Demetrius. Follow! Nay, I'll go with thee, cheek by
   jowl.   [*Exeunt Lysander and Demetrius.*]

Hermia. You, mistress, all this coil is 'long of you:°
Nay, go not back.

Helena.   I will not trust you, I,   *340*
Nor longer stay in your curst company.
Your hands than mine are quicker for a fray,
My legs are longer though, to run away.

Hermia. I am amazed,° and know not what to say.
                    Exeunt [Helena and Hermia].

Oberon. This is thy negligence. Still thou mistak'st,   *345*
Or else committ'st thy knaveries willfully.

Puck. Believe me, king of shadows, I mistook.
Did not you tell me I should know the man
By the Athenian garments he had on?
And so far blameless proves my enterprise,   *350*
That I have 'nointed an Athenian's eyes;
And so far am I glad it so did sort,°
As this their jangling I esteem a sport.

Oberon. Thou see'st these lovers seek a place to fight.
Hie therefore, Robin, overcast the night.   *355*
The starry welkin° cover thou anon

___

3 **intend** give sign, direct (or possibly "pretend")   335 **aby** pay for
9 **all this coil is 'long of you** all this turmoil is brought about
  you   344 **amazed** in confusion   352 **sort** turn out   356 **welkin**
y

With drooping fog, as black as Acheron;°
And lead these testy° rivals so astray,
As° one come not within another's way.
360   Like to Lysander sometime frame thy tongue,
Then stir Demetrius up with bitter wrong;°
And sometime rail thou like Demetrius.
And from each other look thou lead them thus,
Till o'er their brows death-counterfeiting sleep
365   With leaden legs and batty° wings doth creep.
Then crush this herb into Lysander's eye,
Whose liquor hath this virtuous° property,
To take from thence all error with his might,
And make his eyeballs roll with wonted sight.
370   When they next wake, all this derision°
Shall seem a dream and fruitless vision,
And back to Athens shall the lovers wend,
With league whose date° till death shall never end.
Whiles I in this affair do thee employ,
375   I'll to my queen and beg her Indian boy;
And then I will her charmèd eye release
From monster's view, and all things shall be peace.

Puck. My fairy lord, this must be done with haste,
For night's swift dragons cut the clouds full fast,
380   And yonder shines Aurora's harbinger;°
At whose approach, ghosts, wand'ring here and
    there,
Troop home to churchyards: damnèd spirits all,
That in crossways and floods have burial,
Already to their wormy beds are gone.
385   For fear lest day should look their shames upon,
They willfully themselves exile from light,
And must for aye consort with black-browed night.

Oberon. But we are spirits of another sort.

---

357 **Acheron** one of the rivers of the underworld 358 **testy** excitable,
angry 359 **As** that 361 **wrong** insult 365 **batty** bat-like 367
virtuous potent 370 **derision** i.e., ludicrous delusion 373 **With**
league whose date in union whose term 380 **Aurora's harbinger**
dawn's herald (i.e., the morning star)

I with the Morning's love° have oft made sport;
And, like a forester, the groves may tread,   390
Even till the eastern gate, all fiery-red,
Opening on Neptune with fair blessèd beams,
Turns into yellow gold his salt green streams.
But, notwithstanding, haste; make no delay.
We may effect this business yet ere day.   [*Exit.*]   395

uck.   Up and down, up and down,
             I will lead them up and down:
             I am feared in field and town:
             Goblin,° lead them up and down.
             Here comes one.   400

Enter Lysander.

,ysander. Where art thou, proud Demetrius? Speak
    thou now.

'uck. Here, villain; drawn° and ready. Where art
    thou?

,ysander. I will be with thee straight.

'uck.   Follow me, then,
    To plainer° ground.   [*Exit Lysander.*]

Enter Demetrius.

)emetrius.   Lysander! Speak again!
    Thou runaway, thou coward, art thou fled?   405
    Speak! In some bush? Where dost thou hide thy
        head?

'uck. Thou coward, art thou bragging to the stars,
    Telling the bushes that thou look'st for wars,
    And wilt not come? Come, recreant! Come, thou
        child!

---

89 **the Morning's love** Aurora (or possibly her lover Cephalus)
99 **Goblin** Hobgoblin (one of Puck's names) 402 **drawn** with
rawn sword   404 **plainer** more level

410   I'll whip thee with a rod. He is defiled
        That draws a sword on thee.

Demetrius.   Yea, art thou there

Puck. Follow my voice. We'll try no manhood° here.
                                                    Exeun

[*Enter Lysander.*]

Lysander. He goes before me and still dares me on:
        When I come where he calls, then he is gone.
415   The villain is much lighter-heeled than I.
        I followed fast, but faster he did fly,
        That fallen am I in dark uneven way,
        And here will rest me. [*Lies down.*] Come, thou
            gentle day!
        For if but once thou show me thy gray light,
420   I'll find Demetrius, and revenge this spite.   [*Sleeps.*

[*Enter*] *Robin* [*Puck*] *and Demetrius.*

Puck. Ho, ho, ho! Coward, why com'st thou not?

Demetrius. Abide me,° if thou dar'st; for well I wot°
        Thou runn'st before me, shifting every place,
        And dar'st not stand, nor look me in the face.
        Where art thou now?

425 *Puck.*   Come hither. I am here.

Demetrius. Nay, then, thou mock'st me. Thou shal
            buy this dear,°
        If ever I thy face by daylight see.
        Now, go thy way. Faintness constraineth me
        To measure out my length on this cold bed.
430   By day's approach look to be visited.°
                                [*Lies down and sleeps.*

---

412 **try no manhood** have no test of valor   422 **Abide me** wait for me
422 **wot** know   426 **buy this dear** pay dearly for this   430 **look to be
visited** be sure to be sought out

Enter Helena.

Helena. O weary night, O long and tedious night,
 Abate° thy hours! Shine comforts from the east,
That I may back to Athens by daylight,
 From these that my poor company detest:
And sleep, that sometimes shuts up sorrow's eye,   *435*
Steal me awhile from mine own company.   *Sleeps.*

Puck.   Yet but three? Come one more.
           Two of both kinds makes up four.
           Here she comes, curst° and sad:
           Cupid is a knavish lad,   *440*
           Thus to make poor females mad.

           [*Enter Hermia.*]

Hermia. Never so weary, never so in woe;
 Bedabbled with the dew and torn with briers,
I can no further crawl, no further go;
 My legs can keep no pace with my desires.   *445*
Here will I rest me till the break of day.
Heavens shield Lysander, if they mean a fray!
                    [*Lies down and sleeps.*]

Puck. On the ground
     Sleep sound:
     I'll apply   *450*
     To your eye,
Gentle lover, remedy.
           [*Squeezing the juice on Lysander's eye*]
     When thou wak'st,
     Thou tak'st
     True delight   *455*
     In the sight
Of thy former lady's eye:
And the country proverb known,
That every man should take his own,

---

432 **Abate** make shorter   439 **curst** cross

460   In your waking shall be shown.
         Jack shall have Jill;
         Nought shall go ill;
      The man shall have his mare again, and all shall
      be well.

                                                    [*Exit.*]

[ACT 4

Scene 1. *The wood. Lysander, Demetrius, Helena,*
and Hermia, lying asleep.]

Enter [Titania,] Queen of Fairies, and [Bottom the]
Clown, and Fairies; and [Oberon,] the King, be-
hind them.

Titania. Come, sit thee down upon this flow'ry bed,
    While I thy amiable cheeks do coy,°
And stick musk roses in thy sleek smooth head,
    And kiss thy fair large ears, my gentle joy.

Bottom. Where's Peaseblossom?   5

Peaseblossom. Ready.

Bottom. Scratch my head, Peaseblossom. Where's
    Mounsieur Cobweb?

Cobweb. Ready.

Bottom. Mounsieur Cobweb, good mounsieur, get   10
    you your weapons in your hand, and kill me a red-
    hipped humblebee on the top of a thistle; and, good
    mounsieur, bring me the honey bag. Do not fret
    yourself too much in the action, mounsieur; and,
    good mounsieur, have a care the honey bag break   15

4.1.2 **While I . . . do coy** while I caress your lovely cheeks

59

not; I would be loath to have you overflown with
a honey bag, signior. Where's Mounsieur Mustardseed?

Mustardseed. Ready.

20 *Bottom.* Give me your neaf,° Mounsieur Mustardseed. Pray you, leave your curtsy,° good mounsieur.

Mustardseed. What's your will?

Bottom. Nothing, good mounsieur, but to help Cava-
25   lery° Cobweb to scratch. I must to the barber's,
mounsieur; for methinks I am marvail's° hairy
about the face; and I am such a tender ass, if my
hair do but tickle me, I must scratch.

Titania. What, wilt thou hear some music, my sweet
30   love?

Bottom. I have a reasonable good ear in music. Let's
have the tongs and the bones.°

Titania. Or say, sweet love, what thou desirest to eat.

Bottom. Truly, a peck of provender. I could munch
35   your good dry oats. Methinks I have a great desire
to a bottle° of hay. Good hay, sweet hay, hath no
fellow.°

Titania. I have a venturous fairy that shall seek
The squirrel's hoard, and fetch thee new nuts.

40 *Bottom.* I had rather have a handful or two of dried
peas. But, I pray you, let none of your people stir
me: I have an exposition of° sleep come upon me.

---

20 **neaf** fist, hand   21 **leave your curtsy** i.e., stop bowing, leave your
hat on (a curtsy was any gesture of respect)   24–25 **Cavalery** i.e.,
Cavalier   26 **marvail's** (Bottom means "marvelous")   32 **the tongs
and the bones** rustic music, made by tongs struck with metal and by
bone clappers held between the fingers   36 **bottle** bundle   37 **fellow**
equal   42 **exposition of** (Bottom means "disposition for")

Titania. Sleep thou, and I will wind thee in my arms.
　　Fairies, be gone, and be all ways° away.

　　　　　　　　　　　　　　　　[*Exeunt Fairies.*]

　　So doth the woodbine the sweet honeysuckle　　　　45
　　Gently entwist; the female ivy° so
　　Enrings the barky fingers of the elm.
　　O, how I love thee! How I dote on thee!

　　　　　　　　　　　　　　　　[*They sleep.*]

　　　　Enter Robin Goodfellow [*Puck.*]

Oberon. [*Advancing*] Welcome, good Robin. See'st
　　thou this sweet sight?
　　Her dotage now I do begin to pity:　　　　　　　50
　　For, meeting her of late behind the wood,
　　Seeking sweet favors° for this hateful fool,
　　I did upbraid her, and fall out with her.
　　For she his hairy temples then had rounded
　　With coronet of fresh and fragrant flowers;　　　55
　　And that same dew, which sometime° on the buds
　　Was wont° to swell, like round and orient° pearls,
　　Stood now within the pretty flouriets'° eyes,
　　Like tears, that did their own disgrace bewail.
　　When I had at my pleasure taunted her,　　　　　60
　　And she in mild terms begged my patience,
　　I then did ask of her her changeling child;
　　Which straight she gave me, and her fairy sent
　　To bear him to my bower in fairy land.
　　And now I have the boy, I will undo　　　　　　65
　　This hateful imperfection of her eyes:
　　And, gentle Puck, take this transformèd scalp
　　From off the head of this Athenian swain,
　　That, he awaking when the other° do,
　　May all to Athens back again repair,　　　　　　70
　　And think no more of this night's accidents,°

---

44 **all ways** in every direction   46 **female ivy** (called female because it clings to the elm and is supported by it)   52 **favors** love tokens (probably flowers)   56 **sometime** formerly   57 **Was wont** used to   57 **orient** lustrous   58 **flouriets'** flowerets'   69 **other** others   71 **accidents** happenings

But as the fierce vexation of a dream.
But first I will release the Fairy Queen.
　　　Be as thou wast wont to be;
75　　　See as thou wast wont to see.
　　　Dian's bud o'er Cupid's flower
　　　Hath such force and blessèd power.
Now, my Titania, wake you, my sweet Queen.

Titania. My Oberon, what visions have I seen!
80　　Methought I was enamored of an ass.

Oberon. There lies your love.

Titania.　　　　　　How came these things to pass?
　　O, how mine eyes do loathe his visage now!

Oberon. Silence awhile. Robin, take off this head.
　　Titania, music call; and strike more dead
85　　Than common sleep of all these five the sense.

Titania. Music, ho, music! Such as charmeth sleep!

Puck. Now, when thou wak'st, with thine own fool's
　　eyes peep.

Oberon. Sound, music! [*Music*] Come, my Queen,
　　take hands with me,
　　And rock the ground whereon these sleepers be.
　　　　　　　　　　　　　　　　[*Dance*]
90　　Now thou and I are new in amity,
　　And will tomorrow midnight solemnly°
　　Dance in Duke Theseus' house triumphantly,°
　　And bless it to all fair prosperity.
　　There shall the pairs of faithful lovers be
95　　Wedded, with Theseus, all in jollity.

Puck.　　　Fairy King, attend, and mark:
　　　　I do hear the morning lark.

Oberon.　　Then, my Queen, in silence sad,°
　　　　Trip we after night's shade.

---

91 **solemnly** ceremoniously 92 **triumphantly** in festive procession
98 **sad** serious, solemn

We the globe can compass soon,   *100*
Swifter than the wand'ring moon.

Titania.   Come, my lord; and in our flight,
Tell me how it came this night,
That I sleeping here was found
With these mortals on the ground.   *105*

                                        Exeunt.

Wind horn. Enter Theseus, and all his train;
            [Hippolyta, Egeus].

Theseus. Go, one of you, find out the forester,
For now our observation° is performed;
And since we have the vaward° of the day,
My love shall hear the music of my hounds.
Uncouple in the western valley; let them go.   *110*
Dispatch, I say, and find the forester.

                        [Exit an Attendant.]

We will, fair Queen, up to the mountain's top,
And mark the musical confusion
Of hounds and echo in conjunction.

Hippolyta. I was with Hercules and Cadmus once,   *115*
When in a wood of Crete they bayed° the bear
With hounds of Sparta. Never did I hear
Such gallant chiding; for, besides the groves,
The skies, the fountains, every region near
Seemed all one mutual cry. I never heard   *120*
So musical a discord, such sweet thunder.

Theseus. My hounds are bred out of the Spartan kind,
So flewed, so sanded;° and their heads are hung
With ears that sweep away the morning dew;
Crook-kneed, and dew-lapped like Thessalian bulls; *125*
Slow in pursuit, but matched in mouth like bells,

---

107 **observation** observance, i.e., of the rite of May (cf. 1.1.167)
108 **vaward** vanguard, i.e., morning 116 **bayed** brought to bay
123 **So flewed, so sanded** i.e., like Spartan hounds, with hanging
cheeks and of sandy color

Each under each.° A cry° more tunable
Was never holloed to, nor cheered with horn,
In Crete, in Sparta, nor in Thessaly.
Judge when you hear. But, soft!° What nymphs
130   are these?

Egeus. My lord, this is my daughter here asleep;
And this, Lysander; this Demetrius is;
This Helena, old Nedar's Helena:
I wonder of their being here together.

135 *Theseus.* No doubt they rose up early to observe
The rite of May; and, hearing our intent,
Came here in grace of our solemnity.°
But speak, Egeus. Is not this the day
That Hermia should give answer of her choice?

140 *Egeus.* It is, my lord.

Theseus. Go, bid the huntsmen wake them with their
  horns.

        Shout within. They all start up. Wind horns.

Good morrow, friends. Saint Valentine is past:
Begin these wood birds but to couple now?°

Lysander. Pardon, my lord.

Theseus.   I pray you all, stand up.
145 I know you two are rival enemies.
How comes this gentle concord in the world,
That hatred is so far from jealousy,°
To sleep by hate, and fear no enmity?

Lysander. My lord, I shall reply amazedly,°
150 Half sleep, half waking: but as yet, I swear,
I cannot truly say how I came here.

---

127 **Each under each** of different tone (like the chime of bells)
127 **cry** pack of hounds   130 **soft** stop   137 **in grace of our solemnity** in honor of our festival   143 **Begin these ... couple now** (it was supposed that birds began to mate on February 14, St. Valentine's Day)   147 **jealousy** suspicion   149 **amazedly** confusedly

But, as I think—for truly would I speak,
And now I do bethink me, so it is—
I came with Hermia hither. Out intent
Was to be gone from Athens, where we might,   *155*
Without° the peril of the Athenian law—

Egeus. Enough, enough, my lord; you have enough.
I bet the law, the law, upon his head.
They would have stol'n away; they would, Deme-
    trius,
Thereby to have defeated° you and me,   *160*
You of your wife and me of my consent,
Of my consent that she should be your wife.

Demetrius. My lord, fair Helen told me of their
    stealth,°
Of this their purpose hither to this wood,
And I in fury hither followed them,   *165*
Fair Helena in fancy° following me.
But, my good lord, I wot not by what power—
But by some power it is—my love to Hermia,
Melted as the snow, seems to me now
As the remembrance of an idle gaud,°   *170*
Which in my childhood I did dote upon;
And all the faith, the virtue° of my heart,
The object and the pleasure of mine eye,
Is only Helena. To her, my lord,
Was I betrothed ere I saw Hermia: *175*
But, like a sickness,° did I loathe this food;
But, as in health, come to my natural taste,
Now I do wish it, love it, long for it,
And will for evermore be true to it.

Theseus. Fair lovers, you are fortunately met.   *180*
Of this discourse we more will hear anon.
Egeus, I will overbear your will,
For in the temple, by and by,° with us

156 **Without** outside of 160 **defeated** deprived by fraud 163
stealth stealthy flight 166 **in fancy** in love, doting 170 **idle gaud**
worthless trinket 172 **virtue** power 176 **like a sickness** like one
who is sick 183 **by and by** shortly

These couples shall eternally be knit;
185   And, for the morning now is something worn,°
Our purposed hunting shall be set aside.
Away with us to Athens! Three and three,
We'll hold a feast in great solemnity.
Come, Hippolyta.
[*Exeunt Theseus, Hippolyta, Egeus, and train.*]

Demetrius. These things seem small and undistin-
190   guishable,
Like far-off mountains turnèd into clouds.

Hermia. Methinks I see these things with parted eye,°
When everything seems double.

Helena.   So methinks:
And I have found Demetrius like a jewel,
Mine own, and not mine own.

195 *Demetrius.*   Are you sure
That we are awake? It seems to me
That yet we sleep, we dream. Do not you think
The Duke was here, and bid us follow him?

Hermia. Yea, and my father.

Helena.   And Hippolyta.

200 *Lysander.* And he did bid us follow to the temple.

Demetrius. Why, then, we are awake. Let's follow
       him,
And by the way let us recount our dreams.
                                   [*Exeunt.*]

Bottom. [*Awaking*] When my cue comes, call me,
and I will answer. My next is, "Most fair Pyramus."
205   Heigh-ho! Peter Quince? Flute, the bellows
mender? Snout, the tinker? Starveling? God's my
life,° stol'n hence, and left me asleep? I have had a
most rare vision. I have had a dream, past the

185 **something worn** somewhat spent   192 **with parted eye** i.e., with
the eyes out of focus   206–07 **God's my life** an oath (possibly from
"God bless my life")

wit of man to say what dream it was. Man is but
an ass, if he go about° to expound this dream.   *210*
Methought I was—there is no man can tell what.
Methought I was—and methought I had—but man
is but a patched° fool if he will offer to say what
methought I had. The eye of man hath not heard,
the ear of man hath not seen, man's hand is not   *215*
able to taste, his tongue to conceive, nor his heart
to report, what my dream was. I will get Peter
Quince to write a ballet° of this dream. It shall
be called "Bottom's Dream," because it hath no
bottom; and I will sing it in the latter end of a   *220*
play, before the Duke. Peradventure to make it
the more gracious, I shall sing it at her death.°

                                        [Exit.]

[Scene 2.   *Athens. Quince's house.*]

Enter Quince, Flute,° Thisby and the rabble
[Snout, Starveling].

Quince. Have you sent to Bottom's house? Is he come
home yet?

Starveling. He cannot be heard of. Out of doubt he
is transported.°

Flute. If he come not, then the play is marred. It   *5*
goes not forward, doth it?

Quince. It is not possible. You have not a man in all

---

210 **go about** endeavor   213 **patched** (referring to the patchwork
dress of jesters)   218 **ballet** ballad   222 **her death** i.e., Thisby's
death in the play   4.2.s.d. **Flute** (Shakespeare seems to have forgotten that Flute and Thisby are the same person)   4 **transported**
carried off (by the fairies)

Athens able to discharge° Pyramus but he.

Flute. No, he hath simply the best wit of any handi-
craft man in Athens.

Quince. Yea, and the best person too; and he is a
very paramour for a sweet voice.

Flute. You must say "paragon." A paramour is, God
bless us, a thing of nought.°

Enter Snug the Joiner.

Snug. Masters, the Duke is coming from the temple,
and there is two or three lords and ladies more
married. If our sport had gone forward, we had
all been made men.°

Flute. O sweet bully Bottom! Thus hath he lost sixpence a day° during his life. He could not have
scaped sixpence a day. An the Duke had not given
him sixpence a day for playing Pyramus, I'll be
hanged. He would have deserved it. Sixpence a
day in Pyramus, or nothing.

Enter Bottom.

Bottom. Where are these lads? Where are these
hearts?

Quince. Bottom! O most courageous° day! O most
happy hour!

Bottom. Masters, I am to discourse wonders: but ask
me not what; for if I tell you, I am not true
Athenian. I will tell you everything, right as it fell
out.

Quince. Let us hear, sweet Bottom.

---

8 **discharge** play   14 **a thing of nought** a wicked thing   18 **made
men** men whose fortunes are made   19–20 **sixpence a day** (a pension)
27 **courageous** brave, splendid

Bottom. Not a word of me.° All that I will tell you
is, that the Duke hath dined. Get your apparel   *35*
together, good strings to your beards, new ribbons
to your pumps; meet presently° at the palace; every
man look o'er his part; for the short and the long
is, our play is preferred.° In any case, let Thisby
have clean linen; and let not him that plays the   *40*
lion pare his nails, for they shall hang out for the
lion's claws. And, most dear actors, eat no onions
nor garlic, for we are to utter sweet breath,° and
I do not doubt but to hear them say it is a sweet
comedy. No more words. Away! Go, away!   *45*

                              [*Exeunt.*]

34 **of me** from me   37 **presently** immediately   39 **preferred** put
forward, recommended   43 **breath** (1) exhalation (2) words

[ACT 5

Scene 1. *Athens. The palace of Theseus.*]

*Enter Theseus, Hippolyta, and Philostrate, [Lords,
and Attendants].*

Hippolyta. 'Tis strange, my Theseus, that these lovers
    speak of.

Theseus. More strange than true. I never may believe
    These antique° fables, nor these fairy toys.°
    Lovers and madmen have such seething brains,
5   Such shaping fantasies,° that apprehend
    More than cool reason ever comprehends.
    The lunatic, the lover and the poet
    Are of imagination all compact.°
    One sees more devils than vast hell can hold,
10   That is the madman. The lover, all as frantic,
    Sees Helen's beauty in a brow of Egypt.°
    The poet's eye, in a fine frenzy rolling,
    Doth glance from heaven to earth, from earth to
      heaven;
    And as imagination bodies forth
15   The forms of things unknown, the poet's pen
    Turns them to shapes, and gives to airy nothing
    A local habitation and a name.

5.1.3 **antique** (1) ancient (2) grotesque (antic)   3 **fairy toys** trifles
about fairies   5 **fantasies** imagination   8 **compact** composed   11
brow of Egypt face of a gypsy

Such tricks hath strong imagination,
That, if it would but apprehend some joy,
It comprehends some bringer of that joy;°   20
Or in the night, imagining some fear,°
How easy is a bush supposed a bear!

Hippolyta. But all the story of the night told over,
And all their minds transfigured so together,
More witnesseth than fancy's images,   25
And grows to something of great constancy;°
But, howsoever, strange and admirable.°

> *Enter Lovers: Lysander, Demetrius, Hermia and Helena.*

Theseus. Here come the lovers, full of joy and mirth.
Joy, gentle friends! Joy and fresh days of love
Accompany your hearts!

Lysander.   More than to us   30
Wait in your royal walks, your board, your bed!

Theseus. Come now, what masques,° what dances shall we have,
To wear away this long age of three hours
Between our aftersupper° and bedtime?
Where is our usual manager of mirth?.   35
What revels are in hand? Is there no play,
To ease the anguish of a torturing hour?
Call Philostrate.

Philostrate.   Here, mighty Theseus.

Theseus. Say, what abridgment° have you for this evening?

___

20 **It comprehends . . . that joy** it includes an imagined bringer of the
joy   21 **fear** object of fear   26 **constancy** consistency (and reality)
27 **admirable** wonderful   32 **masques** courtly entertainments with
masked dancers   34 **aftersupper** refreshment served after early supper
39 **abridgment** entertainment (to abridge or shorten the time)

40   What masque? What music? How shall we beguile
        The lazy time, if not with some delight?

        Philostrate. There is a brief° how many sports are
            ripe:°
        Make choice of which your Highness will see first.
                                        [*Giving a paper*]

        Theseus. "The battle with the Centaurs, to be sung
45   By an Athenian eunuch to the harp."
        We'll none of that. That have I told my love,
        In glory of my kinsman Hercules.
        "The riot of the tipsy Bacchanals,
        Tearing the Thracian singer° in their rage."
50   That is an old device;° and it was played
        When I from Thebes came last a conqueror.
        "The thrice three Muses mourning for the death
        Of Learning, late deceased in beggary."
        That is some satire, keen and critical,
55   Not sorting with° a nuptial ceremony.
        "A tedious brief scene of young Pyramus
        And his love Thisby; very tragical mirth."
        Merry and tragical? Tedious and brief?
        That is, hot ice and wondrous strange snow.
60   How shall we find the concord of this discord?

        Philostrate. A play there is, my lord, some ten words
            long,
        Which is as brief as I have known a play;
        But by ten words, my lord, it is too long,
        Which makes it tedious. For in all the play
65   There is not one word apt, one player fitted.
        And tragical, my noble lord, it is,
        For Pyramus therein doth kill himself.
        Which, when I saw rehearsed, I must confess,
        Made mine eyes water; but more merry tears
70   The passion° of loud laughter never shed.

        Theseus. What are they that do play it?

42 **brief** written list   42 **ripe** ready to be presented   49 **Thracian
singer** Orpheus   50 **device** show   55 **sorting with** suited to   70 **passion** strong emotion

Philostrate. Hard-handed men, that work in Athens
  here,
  Which never labored in their minds till now;
  And now have toiled their unbreathed° memories
  With this same play, against° your nuptial.   *75*

Theseus. And we will hear it.

Philostrate.   No, my noble lord;
  It is not for you. I have heard it over,
  And it is nothing, nothing in the world;
  Unless you can find sport in their intents,
  Extremely stretched and conned with cruel pain,   *80*
  To do you service.

Theseus.   I will hear that play;
  For never anything can be amiss,
  When simpleness and duty tender it.
  Go, bring them in: and take your places, ladies.

                              [*Exit Philostrate.*]

Hippolyta. I love not to see wretchedness o'ercharged,°   *85*
  And duty in his service perishing.

Theseus. Why, gentle sweet, you shall see no such
  thing.

Hippolyta. He says they can do nothing in this kind.°

Theseus. The kinder we, to give them thanks for
  nothing.
  Our sport shall be to take what they mistake: *90*
  And what poor duty cannot do, noble respect
  Takes it in might,° not merit.
  Where I have come, great clerks° have purposèd
  To greet me with premeditated welcomes;
  Where I have seen them shiver and look pale,   *95*
  Make periods in the midst of sentences,
  Throttle their practiced accent in their fears,

---

74 **unbreathed** unexercised 75 **against** in preparation for 85
wretchedness o'ercharged lowly people overburdened 88 **in this
kind** in this kind of thing (i.e., acting) 92 **Takes it in might** considers the ability and the effort made 93 **clerks** scholars

And, in conclusion, dumbly have broke off,
Not paying me a welcome. Trust me, sweet,
100 Out of this silence yet I picked a welcome;
And in the modesty of fearful duty
I read as much as from the rattling tongue
Of saucy and audacious eloquence.
Love, therefore, and tongue-tied simplicity
105 In least speak most, to my capacity.°

[*Enter Philostrate.*]

Philostrate. So please your Grace, the Prologue is
addressed.°

Theseus. Let him approach.   [*Flourish trumpets.*]

Enter the Prologue [*Quince*].

Prologue. If we offend, it is with our good will.
That you should think, we come not to offend,
110 But with good will. To show our simple skill,
That is the true beginning of our end.°
Consider, then, we come but in despite.
We do not come, as minding to content you,
Our true intent is. All for your delight,
We are not here. That you should here repent
115   you,
The actors are at hand; and, by their show,°
You shall know all, that you are like to know.

Theseus. This fellow doth not stand upon points.°

Lysander. He hath rid his prologue like a rough colt;
120 he knows not the stop.° A good moral, my lord:
it is not enough to speak, but to speak true.

---

105 **to my capacity** according to my understanding   106 **addressed**
ready   111 **end** aim   116 **show** (probably referring to a kind of
pantomime—"dumb show"—that was to follow, in which the
action of the play was acted without words while the Prologue gave
his account)   118 **stand upon points** (1) care about punctuation
(2) worry about niceties   120 **stop** (1) technical term for the checking of a horse (2) mark of punctuation

Hippolyta. Indeed he hath played on this prologue
   like a child on a recorder;° a sound, but not in
   government.°

Theseus. His speech was like a tangled chain; noth-   *125*
   ing impaired, but all disordered. Who is next?

*Enter Pyramus and Thisby and Wall and Moonshine
   and Lion [as in dumbshow].*

Prologue. Gentles, perchance you wonder at this show;
   But wonder on, till truth make all things plain.
   This man is Pyramus, if you would know;
     This beauteous lady Thisby is certain.   *130*
   This man, with lime and roughcast, doth present
     Wall, that vile Wall which did these lovers
       sunder;
   And through Wall's chink, poor souls, they are
       content
     To whisper. At the which let no man wonder.
   This man, with lantern, dog, and bush of thorn,   *135*
     Presenteth Moonshine; for, if you will know,
   By moonshine did these lovers think no scorn
     To meet at Ninus' tomb, there, there to woo.
   This grisly beast, which Lion hight° by name,
   The trusty Thisby, coming first by night,   *140*
   Did scare away, or rather did affright;
   And, as she fled, her mantle she did fall,°
     Which Lion vile with bloody mouth did stain.
   Anon comes Pyramus, sweet youth and tall,°
     And finds his trusty Thisby's mantle slain: *145*
   Whereat, with blade, with bloody blameful blade,
     He bravely broached° his boiling bloody breast;
   And Thisby, tarrying in mulberry shade,
     His dagger drew, and died. For all the rest,

---

123 **recorder** flutelike instrument   124 **government** control   139
hight is called   142 **fall** let fall   144 **tall** brave   147 **bravely**
broached gallantly stabbed

150   Let Lion, Moonshine, Wall, and lovers twain
         At large° discourse, while here they do remain.

Theseus. I wonder if the lion be to speak.

Demetrius. No wonder, my lord. One lion may, when
many asses do.

Exit Lion, Thisby and Moonshine.

155   *Wall.* In this same interlude it doth befall
         That I, one Snout by name, present a wall;
         And such a wall, as I would have you think,
         That had in it a crannied hole or chink,
         Through which the lovers, Pyramus and Thisby,
160   Did whisper often very secretly.
         This loam, this roughcast, and this stone, doth
            show
         That I am that same wall; the truth is so;
         And this the cranny is, right and sinister,°
         Through which the fearful lovers are to whisper.

165   *Theseus.* Would you desire lime and hair to speak
better?

Demetrius. It is the wittiest partition° that ever I
heard discourse, my lord.

Theseus. Pyramus draws near the wall. Silence!

Pyramus. O grim-looked night! O night with hue so
170   black!
         O night, which ever art when day is not!
         O night, O night! Alack, alack, alack,
         I fear my Thisby's promise is forgot!
         And thou, O wall, O sweet, O lovely wall,
         That stand'st between her father's ground and
175   mine!
         Thou wall, O wall, O sweet and lovely wall,

---

151 **At large** at length   163 **right and sinister** i.e., running right and
left, horizontal   167 **wittiest partition** most intelligent wall (with a
pun on "partition," a section of a book or of an oration)

Show me thy chink, to blink through with mine
    eyne!
                [*Wall holds up his fingers.*]
Thanks, courteous wall. Jove shield thee well for
    this!
But what see I? No Thisby do I see.
O wicked wall, through whom I see no bliss!   *180*
Cursed be thy stones for thus deceiving me!

Theseus. The wall, methinks, being sensible,° should
curse again.°

Pyramus. No, in truth, sir, he should not. "Deceiving
me" is Thisby's cue. She is to enter now, and I *185*
am to spy her through the wall. You shall see it
will fall pat° as I told you. Yonder she comes.

Enter Thisby.

Thisby. O wall, full often hast thou heard my moans,
    For parting my fair Pyramus and me!
My cherry lips have often kissed thy stones,   *190*
    Thy stones with lime and hair knit up in thee.

Pyramus. I see a voice: now will I to the chink,
    To spy an I can hear my Thisby's face.
    Thisby!

Thisby. My love thou art, my love I think.   *195*

Pyramus. Think what thou wilt, I am thy lover's
    grace;°
And, like Limander,° am I trusty still.

Thisby. And I like Helen,° till the Fates me kill.

Pyramus. Not Shafalus to Procrus° was so true.

---

182 **sensible** conscious 183 **again** in return 187 **pat** exactly 196
thy lover's grace thy gracious lover 197 **Limander** (Bottom means
Leander, but blends him with Alexander) 198 **Helen** (Hero, beloved of Leander, is probably meant) 199 **Shafalus to Procrus**
(Cephalus and Procris are meant, legendary lovers)

200 *Thisby.* As Shafalus to Procrus, I to you.

Pyramus. O kiss me through the hole of this vile wall!

Thisby. I kiss the wall's hole, not your lips at all.

Pyramus. Wilt thou at Ninny's tomb meet me straightway?

Thisby. 'Tide life, 'tide death,° I come without delay.
[*Exeunt Pyramus and Thisby.*]

205 *Wall.* Thus have I, Wall, my part dischargèd so;
And, being done, thus wall away doth go.   [*Exit.*]

Theseus. Now is the moon used° between the two neighbors.

Demetrius. No remedy, my lord, when walls are so
210 willful to hear without warning.°

Hippolyta. This is the silliest stuff that ever I heard.

Theseus. The best in this kind° are but shadows; and
the worst are no worse, if imagination amend them.

Hippolyta. It must be your imagination then, and
215 not theirs.

Theseus. If we imagine no worse of them than they
of themselves, they may pass for excellent men.
Here come two noble beasts in, a man and a lion.

Enter Lion and Moonshine.

Lion. You, ladies, you, whose gentle hearts do fear
The smallest monstrous mouse that creeps on
220   floor,

---

204 **'Tide life, 'tide death** come (betide) life or death   207 **moon used** (the quartos read thus, the Folio reads **morall downe**. Among suggested emendations are "mural down," and "moon to see")   209–10 **when walls ... without warning** i.e., when walls are so eager to listen without warning the parents (?)   212 **in this kind** of this sort, i.e., plays (or players?)

May now perchance both quake and tremble here,
   When lion rough in wildest rage doth roar.
Then know that I, as Snug the joiner, am
A lion fell,° nor else no lion's dam;
For, if I should as lion come in strife   225
Into this place, 'twere pity on my life.°

Theseus. A very gentle° beast, and of a good con-
science.

Demetrius. The very best at a beast, my lord, that
e'er I saw.   230

Lysander. This lion is a very fox for his valor.

Theseus. True; and a goose for his discretion.

Demetrius. Not so, my lord; for his valor cannot
carry° his discretion, and the fox carries the goose.

Theseus. His discretion, I am sure, cannot carry his   235
valor; for the goose carries not the fox. It is well.
Leave it to his discretion, and let us listen to the
moon.

Moonshine. This lanthorn° doth the hornèd moon
present—

Demetrius. He should have worn the horns on his
head.°   240

Theseus. He is no crescent, and his horns are invisible
within the circumference.

Moonshine. This lanthorn doth the hornèd moon
present;
Myself the man i' th' moon do seem to be.   245

Theseus. This is the greatest error of all the rest.

---

224 **lion fell** fierce lion (perhaps with a pun on *fell* = "skin")
226 **pity on my life** a dangerous thing for me   227 **gentle** gentle-
manly, courteous   234 **carry** carry away   239 **lanthorn** (so spelled,
and perhaps pronounced "lant-horn," because lanterns were commonly made of horn)   240 **horns on his head** (cuckolds were said
to have horns)

The man should be put into the lanthorn. How is
it else the man i' th' moon?

Demetrius. He dares not come there for the candle;
250   for, you see, it is already in snuff.°

Hippolyta. I am aweary of this moon. Would he would
change!

Theseus. It appears, by his small light of discretion,
that he is in the wane; but yet, in courtesy, in all
255   reason, we must stay the time.

Lysander. Proceed, Moon.

Moonshine. All that I have to say is to tell you that
the lanthorn is the moon; I, the man i' th' moon;
this thorn bush, my thorn bush; and this dog, my
260   dog.

Demetrius. Why, all these should be in the lanthorn;
for all these are in the moon. But, silence! Here
comes Thisby.

Enter Thisby.

Thisby. This is old Ninny's tomb. Where is my love?

265 *Lion.* Oh—   [*The lion roars. Thisby runs off.*]

Demetrius. Well roared, Lion.

Theseus. Well run, Thisby.

Hippolyta. Well shone, Moon. Truly, the moon shines
with a good grace.
              [*The Lion shakes Thisby's mantle, and exits.*]

270 *Theseus.* Well moused,° Lion.

Demetrius. And then came Pyramus.

Lysander. And so the lion vanished.

---

250 **in snuff** (1) in need of snuffing (2) resentful   270 **moused**
shaken (like a mouse)

Enter Pyramus.

Pyramus. Sweet Moon, I thank thee for thy sunny
   beams;
  I thank thee, Moon, for shining now so bright;
  For, by thy gracious, golden, glittering gleams,   *275*
      I trust to take of truest Thisby sight.
        But stay, O spite!°
        But mark, poor knight,
    What dreadful dole° is here!
      Eyes, do you see   *280*
      How can it be?
    O dainty duck! O dear!
      Thy mantle good,
      What, stained with blood!
    Approach, ye Furies fell!°   *285*
      O Fates, come, come,
      Cut thread and thrum;°
    Quail,° crush, conclude, and quell!°

Theseus. This passion, and the death of a dear friend,
  would go near to make a man look sad.   *290*

Hippolyta. Beshrew° my heart, but I pity the man.

Pyramus. O wherefore, Nature, didst thou lions frame?
   Since lion vile hath here deflow'red my dear:
  Which is—no, no—which was the fairest dame
    That lived, that loved, that liked, that looked
      with cheer.°   *295*
        Come, tears, confound;
        Out, sword, and wound
      The pap of Pyramus;
        Ay, that left pap,
        Where heart doth hop. [*Stabs himself.*]   *300*
      Thus die I, thus, thus, thus.
        Now am I dead,

---

277 **spite** vexation   279 **dole** sorrowful thing   285 **fell** fierce   287
thread and thrum i.e., everything (*thrum* = the end of the warp thread)
288 **Quail** destroy   288 **quell** kill   291 **Beshrew** curse (but a mild
word)   295 **cheer** countenance

                    Now am I fled;
                 My soul is in the sky.
305   Tongue, lose thy light;
                 Moon, take thy flight.

                                    [*Exit Moonshine.*]
                 Now die, die, die, die, die.   [*Dies.*]

Demetrius. No die, but an ace,° for him; for he is but
    one.

310 *Lysander.* Less than an ace, man; for he is dead, he is
    nothing.

Theseus. With the help of a surgeon he might yet re-
    cover, and yet prove an ass.

Hippolyta. How chance° Moonshine is gone before
315   Thisby comes back and finds her lover?

Theseus. She will find him by starlight. Here she
    comes; and her passion° ends the play.

                 [*Enter Thisby.*]

Hippolyta. Methinks she should not use a long one
    for such a Pyramus. I hope she will be brief.

320 *Demetrius.* A mote will turn the balance, which Pyra-
    mus, which Thisby, is the better; he for a man,
    God warr'nt us; she for a woman, God bless us!

Lysander. She hath spied him already with those
    sweet eyes.

325 *Demetrius.* And thus she means,° videlicet:

Thisby.   Asleep, my love?
                 What, dead, my dove?
             O Pyramus, arise!
                 Speak, speak. Quite dumb?
330   Dead, dead? A tomb

---

308 **No die, but an ace** not a die (singular of "dice"), but a one-spot
on a die   314 **How chance** how does it come that   317 **passion**
passionate speech   325 **means** laments

    Must cover thy sweet eyes.
      These lily lips,
      This cherry nose,
    These yellow cowslip cheeks,
      Are gone, are gone.   *335*
      Lovers, make moan.
    His eyes were green as leeks.
      O Sisters Three,°
      Come, come to me,
    With hands as pale as milk;   *340*
      Lay them in gore,
      Since you have shore°
    With shears his thread of silk.
      Tongue, not a word.
      Come, trusty sword,   *345*
    Come, blade, my breast imbrue!°
                                [Stabs herself.]
    And, farewell, friends.
    Thus Thisby ends.
    Adieu, adieu, adieu.   *[Dies.]*

Theseus. Moonshine and Lion are left to bury the *350*
dead.

Demetrius. Ay, and Wall too.

Bottom. [*Starting up*] No, I assure you; the wall is
down that parted their fathers. Will it please you
to see the epilogue, or to hear a Bergomask dance° *355*
between two of our company?

Theseus. No epilogue, I pray you; for your play needs
no excuse. Never excuse, for when the players are
all dead, there need none to be blamed. Marry, if
he that writ it had played Pyramus and hanged *360*
himself in Thisby's garter, it would have been a
fine tragedy: and so it is, truly; and very notably
discharged. But, come, your Bergomask. Let your
epilogue alone.   *[A dance.]*

---

338 **Sisters Three** i.e., the three Fates   342 **shore** shorn   346 **imbrue**
stain with blood   355 **Bergomask dance** rustic dance

365   The iron tongue of midnight hath told° twelve.
       Lovers, to bed; 'tis almost fairy time.
       I fear we shall outsleep the coming morn,
       As much as we this night have overwatched.
       This palpable-gross° play hath well beguiled
370   The heavy gait of night. Sweet friends, to bed.
       A fortnight hold we this solemnity,
       In nightly revels and new jollity.   *Exeunt.*

                    Enter Puck [with a broom].

       Puck. Now the hungry lion roars,
              And the wolf behowls the moon;
375   Whilst the heavy plowman snores,
              All with weary task fordone.°
       Now the wasted° brands do glow,
              Whilst the screech owl, screeching loud,
       Puts the wretch that lies in woe
380   In remembrance of a shroud.
       Now it is the time of night,
              That the graves, all gaping wide,
       Every one lets forth his sprite,
              In the churchway paths to glide:
385   And we fairies, that do run
              By the triple Hecate's team,°
       From the presence of the sun,
              Following darkness like a dream,
       Now are frolic.° Not a mouse
390   Shall disturb this hallowed house:
       I am sent, with broom, before,
       To sweep the dust behind the door.°

---

365 **told** counted, tolled   369 **palpable-gross** obviously grotesque
376 **fordone** worn out   377 **wasted** used-up   386 **triple Hecate's
team** i.e., because she had three names: Phoebe in Heaven, Diana
on Earth, Hecate in Hades. (Like her chariot—drawn by black
horses or dragons—the elves were abroad only at night; but
3.2.388–91 says differently)   389 **frolic** frolicsome   392 **behind
the door** i.e., from behind the door (Puck traditionally helped with
household chores)

Enter King and Queen of Fairies with all their train.

Oberon. Through the house give glimmering light,
    By the dead and drowsy fire:
  Every elf and fairy sprite   395
    Hop as light as bird from brier;
  And this ditty, after me,
  Sing, and dance it trippingly.

Titania. First, rehearse your song by rote,
  To each word a warbling note: 400
  Hand in hand, with fairy grace,
  Will we sing, and bless this place.

                           [Song and dance.]

Oberon. Now, until the break of day,
  Through this house each fairy stray.
  To the best bride-bed will we,   405
  Which by us shall blessèd be;
  And the issue there create°
  Ever shall be fortunate.
  So shall all the couples three
  Ever true in loving be;   410
  And the blots of Nature's hand
  Shall not in their issue stand.
  Never mole, harelip, nor scar,
  Nor mark prodigious,° such as are
  Despisèd in nativity,   415
  Shall upon their children be.
  With this field-dew consecrate,
  Every fairy take his gait,°
  And each several° chamber bless,
  Through this palace, with sweet peace,   420
  And the owner of it blest
  Ever shall in safety rest.
  Trip away; make no stay;
  Meet me all by break of day.

                     Exeunt [all but Puck].

407 **create** created   414 **mark prodigious** ominous birthmark   418
take his gait proceed   419 **several** individual

425 *Puck.* If we shadows have offended,
    Think but this, and all is mended:
    That you have but slumb'red here,
    While these visions did appear.
    And this weak and idle° theme,
430   No more yielding but° a dream,
    Gentles, do not reprehend:
    If you pardon, we will mend.
    And, as I am an honest Puck,
    If we have unearnèd luck
435   Now to scape the serpent's tongue,°
    We will make amends ere long;
    Else the Puck a liar call:
    So, good night unto you all.
    Give me your hands,° if we be friends,
440   And Robin shall restore amends.°   [*Exit.*]

FINIS

429 **idle** foolish   430 **No more yielding but** yielding no more than
435 **to scape the serpent's tongue** i.e., to escape hisses from the
audience   439 **Give me your hands** applaud   440 **restore amends**
make amends

Textual Note

Our chief authority for the text of *A Midsummer Night's
eam* is the First Quarto of 1600 (Q1), possibly printed
m Shakespeare's own manuscript. The Second Quarto of
19 (Q2), fraudulently dated 1600, and the First Folio of
23 (F) correct a few obvious mistakes of Q1 and add some
w ones. The Folio introduces division into acts. The pres-
t text follows Q1 as closely as possible, but modernizes
nctuation and spelling (and prints "and" as "an" when it
ans "if"), occasionally alters the lineation (e.g., prints as
ose some lines that were mistakenly set as verse), expands
d regularizes the speech prefixes, slightly alters the posi-
n of stage directions where necessary, and corrects
vious typographical errors. Other departures from Q1 are
ted below, the adopted reading first in italics, and then
's reading in roman. If the adopted reading is derived
m Q2 or from F, the fact is noted in a bracket following
reading.

.4 *wanes* [Q2] waues   10 *New-bent* Now bent   19 s.d. *Lysander* [F]
ander and Helena   24 *Stand forth, Demetrius* [printed as s.d. in Q1, Q2,
  26 *Stand   forth,   Lysander* [printed   as   s.d.   in   Q1,   Q2,
102 *Demetrius'* Demetrius   136 *low* loue   187 *Yours would* Your
rds   191 *I'd* ile   216 *sweet* sweld   219 *stranger companies* strange
npanions

.69 *steep* [Q2] steppe   79 *Aegles* Eagles   109 *thin* chinne   158 *the*
t [F] west   190 *slay . . . slayeth* stay . . . stayeth   201 *not nor* [F] not not

9, 13, 24 [speech prefixes added by editor]   39 *Be't* Bet it   47 *is* [Q2] it

13 *By'r lakin* Berlakin   29-30 *yourselves* [F] your selfe   56 *Bottom*
] Cet 70 *and   let* or   let 84 *Odors,   odors* [F]   odours,
rous   89 *Puck* [F] Quin   164 *Peaseblossom . . . All* [Q1, Q2, and F
t as a single speech, attributed to "Fairies"]   176 *Peaseblossom . . .
stardseed. Hail* [Q1, Q2, and F print thus: 1 Fai. Haile mortall, haile./2.
. Haile./3. Fai. Haile]   195 *you of* you

87

3.2.19 *mimic* [F] Minnick   80 *part I so* part I   85 *sleep* slippe   213 *f*
like   first   life   220 *passionate words* [F]   words   250 *pra*
praise   299 *gentlemen*   [Q2]   gentleman   323 *she's*   [Q2]
is   406 *Speak! In some bush?* Speake in some bush   426 *shalt* [
shat   451 *To your eye* your eye

4.1.76 *o'er* or   85 *sleep of all these five* sleepe: of all th
fine   120 *seemed* seeme   131 *this is my* [Q2] this my   175
see   202 *let us* [Q2] lets   210 *to expound* [Q2] expound   213 *a patc*
[F] patcht a

4.2.3 *Starveling* [F] Flute

5.1.34 *our* [F] or   156 *Snout* [F] Flute   19 *up in thee* [F]
againe   275 *gleams* beams   320 *mote* moth   353 *Bottom*
Lion   373 *lion* Lyons   374 *behowls* beholds   421–22 *And the owner*
rest [these two lines are transposed in Q1, Q2, and F]

A Note on the Source of
A Midsummer Night's Dream

A *Midsummer Night's Dream* is, together with *Love's Labor's Lost* and *The Tempest*, one of those few plays for which no specific source appears to exist. The plot, with its skillful interplay of four different actions, is of Shakespeare's own making, although single incidents and motives as well as some names and details come from widely different origins.

Thus, the enveloping action of Theseus and Hippolyta derives in part from Chaucer's *The Knight's Tale*. This tale begins, as our play does, with Theseus' victorious return from war with Hippolyta and also ends with a celebration at court. Moreover, the story of Palamon and Arcite in *The Knight's Tale* is linked with the Theseus story in a similar way and also illustrates how friendship is broken by love. But Shakespeare has modified this motif in a characteristic way, replacing the two men by two young women and adding a fourth lover, thereby not only establishing symmetry but also providing for those multiple combinations and varying relationships between Lysander, Hermia, Demetrius, and Helena that constitute the *comedy of errors* of the night in the forest. Shakespeare's portrait of Theseus may have been further influenced by the figure of Theseus in Plutarch's *Lives*, which Shakespeare read in Sir Thomas North's translation. Theseus' function as a wise judge as well as his tolerance and benevolence toward the craftsmen are features that find a parallel in Plutarch.

Oberon as the fairy king with a kingdom in the East had been made familiar through the French romance *Huon of Bordeaux*, while the name of Titania for the fairy queen in *A Midsummer Night's Dream* may have been suggested by the epithet given to Diana in Ovid's *Metamorphoses* (III, 173). Diana, however, occurs as the "lady of the fairies" in Reginald Scot's *The Discoverie of Witchcraft* (1584), which supplied Shakespeare with much information about witches, fairies, and transformations and contends at the same time that belief in Robin Goodfellow was declining, and that all those stories about fairies were untrue. Bottom's "assification" may also have been suggested by Scot's account of the spells exercised by the witches but has another parallel in Apuleius' *The Golden Ass*, which had been translated in 1566. For the magic juice, several analogues have been pointed out, the closest being in Montemayor's prose pastoral *Diana Enamorada* (1542).

The story of Pyramus and Thisbe existed in Elizabethan times in many poetical versions, some of them exhibiting those sentimental and melodramatic exaggerations that must have prompted Shakespeare to his subtle and complex parody. It is significant that George Pettie in his *Petite Pallace of Pettie his Pleasure* (1576) sees in this story a parallel with the account of *Romeo and Juliet*. Shakespeare in his "play within the play" obviously creates an ironic and comic parallel to his own tragedy—no matter whether *Romeo and Juliet* was already in existence then or soon to appear. Geoffrey Bullough, in the second volume of his *Narrative and Dramatic Sources of Shakespeare*, reprints eleven pieces from which Shakespeare may have drawn.

The most interesting of our play's sources are, however, the unwritten ones. For the fairy world that is presented by so many graphic details and concrete features owes much to folklore and the living tradition of the Warwickshire countryside. Shakespeare must have been intensely alive to the mass of popular superstition, legend, and folk custom still to be found in his own times. He took what he could use from these sources, adding, however, many details of his own invention and modifying several traditional traits. The fairy world which thus emerges is—if we consider its dramatic function—a new creation of Shakespeare's own poetic imagination, which has at each stage transmuted the source material "into something rich and strange."

Commentaries

WILLIAM HAZLITT

From The Characters of Shakespear's Plays

Bottom the Weaver is a character that has not had justice done him. He is the most romantic of mechanics. And what a list of companions he has—Quince the Carpenter, Snug the Joiner, Flute the Bellows Mender, Snout the Tinker, Starveling the Tailor; and then again, what a group of fairy attendants, Puck, Peaseblossom, Cobweb, Moth, and Mustardseed! It has been observed that Shakespeare's characters are constructed upon deep physiological principles; and there is something in this play which looks very like it. Bottom the Weaver, who takes the lead of

> This crew of patches, rude mechanicals,
> That work for bread upon Athenian stalls,

follows a sedentary trade, and he is accordingly represented as conceited, serious, and fantastical. He is ready to undertake anything and everything, as if it was as much a matter of course as the motion of his loom and shuttle. He is for playing the tyrant, the lover, the lady, the lion. "He will roar that it shall do any man's heart good to hear him"; and this being objected to as improper, he still has a resource in his good opinion of himself, and "will roar you an 'twere any nightingale." Snug the Joiner is the moral man of the piece,

From *The Characters of Shakespear's Plays* by William Hazlitt. 2nd ed. London: Taylor & Hessey, 1818.

who proceeds by measurement and discretion in all things. You see him with his rule and compasses in his hand. "Have you the lion's part written? Pray you, if it be, give it me, for I am slow of study." —"You may do it extempore," says Quince, "for it is nothing but roaring." Starveling the Tailor keeps the peace, and objects to the lion and the drawn sword. "I believe we must leave the killing out when all's done." Starveling, however, does not start the objections himself, but seconds them when made by others, as if he had not spirit to express his fears without encouragement. It is too much to suppose all this intentional: but it very luckily falls out so. Nature includes all that is implied in the most subtle analytical distinctions; and the same distinctions will be found in Shakespear. Bottom, who is not only chief actor, but stage manager for the occasion, has a device to obviate the danger of frightening the ladies: "Write me a prologue, and let the prologue seem to say, we will do no harm with our swords, and that Pyramus is not killed indeed; and for better assurance, tell them that I, Pyramus, am not Pyramus, but Bottom the Weaver: this will put them out of fear." Bottom seems to have understood the subject of dramatic illusion at least as well as any modern essayist. If our holiday mechanic rules the roost among his fellows, he is no less at home in his new character of an ass, "with amiable cheeks, and fair large ears." He instinctively acquires a most learned taste, and grows fastidious in the choice of dried peas and bottled hay. He is quite familiar with his new attendants, and assigns them their parts with all due gravity. "Monsieur Cobweb, good Monsieur, get your weapon in your hand, and kill me a red-hipt humblebee on the top of a thistle, and, good Monsieur, bring me the honey bag." What an exact knowledge is here shown of natural history!

Puck, or Robin Goodfellow, is the leader of the fairy band. He is the Ariel of the *Midsummer Night's Dream*; and yet as unlike as can be to the Ariel in *The Tempest*. No other poet could have made two such different characters out of the same fanciful materials and situations. Ariel is a minister of retribution, who is touched with the sense of pity at the woes he inflicts. Puck is a madcap sprite, full of wantonness and mischief, who laughs at those whom he misleads— "Lord, what fools these mortals be!" Ariel cleaves the air, and executes his mission with the zeal of a winged messenger; Puck is borne along on his fairy errand like the light and glittering gossamer before the breeze. He is, indeed, a most Epicurean little gentleman, dealing in quaint devices, and faring in dainty delights. Prospero and his world of spirits are a set of moralists: but with Oberon and his fairies we are launched at once into the empire of the butterflies. How beautifully is this race of beings contrasted with the men and women actors in the scene, by a single epithet which Titania gives to the latter, "the human mortals!" It is astonishing that Shakespear should be considered, not only by foreigners, but by many of our own critics, as a gloomy and heavy writer, who painted nothing but "gorgons and hydras, and chimeras dire." His subtlety exceeds that of all other dramatic writers, insomuch that a celebrated person of the present day said that he regarded him rather as a metaphysician than a poet. His delicacy and sportive gaiety are infinite. In the *Midsummer Night's Dream* alone, we should imagine, there is more sweetness and beauty of description than in the whole range of French poetry put together. What we mean is this, that we will produce out of that single play ten passages, to which we do not think any ten passages in the works of the French poets can be opposed, displaying equal fancy and imagery. Shall we mention the remonstrance of Helena to Hermia, or Titania's description of her fairy train, or her disputes with Oberon about the Indian boy, or Puck's account of himself and his employments, or the Fairy Queen's exhortation to the elves to pay due attendance upon her favorite, Bottom; or Hippolita's description of a chase, or Theseus's answer? The two last are as heroical and spirited as the others are full of luscious tenderness. The reading of this play is like wandering in a grove by moonlight: the descriptions breathe a sweetness like odors thrown from beds of flowers.

Titania's exhortation to the fairies to wait upon Bottom, which is remarkable for a certain cloying sweetness in the repetition of the rhymes, is as follows:

> Be kind and courteous to this gentleman.
> Hop in his walks, and gambol in his eyes,

> Feed him with apricocks and dewberries,
> With purple grapes, green figs and mulberries;
> The honey bags steal from the humblebees,
> And for night tapers crop their waxen thighs,
> And light them at the fiery glowworm's eyes,
> To have my love to bed, and to arise:
> And pluck the wings from painted butterflies,
> To fan the moonbeams from his sleeping eyes;
> Nod to him, elves, and do him courtesies.

The sounds of the lute and of the trumpet are not more distinct than the poetry of the foregoing passage, and of the conversation between Theseus and Hippolita.

> *Theseus.* Go, one of you, find out the forester,
>   For now our observation is perform'd;
>   And since we have the vaward of the day,
>   My love shall hear the music of my hounds.
>   Uncouple in the western valley, go,
>   Dispatch, I say, and find the forester.
>   We will, fair Queen, up to the mountain's top,
>   And mark the musical confusion
>   Of hounds and echo in conjunction.

> *Hippolyta.* I was with Hercules and Cadmus once,
>   When in a wood of Crete they bay'd the bear
>   With hounds of Sparta; never did I hear
>   Such gallant chiding. For besides the groves,
>   The skies, the fountains, every region near
>   Seem'd all one mutual cry. I never heard
>   So musical a discord, such sweet thunder.

> *Theseus.* My hounds are bred out of the Spartan kind,
>   So flew'd, so sanded, and their heads are hung
>   With ears that sweep away the morning dew;
>   Crook-knee'd and dew-lap'd, like Thessalian bulls.
>   Slow in pursuit, but matched in mouth like bells,
>   Each under each. A cry more tunable
>   Was never halloo'd to, nor cheer'd with horn,
>   In Crete, in Sparta, nor in Thessaly:
>   Judge when you hear.

Even Titian never made a hunting piece of a *gusto* so fresh and lusty, and so near the first ages of the world as this.

It had been suggested to us, that the *Midsummer Night's Dream* would do admirably to get up as a Christmas afterpiece; and our prompter proposed that Mr. Kean should play the part of Bottom, as worthy of his great talents. He might, in the discharge of his duty, offer to play the lady like any of our actresses that he pleased, the lover or the tyrant like any of our actors that he pleased, and the lion like "the most fearful wildfowl living." The carpenter, the tailor, and joiner, it was thought, would hit the galleries. The young ladies in love would interest the side boxes; and Robin Goodfellow and his companions excite a lively fellow feeling in the children from school. There would be two courts, an empire within an empire, the Athenian and the Fairy King and Queen, with their attendants, and with all their finery. What an opportunity for processions, for the sound of trumpets and glittering of spears! What a fluttering of urchins' painted wings; what a delightful profusion of gauze clouds and airy spirits floating on them!

Alas the experiment has been tried, and has failed; not through the fault of Mr. Kean, who did not play the part of Bottom, nor of Mr. Liston, who did, and who played it well, but from the nature of things. The *Midsummer Night's Dream*, when acted, is converted from a delightful fiction into a dull pantomime. All that is finest in the play is lost in the representation. The spectacle was grand: but the spirit was evaporated, the genius was fled. Poetry and the stage do not agree well together. The attempt to reconcile them in this instance fails not only of effect, but of decorum. The *ideal* can have no place upon the stage, which is a picture without perspective; everything there is in the foreground. That which was merely an airy shape, a dream, a passing thought, immediately becomes an unmanageable reality. Where all is left to the imagination (as is the case in reading) every circumstance, near or remote, has an equal chance of being kept in mind, and tells according to the mixed impression of all that has been suggested. But the imagination cannot sufficiently qualify the actual impressions of the senses. Any offense given to the eye is not to be got rid of by explanation.

Thus Bottom's head in the play is a fantastic illusion, produced by magic spells: on the stage it is an ass's head, and nothing more; certainly a very strange costume for a gentleman to appear in. Fancy cannot be embodied any more than a simile can be painted; and it is as idle to attempt it as to personate *Wall* or *Moonshine*. Fairies are not incredible, but fairies six feet high are so. Monsters are not shocking, if they are seen at a proper distance. When ghosts appear at midday, when apparitions stalk along Cheapside, then may the *Midsummer Night's Dream* be represented without injury at Covent Garden or at Drury Lane. The boards of a theater and the regions of fancy are not the same thing.

HENRY ALONZO MYERS

"Romeo and Juliet" and *"A Midsummer Night's Dream"*: Tragedy and Comedy

At the end of Plato's *Symposium* we find an amusing picture of a great philosopher putting Agathon, the tragic poet, and Aristophanes, the greatest comic poet of Athens, to sleep with his discourse on the nature of tragedy and comedy. As Plato tells the story, it happened in the early hours of the morning, after a night spent in feasting and singing the praises of love:

> There remained [of the company] only Socrates, Aristophanes, and Agathon, who were drinking out of a large goblet which they passed round, and Socrates was discoursing to them. Aristodemus was only half awake, and he did not hear the beginning of the discourse; the chief thing which he remembered was Socrates compelling the other two to acknowledge that the genius of comedy was the same with that of tragedy, and that the true artist in tragedy was an artist in comedy also. To this they were constrained to assent, being drowsy, and not quite following the argument. And first of all Aristophanes dropped off, then, when the day was already dawning, Agathon. Socrates, having laid them to sleep, rose to depart. [Jowett translation]

Like all good comedy, this scene is entertaining as well as instructive. It is entertaining because it presents the opposite of the order we naturally expect: a tragic poet and

From *Tragedy: A View of Life* by Henry Alonzo Myers. Ithaca, N.Y.: Cornell University Press, 1956. Copyright 1956 by Cornell University Press. Reprinted by permission of the publishers.

a comic poet, whom we expect to be interested in a discourse on the nature of tragedy and comedy, fall asleep; it is instructive because it makes the point, evident elsewhere in literary history, that tragic and comic poets do not need explicitly formulated theories of tragedy and comedy, that they are often indifferent to such abstract speculations.

The distinctive form and significance of tragedies and comedies indicate, however, that the successful poets have had an adequate sense of the tragic and the comic. Apparently the appreciative reader or spectator also possessed this mysterious but adequate sense of the nature of tragedy and comedy, for as the artist can create without an explicitly formulated theory, so the reader can appreciate and enjoy the specific work of art without the benefit of definitions and generalizations. But although speculation about the nature of tragedy and comedy is not indispensable to either creation or appreciation, it is, nevertheless, a natural and, indeed, inevitable result of our curiosity as rational beings. If it did not begin before, dramatic theory began as the first spectators were leaving the first performance in the first theater. When we have had an intensely interesting experience, we are eager to know its nature and its causes. Why do we enjoy the spectacle of a man who falls from prosperity to adversity? Why do we laugh at fools? As long as we are interested in drama and in its sources in life, we shall be asking these questions and trying to answer them.

The assertion that the genius of tragedy is the same as that of comedy and that the true artist in tragedy is an artist in comedy also is the kind of provocative conundrum or apparent paradox which Socrates loved to discuss. It was a bold speculative assertion rather than a description of known facts, for the Greek dramatic poets, as we know them, kept tragedy and comedy apart and excelled in one or the other, not in both. Plato, who recorded the assertion, supported it in practice by displaying a sharp comic sense in the *Symposium* and a deep tragic sense in the dialogues which describe the trial and death of Socrates. But its support in drama did not come until the 1590's, when Shakespeare wrote *Romeo and Juliet* and *A Midsummer Night's Dream*, displaying genius in both tragedy and comedy.

What did Socrates have in mind? If the genius of tragedy

is the same as that of comedy, what is the difference between the two? Certainly, he rejected the popular choice of the distinction between an unhappy and a happy ending as the difference between tragedy and comedy: in Plato's *Philebus* he maintains that we view both forms of drama with mingled pleasure and pain, smiling through our tears at tragedy and responding to the ridiculous in others with laughter, which is pleasant, tinged with envy, which is unpleasant. But this view, although it supports the assertion that tragedy and comedy are similar, leaves us, if both have the same effect, with no way of distinguishing one from the other. It can hardly be all that Socrates had in mind.

After years of wondering what he had in mind when his audience at the symposium failed him, I do not know the answer, but I have reached the point where I know what I should have said if I had been Socrates and if I had been more fortunate than he in holding my audience.

Man, I should have said, is a rational animal: he is always looking for meaning in his experience. He looks for meaning and order everywhere, but since the desire to find some significant pattern in his joys and sorrows, some just relation between good and evil, is closest to his heart, surpassing even his desire to grasp the order of the physical world, he looks most intently for meaning in the realm of values. That is why tragedy, which is an artistic demonstration that justice governs our joys and sorrows, has always seemed to most critics to be the highest form of art.

Since man has only a finite intelligence, he cannot always find the order he craves, either in the inner world of values or in the outer world of science and external description. In his search for order he is everywhere confronted by disorder, absurdity, nonsense, and incongruity. Fortunately, however, he finds in laughter, at least in his relaxed moments, an enjoyable emotional reaction to these disappointments to his reason. We rightly honor the comic poet, who by presenting nonsense in contrast to sense points up the difference between the two and who through laughter reconciles us to those experiences which frustrate the effort of reason to find meaningful patterns in all experience.

Order and disorder, the congruous and the incongruous, sense and nonsense, profundity and absurdity are pairs of opposites; each member of each pair throws light on the other so that whoever has a keen sense of order, congruity, sense, and profundity must also have a keen sense of disorder, incongruity, nonsense, and absurdity. Clearly, then, if the discovery of order in the realm of good and evil is the glory of tragedy, which finds intelligibility and justice in our seemingly chance joys and sorrows, and if the glory of comedy lies in its transformation of the frustrations of reasoning into soothing laughter, the artist in tragedy may also be an artist in comedy, and vice versa; and it may also be said that the genius of tragedy is similar to that of comedy.

Socrates, who was a rationalist, might well have expounded his apparent paradox in this fashion; very probably, however, the rivalry between philosophers and poets in his time would have made it difficult for him to recognize the tragic poets as the discoverers of justice in our joys and sorrows and the comic poets as the teachers of the difference between sense and nonsense. Since we can never know what Socrates had in mind, the final episode of the *Symposium* must remain, as Plato intended, a frustration of reason made pleasant by laughter at the absurdity of the ideal audience falling asleep in the presence of the right speaker on the right subject. This pleasant frustration does not prevent us, however, from determining for ourselves whether the great teacher's provocative conundrum will serve as a key to the meaning of tragedy and comedy.

The hypothesis which I have offered as a substitute for the slumber-stifled discussion needs amplification and verification by specific examples. What better test can be found than the first test afforded by the history of dramatic literature— the appearance of *Romeo and Juliet* and *A Midsummer Night's Dream* as the works of one author? These plays prove that Shakespeare, at least, was an artist in both tragedy and comedy. Do they indicate also that the genius of tragedy is similar to that of comedy? Do they indicate that the two are related as order is related to disorder—that the function of tragedy is to reveal a just order in our joys and sorrows and the function of comedy to turn disorder into soothing laughter?

II

The answers to two questions lead us directly to the heart of the tragic meaning of *Romeo and Juliet*. The first question is, What causes the downfall of the hero and of the heroine who shares his fate? The second question is, In what sense does the play have universality: does the fate of Romeo and Juliet represent the fate of all lovers?

Shakespeare himself could not have correctly answered the first question—What causes the downfall of the hero and heroine?—before he finished the play. *Romeo and Juliet* is Shakespeare's first true tragedy; as he wrote it, he was developing his own sense of the tragic. He started the play with a view which he found unsatisfactory as he went on writing and ended with a view which he upheld in all his later tragedies. He started with the view that something outside the hero is the cause of his downfall, that something outside man is the cause of the individual's particular fate.

His first view is stressed in the Prologue, which announces that "a pair of star-cross'd lovers take their life." This forecast points ahead to Romeo's exclamation, when he hears and believes the report of Juliet's death:

Is it even so? then I defy you, stars!

(5.1.24)

From this point on, every step he takes leads to his downfall. He buys poison from the apothecary, goes to Juliet's tomb, drinks the poison, and dies—while Juliet still lives. The stars are triumphant. Romeo's defiance of his fate hastens its fulfillment.

The stars are symbolic of the elements of bad luck and chance in the action of the play, of the bad luck which involves Romeo in a renewal of the feud and of the chance delay of the messenger who would have told him that Juliet lived. But do the stars, do chance and bad luck, determine the particular fate of the individual? Bad luck and chance are facts of life, but is there a deeper fact than chance and bad luck, a truer cause of the individual's fate? Like Romeo, we all suffer at times from bad luck. Like Romeo, we all hear rumors and alarms and false warnings and reports of danger and disaster. We know from experience that our response to these chance and unlucky events is more important than the events themselves; and our responses depend upon our characters. Character is a deeper and more important influence in human affairs than luck or chance.

Some time ago a radio program presented, as a remarkable illustration of chance and bad luck, the story of a man from Pennsylvania who had been hit by a train three times at the same crossing. When we reflect upon his story, we are likely to conclude that it is a revelation of character rather than an illustration of chance. If we had been in his place, most of us, after the first accident, would have taken all possible precautionary measures to see that it did not happen again; and if by chance we were struck again by an unscheduled train on a day when the crossing signals were not working, it seems likely that we would never again cross the tracks at that point. It is difficult for us to avoid the conclusion that the man from Pennsylvania was the kind of man who gets hit by trains.

Examples of "chance" and "bad luck" are common in the news. The following is representative of many: "A year to the day after he broke his left leg in a fall caused by a loose plank in his doorstep, John Jones, 47, of . . . , broke his right leg when he tripped over the same plank." Obviously, this is another revelation of character: Jones is the kind of man who will risk another leg rather than fix the plank.

While writing his first tragedy, Shakespeare discovered that the individual's fate is determined from within, by character, and not from without, by chance or bad luck. Although the character of Romeo is not as clearly revealed as the characters of Lear, Hamlet, Macbeth, and Othello, it is nevertheless certain from a point early in the play that Romeo is the kind of person who is inclined to accept bad news at its face value and who is inclined, when he is confronted by apparent disaster, toward some despairing deed. In his despair when the feud broke out—at a time when he knew that Juliet lived—he would have killed himself if the Nurse and Friar Laurence had not prevented him from so doing. Since the Nurse and Friar Laurence could not always be present in his despairing moments and since the temptations to despair are all too common in life, it was with Romeo only a matter of time.

The stars remain in *Romeo and Juliet*, as well as the chance and bad luck of which they are symbols, but the play also offers a better explanation for the downfall of Romeo. It suggests that "a man's character is his fate," as Heraclitus said—a dictum which sums up one pattern of tragic meaning, one aspect of the tragic poet's vision of order in the universe.

In all his later plays, Shakespeare looked within to character, and not to the stars or to chance or luck, for the causes of individual fates:

> The fault, dear Brutus, is not in our stars,
> But in ourselves, that we are underlings.
>
> (*Caesar*, 1.2.140–41)

We come now to the second question: How is the fate of Romeo and Juliet representative of the fate of all lovers: in what sense does the play have universality?

In looking for the answer to this question, we should first notice how neatly balanced are the feelings of the principals in the play. Taking love as a representative emotional experience, Shakespeare stresses both sides of the experience— the joy and exaltation of the lovers when they are united and their anxiety and unhappiness when they are separated. We see the lovers at both extremes of feeling. The balanced pyramidal form of the play, the five-act structure with the turn at the middle following the rise and fall of the fortunes of the principals, parallels the balance between joy and sorrow which Shakespeare's insight finds in human experience. The artistic structure of the play is an outward show of its inner meaning.

In *Romeo and Juliet* the ending is a dramatic summing up of the whole action: the death of the lovers is symbolical of their lives. Each realizes at the end the extremes of good and evil. In one sense they are united forever, as they wished to be; in another sense they are separated forever in death. Here we see not a happy ending, as in a fairy story, and not an unhappy ending, as in some grim naturalistic tale, in which the worm finally is stilled after wriggling on the hook, but a truly tragic ending, in which joy and sorrow are inevitably joined together—a victory in defeat, a victory of the human spirit accompanied by the inevitable defeat of finite human beings.

Shakespearean tragedy is an artistic vision and revelation of a kind of divine justice which regulates the lives of men and women. Through poetic insight, Shakespeare finds a pattern, an order, in the realm of values; through insight he measures the extremes of feeling, which cannot be measured in any other way. Whoever sees in Shakespearean tragedy only a spectacle of suffering, only an unhappy ending, is seeing only half the story, only one side of life. The artist has done his best to present the whole story and both sides of life. For in the relation between the poles of experience, good and evil, he finds order in the universe. First, he finds that the individual fate of the hero is determined by character, not by chance. Second, he finds that the universality of the hero rests on the fact that, like all of us, the hero is fated to experience the extremes of feeling; and, in accordance with his capacity for feeling, in something like balanced and equal measures, when we follow the rise and fall of the hero's fortunes, we feel ourselves joined to him and to all mankind in the justice of a common fate: this is the secret of the reconciliation to suffering which we find in tragedy.

III

At the time of writing *Romeo and Juliet* and *A Midsummer Night's Dream*, Shakespeare must have been deeply impressed by the thought that the same material—the theme of love, for example, or life itself—may be treated as either tragic or comic. At the beginning of *A Midsummer Night's Dream*, the Athenian lovers, Hermia and Lysander, are in a predicament as serious as the plight of Romeo and Juliet; well may Lysander say, "The course of true love never did run smooth." But the roughness in the course of their love turns out to be the laughable ups and downs of comedy while the roughness in the course of Romeo's love turns into a profoundly tragic change of fortune. The story of Pyramus and Thisbe, the play within a play in *A Midsummer Night's Dream* is, in its main outlines, the same as the story of Romeo and Juliet, yet it becomes in production, as Hippolyta says, "the silliest stuff that ever I heard," while the story of Romeo and Juliet becomes in production a great demonstration that order and justice prevail.

What difference in treatment of the same material—what difference in point of view toward the same material—makes possible the difference between comedy and tragedy?

A Midsummer Night's Dream presents the theme of love on three levels: the level of common sense; the level of nonsense, incongruity, and absurdity; and the level of fantasy. The level of common sense is represented by the love and marriage of Theseus and Hippolyta, who provide the necessary contrast to nonsense. The level of nonsense is represented by the Athenian lovers, Lysander, Demetrius, Helena, and Hermia, and by the workmen, Quince, Snug, Bottom, Flute, Snout, and Starveling, who turn the tragic story of Pyramus and Thisbe into a comic revelation of their own inadequacies. The level of fantasy is represented by the loves of Titania and Oberon, and by the juice of the flower called love-in-idleness, which here serves Shakespeare as an explanation of the influence of chance, caprice, and propinquity on love between the sexes. Since two of these levels, sense and nonsense, are always represented in all comedies, they deserve a few words of comment and definition.

The world of sense is the world of orderly and meaningful patterns, both rational and conventional. Its first law is the law of identity, namely, A is A, which "simply expresses the fact that every term and idea which we use in our reasonings" and practical calculations "must remain what it is." Shakespeare, for example, can make "sense" of the world of human values and find a just order in it only if the law of identity holds true. A is A; and if Romeo is Romeo—that is, if we can be sure that Romeo's character does not change or will not change, then we can understand his fate or even in a general way predict it. Similarly, if for Romeo good is to-be-united-with-Juliet and evil is to-be-separated-from-her—if his values do not change—then we can see in the rise and fall of his fortunes a just balance between good and evil.

The world of nonsense is, in contrast, governed by a law

which is the exact opposite of the law of identity. A is not always A; A is sometimes B, or C, or D; and for this reason the world of nonsense is a world of disorder and incongruities. The laughable absurdities and incongruities in *A Midsummer Night's Dream* are for the most part direct consequences of this law of change of identity. Every change of identity leads to incongruities or comic ups and downs. Lysander, for example, is first presented to us as the lover of Hermia; later, touched by the juice of the magic flower, he becomes the lover of Helena; still later through magic he becomes the lover of Hermia again: A becomes B, and then becomes A again. Helena, we are told, was once the object of Demetrius' love; she is first presented to us as an unloved maiden; later through magic she is the object of Lysander's love, later still the object of the love of both Lysander and Demetrius; and finally the object of Demetrius' love only. A becomes B, and then becomes C, and then becomes D, and finally becomes A again. And so on with the Athenian lovers.

In contrast, Theseus and Hippolyta, who represent sense, remain what they are throughout the play.

Bottom, that king of the world of nonsense, undergoes a series of "translations." An ass in the eyes of the audience from the beginning, but a man of parts to his fellows, he later becomes through magic an ass in appearance, later the object of Titania's doting, later still the object of her loathing, and later still Bottom once more. Meanwhile, to complicate the scheme, he wishes to become Pyramus in the play, and also Thisbe, and also Lion. (I'll spare you the working out of his "translations" in ABC's.)

The most effective comedy in *A Midsummer Night's Dream* comes from the subtle use of change of identity in the production of the play within the play, "Pyramus and Thisbe." In the world of sense we accept the convention whereby the actor assumes the identity of the part he plays. In the theater Brian Aherne is Romeo, Katharine Cornell is Juliet. Not so in "Pyramus and Thisbe": Shakespeare reverses the convention and changes order into disorder and incongruity, so that the production excites in us uproarious laughter rather than sympathy and insight. Following the convention of the theater, we would accept Lion and forget the actor, but Lion insists on telling us that he is not Lion but Snug the joiner. Similarly, by every device at his command, Shakespeare makes certain that we cannot see Pyramus, Thisbe, Wall, Moonshine, and Lion because we must see Snug, Bottom, Flute, Snout, and Starveling. By such devices, based on change of identity, first principle in the world of nonsense and incongruity, what might be seen as tragedy must be seen as comedy.

If tragedy reveals significant patterns in experience, demonstrating that character is fate and that men are united in the justice which apportions equal measures of joy and sorrow to each individual, and if comedy reconciles us through laughter to the disorder, the nonsense, the incongruities and absurdities which we meet everywhere in experience, how does the artist, working with the same material, with love or with life itself, make the choice between comedy and tragedy and determine whether we shall respond to his work of art with laughter or with tragic insight? Shakespeare must have thought of this question in some form while he was writing *Romeo and Juliet* and *A Midsummer Night's Dream*; and possibly his answer is to be found in the reply of Theseus to Hippolyta's verdict on the workers' production of "Pyramus and Thisbe": Hippolyta exclaimed, "This is the silliest stuff that ever I heard." And Theseus replied, "The best in this kind are but shadows, and the worst are no worse, if imagination amend them" (5.1.211–13). If there exists anywhere a wiser comment on drama and the theater, I have not read or heard it.

Undoubtedly Shakespeare must have been thinking, as he wrote the reply of Theseus to Hippolyta, that the same imagination which willingly accepts actors as Romeo, or Hamlet, or Macbeth, or Lear, that accepts the past as the present, the stage as a series of faraway places, and fiction as life itself, could also accept, if it were permitted to do so, his "Pyramus and Thisbe." He knew that his "Pyramus and Thisbe," with the incongruities in the diction removed, and with competent actors losing themselves in their parts (including Lion, Moonshine, and Wall), could be successfully presented as tragedy. For he knew that the chief difference between "silly stuff" and profound art is caused by the artist's power to enlist the spectator's imagination. We can be sure that he knew this because in "Pyramus and Thisbe," as we see it, he has deliberately frustrated, for the sake of laughter, our imagination and prevented us at every point from amending the inherent limitations of drama.

Perhaps he was thinking also of the wider question of what difference in the artist's point of view determines whether we shall focus our attention on the underlying order in experience or on its superficial disorder and incongruities. Can the answer be found in imagination understood as sympathetic insight?

In "Pyramus and Thisbe" we are never permitted to see the story from the point of view of the lovers themselves; we see it only from the outside, as detached and unsympathetic observers. Indeed, we are not permitted to see the lovers at all: we see only the incongruity of the workers presuming to play the parts of a highborn couple. Again, we see the Athenian lovers only from the outside. Hermia, Lysander, Demetrius, and Helena—each is identified for us only as the object of another's affection. They have no inwards for us, and since this is so, how can we possibly tell, from watching them, whether character is fate or whether each suffers and enjoys in equal measures?

Our experience in witnessing *Romeo and Juliet* is altogether different. Soon after the beginning, we follow the action with sympathetic insight from within, from the point of view of the lovers themselves. Inwardness—where character and values may be found and measured by insight—becomes for us the only reality. We live with Romeo and Juliet, seeing the world with their eyes, and as we rise and fall with their fortunes, we are carried finally beyond envy and pity and filled with a sense that all men share a common fate.

IV

Can we say, then, that life is comic if we view it chiefly from the outside, as detached observers whose attention is focused mainly on the disorder and incongruities of the surface? And can we say that life is tragic when we view it from within, from the point of view of an individual—our own point of view or that of someone with whom we identify ourselves by sympathetic insight, as we do with Romeo and Juliet?

Walpole's famous dictum that "the world is a comedy to those that think, a tragedy to those who feel" on first consideration may seem to sum up satisfactorily at this point, for the detached, outer view of man, which permits us to smile at nonsense and incongruity, is at least partially the kind of objectivity which we associate with thought. And sympathetic insight, indispensable in the appreciation of tragedy, obviously involves us in the world of feelings and values. But Walpole's equation of the difference between comedy and tragedy with the difference between thought and feeling does not take into account that, in the first place, laughter is itself an emotion and that, therefore, our response even to "pure" comedy is emotional. Secondly, the emotion of laughter mixes freely with other emotions, and this fact explains the existence of various kinds of comedy.

When the comic poet is amused by someone or something that he dislikes, the result is satire; when he is amused by someone or something that he likes, the result is humor. The spirit of *A Midsummer Night's Dream*, for example, is one of good humor rather than of satire. Shakespeare, we feel, likes human beings even while he laughs at them and is not motivated by a desire to change their ways. Their ways, especially the ways of lovers, are often absurd and nonsensical, but Shakespeare does not view these absurdities as a stern moralist or a cynic might.

A Midsummer Night's Dream is saved from cynicism by the third level of the comedy—the level of fantasy, the imaginative level which softens the sharp distinctions between the world of sense and the world of nonsense. If all the changes of identity on the part of the lovers were attributed to caprice and propinquity, the result would be cynicism, but most of them are attributed to magic in the world of fantasy, and the result is a softer, kindlier humor, which transforms our rational distress at chance and disorder into soothing laughter. There is insight in the background of *A Midsummer Night's Dream*, as in all great comedy. The magic juice of the flower called love-in-idleness seems to tell us that if only we knew the true causes of what seems to be mere chance and caprice in affairs of the heart, then even these apparent absurdities would make sense to us. The fact that it is a creature from fairyland, not a man, who exclaims: "Lord, what fools these mortals be!" takes the poison out of the comment.

Nor can tragedy be satisfactorily explained as the view of a man who is only a man of feeling—if such a man exists. Tragedy can best be explained by its appeal to our rational craving for order, for patterns of meaning; it satisfies this craving at the important point where our reason and our feelings unite. Tragedy offers a vision of order in the universe, which we grasp with sympathetic insight and respond to emotionally as we rise and fall, or fall and rise, with the hero's fortunes. Furthermore, tragedy requires artistic objectivity as well as insight. Sympathetic insight alone might tempt Shakespeare—who as artist enjoys the omnipotence of a creator—to save Romeo from the fate which inevitably flows from his character, but artistic objectivity will not permit him to do so. Even Zeus must bow to necessity.

The spectator also views serious drama with a combination of insight and artistic objectivity, and he applauds the tragic artist who offers both as greater than the writer who is tempted by sympathy to sacrifice objectivity and provide us with a happy ending. We readily recognize such writings as one-sided, as untrue to life, as appeals to our weakness.

Thought and feeling are involved in the creation and appreciation of both comedy and tragedy. In seeing each, we experience an intellectual awareness accompanied by appropriate emotional responses. The main difference is that in tragedy our intelligence is directed toward order in the universe; in comedy, toward disorder and incongruity. Without sympathetic insight, we cannot behold the tragic vision of the fate common to all men. Without detachment, we cannot realize the effect of comedy, which transforms the frustrations of reason into laughter. But there is objectivity as well as insight in the tragic vision, and there is always insight in the background of great comedy. The difference between the point of view of tragedy and that of comedy cannot, therefore, be equated simply with the difference between insight and detachment, but rather is to be found in a subtler proportion whereby insight is stressed in tragedy and detachment is stressed in comedy.

JOHN RUSSELL BROWN

From Shakespeare and His Comedies

The commonest form in which Shakespeare presents the mutual recognition of two lovers is the realization of each other's beauty. For the young lovers in *A Midsummer Night's Dream*, such realization carries its own conviction of exclusive truth; Hermia will not "choose love by another's eyes" (1.1.140), and when Duke Theseus orders her to marry Demetrius whom her father favors, she answers in a single line:

> I would my father looked but with my eyes.
>
> (56)

Even if a lover is inconstant he will always demand the use of his own eyes,[1] and neither the authority of a father nor the force of general opinion can displace a conviction based on such experience.[2] Some lovers, like Helena, may live by such a "truth" even though they recognize that it is exclusive and irrational:

> Things base and vile, holding no quantity,
> Love can transpose to form and dignity.
> Love looks not with the eyes, but with the mind,
> And therefore is winged Cupid painted blind: . . .
>
> (232–35)

In this comedy the irrationality of love's choice provides sport rather than grief. The action takes place in a wood

From *Shakespeare and His Comedies* by John Russell Brown. London: Methuen and Company Ltd., 1957. Reprinted by permission of the publishers.
[1] Cf. *All's Well That Ends Well*, 2.3.115.
[2] Cf. 1.1.227–29.

where moonlight and fairy influence suspend our belief in lasting hardship; sometimes a bush may seem to be a bear, but contrariwise even a bear may seem to have no more awful reality than a shadow and may vanish as easily. Moreover the dialogue of the lovers is light and agile so that we are not allowed to dwell upon frustration or suffering. When the sport natural to blind Cupid is heightened by Oberon's enchantment of the lovers' eyes and when events befall preposterously, we find that, even in the telling of the "saddest tale," a "merrier hour was never wasted" (2.1.51–57).

But our laughter is not thoughtless, for, by bringing Bottom and his fellows to the wood to rehearse a play for the Duke's nuptials, Shakespeare has contrived a contrast to the lovers' single-minded pursuit of their own visions of beauty. Once more Shakespeare's comic vision is expressed in contrasts and relationships; Bottom is the sober man by whom we judge the intoxicated. When Lysander's eyes have been touched with the magic herb, he rationalizes his new love for Helena in the loftiest terms:

> Not Hermia but Helena I love:
> Who will not change a raven for a dove?
> The will of man is by his *reason* swayed
> And *reason* says you are the worthier maid.
>
> (2.2.113–16)

Without the agency of magic but simply because Demetrius scorns her, Helena has come to believe that she is as "ugly as a bear" (94), and protests, as if it were self-evident:

> . . . I did never, no, nor never can,
> Deserve a sweet look from Demetrius' eye.
>
> (126–27)

Helena rationally judges that Lysander's love is a "flout" for her own "insufficiency." And when, in the next scene, Titania is charmed to love Bottom whom Puck has disfigured with an ass's head, she too declares her love as if she were convinced by the best of reasons:

> I pray thee, gentle mortal, sing again:
> Mine ear is much enamored of thy note;
> So is mine eye enthrallèd to thy shape;
> And thy fair virtue's force perforce doth move me
> On the first view to say, to swear, I love thee.
>
> (3.1.138–42)

With more modesty in judgment, Bottom answers the other lovers as well as Titania:

> Methinks, mistress, you should have little reason for that. And yet, to say the truth, *reason* and love keep little company together nowadays; the more the pity, that some honest neighbors will not make them friends.   (143–47)

Bottom's modesty in judgment is well placed, for life makes fewer demands on him—"if I had wit enough to get out of this wood, I have enough to serve mine own turn" (150–52)—he is not asked to love and also to be wise; his judgment is not at the mercy of his eyes.

When Oberon's spell is broken, Bottom seems to have had a strange dream, but it does not count for so much as the helpless game the lovers have played; much as he would like to, Bottom dares not tell his dream, but the lovers must tell theirs, even to the skeptical ear of Theseus. As the vagaries of love and enchantment had seemed perfectly reasonable to those who were involved, and unreasonable or ridiculous to those who had only observed, so the whole action in the wood, once the first sight of day has passed, will seem more real or more fantastic.

Such reflections are made explicit at the beginning of Act 5, in the dialogue of Theseus and his bride, Hippolyta. And at this point the play is given a new dimension; previously we had watched the action as if we were Olympians laughing at the strutting seriousness of mortals; now we seem to take a step backwards and watch others watching the action:

> 'Tis strange, my Theseus, that these lovers speak of.
>
> More strange than *true*. I never may believe
> These antique fables, nor these fairy toys.

Lovers and madmen have such seething brains,
Such shaping fantasies, that apprehend
More than cool reason ever comprehends.

(5.1.1–6)

And not content with likening a lover's truth to that of a madman, Theseus equates these with the poet's:

The lunatic, the lover and the poet
Are of imagination all compact.
One sees more devils than vast hell can hold,
That is the madman. The lover, all as frantic,
Sees Helen's beauty in a brow of Egypt.
The poet's eye, in a fine frenzy rolling,
Doth glance from heaven to earth, from earth to heaven;
And as imagination bodies forth
The forms of things unknown, the poet's pen
Turns them to shapes, and gives to airy nothing
A local habitation and a name.

(7–17)

For a moment, the image in the glass of the stage is strangely lightened; has the action we have witnessed the inconsequence of mere contrivance, or has it the constancy of a poet's[3] imagination? Is it "more strange than true," or is there some "truth" in the lovers' visions of beauty, in the moonlight and enchantments, in Oberon's jealousy and Puck's mistaking? Our judgment hesitates with Hippolyta's:

. . . all the story of the night told over,
And all their minds transfigured so together,
More witnesseth than fancy's images,
And grows to something of great constancy;
But, howsoever, strange and admirable.

(23–27)

[3] In Shakespeare's day "poet" was used in a general sense after Greek and Latin usage: "One who makes or composes works of literature; an author, writer" (*N.E.D.*, s.v. Ib); it is used for "dramatist" in *Hamlet*, 2.2. See also B. Jonson, "To the memory of my beloved, The Author" prefixed to the Shakespeare 1623 Folio.

Possibly we know no more than Demetrius, rubbing his eyes in the daylight:

> . . . I wot not by what power—
> But by some power it is. . . .

> (4.1.167–68)

Our reactions will vary, depending on whether we are stalwart like Bottom, disengaged like Puck, or fanciful like lovers, madmen, and poets. From telling an idle story of magic and love's entangling eyes, Shakespeare has led us to contemplate the relationship between nature and the "art" of lovers and poets; he has led us to recognize the absurdity, privacy, and "truth" of human imagination.[4]

Hard on the heels of this questioning moment, comes talk of a masque or a play to "beguile / The lazy time" (5.1.40–41); this, it seems, is "where we came in." But for the "second time round" the perspective will be changed and we shall watch others watching the play. For us this will be the chief interest of the performance, for, having watched rehearsals, we know precisely the kind of play to expect; again it will be about love and again it will take place by moonlight, but this time the plot will end disastrously. Our interest will lie in whether or not the performance will also be disastrous.

The actors are fully confident; they are so sure of their make-believe that, for fear of frightening the ladies, they must take special precautions before they draw a sword or let their lion roar.[5] But we may doubt whether they will get any help from their text:

> . . . For in all the play
> There is not one word apt, one player fitted.

> (64–65)

As with the pageant at the end of *Love's Labor's Lost*, the actors are at the mercy of their audience, their success

---

[4] The beginning of Act 5, which gives this new perspective, shows signs of revision; Sir Walter Greg believes that it represents Shakespeare's last touches to his play before handing it over to the book-keeper in the theater (*First Folio* [1955], p. 242).

[5] Cf.3.1.9–46.

depending on the audience's ability to be sufficiently generous, gentle, and humble to "bestow . . . the sense of hearing."[6] We cannot be confident of the outcome. Theseus has previously "pick'd a welcome" from the silence of those who, having prepared entertainment for him, have throttled

> . . . their practiced accent in their fears,
> And, in conclusion, dumbly have broke off,
> Not paying me a welcome.
>
> (97–99)

but he is also apt to measure lovers' fancies and "antique fables" by the comprehension of "cool reason." As for the young lovers, we know that they are inclined to believe their own dreams, but we have no proof that they will accept in generosity all that "simpleness and duty tender" (83).

In the event the actors put their faith, as the lovers had done before them, in the "truth" of their fiction:

> Gentles, perchance you wonder at this show;
> But wonder on, till *truth* make all things plain.
>
> (127–28)

and again:

> This loam, this roughcast, and this stone, doth show
> That I am that same wall; the *truth* is so. . . .
>
> (161–62)

But the response wavers, and Bottom has to interfere to correct a wrong impression:

> The wall, methinks, being sensible, should curse again.

> No, in *truth,* sir, he should not. "Deceiving me" is Thisby's cue. She is to enter now, . . . You shall see it will fall pat as I told you.
>
> (182–87)

---

[6] *Love's Labor's Lost*, 5.2.669–70.

Bottom's faith is invincible, but he cannot ensure success, and Hippolyta judges frankly that the play is "the silliest stuff" that she has ever heard (211).

At this point Theseus reminds them all of the nature of their entertainment:

> The best in this kind are but shadows; and the worst are no worse, if imagination amend them.
>
> It must be your imagination then, and not theirs.
>
> If we imagine no worse of them than they of themselves, they may pass for excellent men.   (212–17)

In this spirit, Theseus welcomes the entering actors:

> Here come two noble beasts in, a man and a lion.   (218)

The actors struggle to the end of their play: Moon, unable to complete his prepared speech by reason of the reception he is given, gamely, if somewhat tetchily, substitutes his own less fanciful words; Bottom, with even more fortitude, leaves off talking once, as Pyramus, he is supposed to be dead, and he waits until the play is done before he rises to correct his audience and offer an epilogue.

So, unlike the pageant of the Worthies, the "tedious brief scene" of Pyramus and Thisbe is completed. Theseus refused the epilogue:

> No epilogue, I pray you; for your play needs no excuse. Never excuse, for when the players are all dead, there need none to be blamed.   (357–59)

"Truly" it has been a "fine tragedy" (362) and the players can celebrate with a Bergomask, a joyful country dance which is natural to their elation and abilities. Then Theseus must recall the lovers from the fiction they have been watching:

> The iron tongue of midnight hath told twelve.
> Lovers, to bed; 'tis almost fairy time.
>
>   (365–66)

The "palpable-gross play" has beguiled the time, and they must now to their own parts. And as they file off in due order for the next scene, the fairies enter from the enchanted wood and, following them, bring blessing on their action.

If one wished to describe the judgment which informs *A Midsummer Night's Dream*, one might do so very simply: the play suggests that lovers, like lunatics, poets, and actors, have their own "truth" which is established as they see the beauty of their beloved, and that they are confident in this truth for, although it seems the "silliest stuff" to an outsider, to them it is quite reasonable; it also suggests that lovers, like actors, need, and sometimes ask for, our belief, and that this belief can only be given if we have the generosity and imagination to think "no worse of them than they of themselves."

The play's greatest triumph is the manner in which our wavering acceptance of the illusion of drama is used as a kind of flesh-and-blood image of the acceptance which is appropriate to the strange and private "truth" of those who enact the play of love. By using this living image, Shakespeare has gone beyond direct statement in words or action and has presented his judgment in terms of a mode of being, a relationship, in which we, the audience, are actually involved. And he has ensured that this image is experienced at first hand, for the audience of the play-within-the-play does not make the perfect reaction; one of them describes what this entails but it is left for us to make that description good. The success of the play will, finally, depend upon our reaction to its shadows.[7]

---

[7] So Puck assures us; cf.5.1.425–40.

FRANK KERMODE

A Midsummer Night's Dream

A Midsummer Night's Dream opens with a masterly
scene which, as usual in the earlier Shakespeare, establishes
and develops a central thematic interest. The accusation
against Lysander is that he has corrupted the fantasy of
Hermia (32), and the disorders of fantasy (imagination) are
the main topic of the play. Hermia complains that her father
cannot see Lysander with her eyes; Theseus in reply requires
her to subordinate her eyes to her father's judgment (56–57)
or pay the penalty. She is required to 'fit her fancies to her
father's will'. All withdraw save Lysander and Hermia, who
utter a small litany of complaint against the misfortunes of
love: 'So quick bright things come to confusion'(149). This
recalls not only *Romeo and Juliet* but also *Venus and Adonis*
(the whole passage from 1.720 to 1.756 is related to *Midsummer Night's Dream*). This lament of 'poor Fancy's followers' (155) gives way easily to their plot of elopement.
Helena enters, in her turn complaining of ill-fortune; for
Demetrius prefers Hermia's eyes to hers. Hermia leaves:
'We must starve our sight / From lovers' food till morrow
deep midnight' (222–23). Lysander, remembering that Helena 'dotes / Devoutly dotes, dotes in idolatry' (108–09) on
Demetrius, departs, expressing a wish that Demetrius will
come to 'dote' on Helena as she on him (225). The repetition
of the word 'dote', the insistence that the disordered con-
dition of the imagination which is called 'love' originates
in eyes uncontrolled by judgment; these are hammered
home in the first scene, and the characteristic lamentations
about the brevity and mortality of love are introduced like

Pp. 214–20 of Kermode's "The Mature Comedies," in *Stratford-upon-
Avon Studies: 3, Early Shakespeare*, ed. John Russell Brown and Bernard
Harris (London: Edward Arnold, 1961), pp. 211–27.

a 'second subject' in a sonata. Finally Helena moralizes emblematically:

> And as he [Demetrius] errs, doting on Hermia's eyes,
> So I, admiring of his qualities.
> Things base and vile, holding no quantity,
> Love can transpose to form and dignity.
> Love looks not with the eyes, but with the mind,
> And therefore is wing'd Cupid painted blind.
> Nor hath Love's mind of any judgment taste;
> Wings, and no eyes, figure unheedy haste:
> And therefore is Love said to be a child . . .
>
> (230–38)

In love the eye induces 'doting', not a rational, patient pleasure like that of Theseus and Hippolyta. Helena is making a traditional complaint against the blind Cupid;[1] love has nothing to do with value, is a betrayal of the quality of the high sense of sight, and is therefore depicted blind, irresponsible, without judgment. Later we shall see the base and vile so transformed; love considered as a disease of the eye will be enacted in the plot. But so will the contrary interpretation of 'blind Love'; that it is a higher power than sight; indeed, above intellect. *Amor . . . sine oculis dicitur, quia est supra intellectum.*[2]

The themes of the play are thus set forth in the opening scene. Love-fancy as bred in the eye is called a kind of doting; this is held to end in disasters of the kind that overtook Adonis, Romeo, Pyramus; and the scene ends with an ambiguous emblem of blind love. The next scene introduces the play of the mechanicals, which, in a recognizably Shakespearian manner, gives farcical treatment to an important thematic element; for Bottom and his friends will perform a play to illustrate the disastrous end of doting, of love brought to confusion. Miss Mahood has spoken of Shakespeare's ensuring that in *Romeo and Juliet* 'our final emotion is neither the satisfaction we should feel in the lovers' death if the play were a simple expression of the *Liebestod* theme, nor

---

[1] See E. Panofsky, *Studies in Iconology* (1939), pp. 122–3, and p. 122, n.74.
[2] Pico della Mirandola, quoted in Wind, *Pagan Mysteries of the Renaissance* (1958), p. 56.

the dismay of seeing two lives thwarted and destroyed by vicious fates, but a tragic equilibrium which includes and transcends both these feelings'[3]; and in *Midsummer Night's Dream* we are given a comic equilibrium of a similar kind. The 'moral' of the play is not to be as simple as, say, that of Bacon's essay 'Of Love': there it is said to be unreasonable that a man, 'made for the contemplation of heaven and all noble objects, should do nothing but kneel before a little idol, and make himself subject, though not of the mouth (as beasts are) yet of the eye, which was given them for higher purposes'. Shakespeare's conclusion has not the simplicity of this: 'Nuptial love maketh mankind; friendly love perfecteth it; but wanton love corrupteth and embaseth it.' Yet, for the moment, the theme is blind love; and the beginning of the second act takes us into the dark woods. If we are willing to listen to such critics as C. L. Barber,[4] we shall take a hint from the title of the play and attend to the festival licence of young lovers in midsummer woods. Also we shall remember how far the woods are identified with nature, as against the civility of the city; and then we shall have some understanding of the movement of the plot. Puck is certainly a 'natural' force; a power that takes no account of civility or rational choice. He is, indeed, a blinding Cupid; and the passage in which he is, as it were, cupidinized is so famous for other reasons that its central significance is overlooked:

> That very time I saw, but thou couldst not,
> Flying between the cold moon and the earth,
> Cupid all arm'd. A certain aim he took
> At a fair vestal thronèd by the west,
> And loosed his love shaft smartly from his bow,
> As it should pierce a hundred thousand hearts.
> But I might see young Cupid's fiery shaft
> Quenched in the chaste beams of the wat'ry moon,
> And the imperial vot'ress passèd on,
> In maiden meditation, fancy-free.
> Yet marked I where the bolt of Cupid fell.
> It fell upon a little western flower,

[3] *Shakespeare's Wordplay* (1957), p. 72
[4] *Shakespeare's Festive Comedy* (Princeton U.P. 1959).

> Before milk-white, now purple with love's wound,
> And maidens call it love-in-idleness.
> Fetch me that flow'r; the herb I showed thee once:
> The juice of it on sleeping eyelids laid
> Will make or man or woman madly dote
> Upon the next live creature that it sees.
>
> (2.1. 155–72)

The juice used by Puck to bring confusion to the darkling lovers is possessed of all the force of Cupid's arrow, and is applied with equal randomness. The eye so touched will dote; in it will be engendered a fancy 'for the next live thing it sees'. Puck takes over the role of blind Cupid. The love he causes is a madness; the flower from which he gets his juice is called 'Love-in-*idleness*', and that word has the force of wanton behaviour amounting to madness. The whole object is to punish Titania 'and make her full of hateful fantasies' (258); and to end the naturally intolerable situation of a man's not wanting a girl who wants him (260–61). Puck attacks his task without moral considerations; Hermia and Lysander are lying apart from each other 'in human modesty' (2.2.57) but Puck has no knowledge of this and assumes that Hermia must have been churlishly rejected:

> Pretty soul! She durst not lie
> Near this lack-love, this kill-courtesy.
>
> (76–77)

Lysander awakes; his anointed eyes dote at once on the newly arrived Helena. He ingenuously attributes this sudden change to a sudden maturity:

> The will of man is by his reason swayed
> And reason says you are the worthier maid . . .
> Reason becomes the marshal to my will,
> And leads me to your eyes . . .
>
> (115–16, 120–21)

But in the next scene Bottom knows better: 'Reason and love keep little company nowadays'.

It is scarcely conceivable, though the point is disputed,

that the love-affair between Titania and Bottom is not an allusion to *The Golden Ass*. In the first place, the plot of Oberon is like that of the Cupid and Psyche episode, for Venus then employs Cupid to avenge her by making Psyche (to whom she has lost some followers) fall in love with some base thing. Cupid, at first a naughty and indecent boy, himself becomes Psyche's lover. On this story were founded many rich allegories; out of the wanton plot came truth in unexpected guise. And in the second place, Apuleius, relieved by the hand of Isis from his ass's shape, has a vision of the goddess, and proceeds to initiation in her mysteries. On this narrative of Apuleius, for the Renaissance half-hidden in the enveloping commentary of Beroaldus, great superstructures of platonic and Christian allegory had been raised; and there is every reason to suppose that these mysteries are part of the flesh and bone of *A Midsummer Night's Dream*.

The antidote by which the lovers are all restored 'to wanted sight' is 'virtuous' (3.2.367), being expressed from 'Dian's bud' (4.1.70), which, by keeping men chaste keeps them sane. So far the moral seems to be simple enough; the lovers have been subject to irrational forces; in the dark they have chopped and changed like the 'little dogs' of Dylan Thomas's story, though without injury to virtue. But they will awake, and 'all this derision / Shall seem a dream and fruitless vision' (3.2.370–1). Oberon pities the 'dotage' of Titania, and will 'undo / This hateful imperfection of her eyes' (4.1.65–66); she will awake and think all this 'the fierce vexation of a dream' (72) and Puck undoes the confusions of the young lovers. In the daylight they see well, and Demetrius even abjures the dotage which enslaved him to Hermia; his love for Helena returns as 'natural taste' returns to a man cured of a sickness (168 ff.). They return to the city and civility. All are agreed that their dreams were fantasies; that they have returned to health. But the final awakening of this superbly arranged climax (as so often in the mature Shakespearian comedy it occurs at the end of the fourth act) is Bottom's. And here the 'moral' defies comfortable analysis; we suddenly leave behind the neat love-is-a-kind-of-madness pattern and discover that there is more to ideas-in-poetry than ideas and verse.

I have had a most rare vision. I have had a dream, past the wit
of man to say what dream it was. Man is but an ass, if he go
about to expound this dream . . . The eye of man hath not heard,
the ear of man hath not seen, man's hand is not able to taste, his
tongue to conceive, nor his heart to report, what my dream was.

(207–10, 214–17)

It must be accepted that this is a parody of I Corinthians ii. 9 ff.:

Eye hath not seen, nor ear heard, neither have entered into the
heart of man the things which God hath prepared for them that
love him . . .
Which things also we speak, not in the words which man's
wisdom teacheth, but which the Holy Ghost teacheth . . .

Apuleius, after his transformation, might not speak of the
initiation he underwent; but he was vouchsafed a vision of the
goddess Isis. St. Paul was initiated into the religion he
had persecuted by Ananias in Damascus. What they have in
common is transformation, and an experience of divine love.
Bottom has known the love of the triple goddess in a vision.
His dream is of a different quality from the others'; they
have undergone what in the Macrobian division (*Comm. in
Somm. Scip.*, I. 3) is called the *phantasma*: Brutus glosses
this as 'a hideous dream' (*J. Caesar*, 2.1.65). But Bottom's
dream is *oneiros* or *somnium*; ambiguous, enigmatic, of high
import. And this is the contrary interpretation of blind love;
the love of God or of Isis, a love beyond the power of the
eyes. To Pico, to Cornelius Agrippa, to Bruno, who distinguished nine kinds of fruitful love-blindness, this exaltation
of the blindness of love was both Christian and Orphic;
Orpheus said that love was eyeless; St. Paul and David that
God dwelt in darkness and beyond knowledge.[5] Bottom is
there to tell us that the blindness of love, the dominance of
the mind over the eye, can be interpreted as a means to grace
as well as to irrational animalism; that the two aspects are,
perhaps, inseparable.

The last Act opens with the set piece of Theseus on the
lunatic, the lover, and the poet. St. Paul speaks of the

[5] E. Wind, *op. cit.*, pp. 57 ff.

'hidden wisdom' 'which none of the princes of this world
know', which must be spoken of 'in a mystery'; and which
may come out of the learned ignorance of 'base things of
the world, . . . which . . . God hath chosen' (I Cor., ii). Theseus cannot understand these matters. In lunatics, lovers
and poets, the imagination is out of control; it is the power
that makes 'things unknown', as, so this orthodox psy-
chologist implies, these are the disordered creations of the
faculty when reason, whether because of love or lunacy or
the poetic *furor*, is not in charge of it. The doubts of Hippolyta (5.1.23 ff.) encourage us to believe that this 'prince
of the world' may be wrong. The love of Bottom's vision
complements the rational love of Theseus; Bottom's play,
farcical as it is, speaks of the disasters that do not cease to
happen but only become for a moment farcically irrelevant,
on a marriage day. 'Tragical mirth . . . hot ice and wondrous strange snow' are terms not without their relevance;
and the woods have their wisdom as well as the city.

Thus, without affectation, one may suggest the *skopos* of
A Midsummer Night's Dream—the thematic preoccupation,
the characteristic bursting through into action of what seems
a verbal trick only (the talk of eyes). Unless we see that these
mature comedies are thematically serious we shall never get
them right. And it might even be added that *A Midsummer
Night's Dream* is more serious in this way than *Cymbeline*,
because the patterns of sight and blindness, wood and city,
phantasma and vision, grow into a large and complex statement, or an emblematic presentation not to be resolved into
its component parts, of love, vulgar and celestial. I should
here mention the excellent essay on this play by Paul A.
Olsen[6] who interprets the Macrobian dreams differently, and
pays no attention to Apuleius or the imagery of eyes; on the
other hand he has much to say about Oberon, the themes of
conventional marriage entertainments, and the contrast
between sensuality and married love. My own feeling is that
he sacrifices too much to the view that *A Midsummer Night's*

---

[6] 'A Midsummer Night's Dream and the meaning of court marriage'
(*English Literary History* [1957] pp. 95–119). Many of the points I make
above are made by Mr. Olsen (I may mention that my own reading is one I
have developed in lectures; this is to some extent a concurrence of independent testimony).

Dream is a very courtly play, and I do not think that we ever find in Shakespeare the kind of allegory he is looking for; he makes *A Midsummer Night's Dream* a slightly more diffuse *Hymenaei*. At present, however, the comedies may stand to lose less by over- than by under-interpretation, and Olsen's is one of the best essays on a Shakespearian comedy I have ever read. One may hope that it will be influential, but that others may point to simpler meanings that are overlooked because of our bondage to an old tradition: the tradition of Shakespeare's 'natural' genius, still potent in respect of the earlier comedies, and still capable of preventing us from studying him as an artist.

LINDA BAMBER

The Status of the Feminine
in Shakespearean Comedy

The best example of the relationship between male dominance and the status quo comes in *A Midsummer Night's
Dream*, which begins with a rebellion of the feminine against
the power of masculine authority. Hermia refuses the man both
Aegeus and Theseus order her to marry; her refusal sends us off
into the forest, beyond the power of the father and the masculine state. Once in the forest, of course, we find the social situation metaphorically repeated in this world of imagination and
nature. The fairy king, Oberon, rules the forest. His rule, too, is
troubled by the rebellion of the feminine. Titania has refused to
give him her page, the child of a human friend who died in
childbirth. But by the end of the story Titania is conquered, the
child relinquished, and order restored. Even here the comic
upheavals, whether we see them as May games or bad dreams,
are associated with an uprising of women. David P. Young, in
Something of Great Constancy, has pointed out how firmly this
play connects order with masculine dominance and the disruption of order with the rebellion of the feminine:

> It is appropriate that Theseus, as representative of daylight and
> right reason, should have subdued his bride-to-be to the rule of
> his masculine will. That is the natural order of things. It is
> equally appropriate that Oberon, as king of darkness and fan-
> tasy, should have lost control of his wife, and that the corre-
> sponding natural disorder dscribed by Titania should ensue.

Reprinted (slightly adapted, with the author's permission) from Linda
Bamber, *Cosmic Women, Tragic Men* (Stanford, Cal.: Stanford University
Press, 1982), pp. 29–31.

The natural order, the status quo, is for men to rule women. When they fail to do so, we have the exceptional situation, the festive, disruptive, disorderly moment of comedy.

A Midsummer Night's Dream is actually an anomaly among the festive comedies. It is unusual for the forces of the green world to be directed, as they are here, by a masculine figure. Because the green world here is a partial reproduction of the social world, the feminine is reduced to a kind of first cause of the action while a masculine power directs it. In the other festive comedies the feminine Other presides. She does not *command* the forces of the alternative world, as Oberon does, but since she acts in harmony with these forces her will and desire often prevail.

Where are we to bestow our sympathies? On the forces that make for the disruption of the status quo and therefore for the plot? Or on the force that asserts itself against the disruption and reestablishes a workable social order? Of course we cannot choose. We can only say that in comedy we owe our holiday to such forces as the tendency of the feminine to rebel, whereas to the successful reassertion of masculine power we owe our everyday order. Shakespearean comedy endorses both sides. Holiday is, of course, the subject and the analogue of each play; but the plays always end in a return to everyday life. The optimistic reading of Shakespearean comedy says that everyday life is clarified and enriched by our holiday from it; according to the pessimistic reading the temporary subversion of the social order has revealed how much that order excludes, how high a price we pay for it. But whether our return to everyday life is a comfortable one or not, the return itself is the inevitable conclusion to the journey out.

Does this make the comedies sexist? Is the association of women with the disruption of the social order an unconscious and insulting projection? It seems to begin as such; but the feminine in Shakespearean comedy quickly develops from the shrew (who must be put in her place) to the comic heroine (who is associated with a positive kind of subversion). The shrew's rebellion directly challenges masculine authority, whereas the comic heroine merely presides over areas of experience to which masculine authority is irrelevant. But the shrew is essentially powerless against the social system, whereas the comic heroine is in alliance with forces that can never be finally overcome. The shrew is defeated by the superior strength, physical and social, of a man, or by women who support the status quo. She provokes a battle of the sexes, and the outcome of this battle, from Shakespeare's point of view, is inevitable. The comic heroine, on the other hand, does not fight the system but merely surfaces, again and again, when and where the social system is temporarily subverted. The comic heroine does not actively resist the social and political hegemony of the men, but in alliance with the Saturnalian forces she successfully competes for our favor with the (masculine) representatives of the social Self. The development of the feminine from the shrew to the comic heroine indicates a certain consciousness on the author's part of sexual politics; and it indicates a desire, at least, to create conditions of sexual equality within the drama even while reflecting the unequal conditions of men and women in the society at large.

CAMILLE WELLS SLIGHTS

From Shakespeare's Comic Commonwealths

In *A Midsummer Night's Dream*, distinct groups pursuing their own objectives, influenced by distinct values, largely unaware of each other's existence, yet operating within the same sphere of time and place and interacting occasionally and crucially, enact ... an agreement. Social harmony is achieved not by the triumph of passionate youth over oppressive age nor by the vindication of established hierarchy and the exorcism of disobedience but by unequal voices agreeing together. The social hierarchy disrupted in the first scene is reasserted in the denouement: Theseus assumes control and the young lovers defer to him. But it is the fact that Demetrius has been brought to see differently that has turned hatred and jealousy into 'gentle concord' (4.1.143). Oberon's machinations and Theseus' blessing contribute, but the existence of diversity rather than the benevolence of authority makes possible the consensual marriages that constitute the happy ending.

In addition, while Theseus' authoritative voice is necessary to legitimize these marriages, his overruling of Egeus implicitly acknowledges that his power rests ultimately on the cooperation of those he governs.[1] When Hermia and Lysander are pitted against Egeus and Demetrius, Theseus cannot resolve the conflict and defers to the law, but when

From Camille Wells Slights, *Shakespeare's Comic Commonwealths* (University of Toronto, 1993), pp. 122–24. Reprinted by permission of University of Toronto Press Incorporated.

[1] Simultaneous belief in the need for social hierarchy and in government by consent, or at least government with due respect for community values and customs, was common in early modern England. See J. P. Sommerville, *Politics and Ideology in England, 1603–1640* (London: Longman, 1986), Chapter 2, 'Government by consent'; David Underdown, *Revel, Riot, and Rebellion: Popular Politics and Culture in England, 1603–1660* (Oxford: Clarendon Press, 1985), Chapter 5, 'Popular Politics before the Civil War.'

the lovers have reached a mutually satisfying arrangement, he casually dismisses Egeus' demand for the law. His authoritative voice is a recognition of a *fait accompli,* an articulation of the lovers' desires. The emergence of harmony from discord thus requires mutuality as well as diversity. As La Primaudaye makes the point 'every commonwealth well appointed and ordred ... consisting of many and sundry subjects, is maintained by their unity, being brought to be of one consent and wil, and to communicate their works, artes and exercises together for common benefit and profit.'[2] On the one hand, social harmony depends not on establishing truth but on differing perceptions: what matters is not the objective merits of Hermia and Helena but that Lysander and Demetrius love different women. On the other hand, a sense of community requires a shared perception of reality. As Theseus observes, love, like lunacy and poetry, results from the unverifiable perceptions of individual imagination, but, as Hippolyta reminds him, because the lovers all give the same account of their experience, their testimony represents more than the perception of an individual imagination: their story 'grows to something of great constancy' (5.1.26). Hippolyta's reference to constancy, often cited as an intuitive faith in the lovers' fidelity, taken literally, demonstrates faith in numbers.[3] Bottom's story, which cannot be corroborated, remains untold and inaccessible to the community at large, but the coincidence of the lovers' perceptions increases the probability of truth, or at least of a socially usable version of reality. The resolution of the courtship plot, then, does not endorse established authority: Theseus merely ratifies the arrangement the lovers

[2] La Primaudaye, *French Academie,* 744.
[3] David Young's discussion of the exchange between Theseus and Hippolyta about the lovers' account of their night in the woods argues that the play undercuts the traditional dichotomy between reason and imagination. Young points out the humor of Theseus' dismissing the means by which he himself exists but does not mention the comedy inherent in Hippolyta's argument for the lovers' credibility. Concurring testimony was a criterion associated with the new empirical and probabilistic approach to knowledge, which was often hostile to the fictitious and imaginary. See David Young, *Something of Great Constancy: The Art of 'A Midsummer Night's Dream'* (New Haven: Yale University Press, 1966), 126–41, and Barbara J. Shapiro, *Probability and Certainty in Seventeenth-Century England* (Princeton: Princeton University Press, 1983), passim.

have made. Nor does it constitute a triumph of individual subjectivity: his ratification is contingent on 'all their minds [being] transfigur'd so together' (24).

The performance of *The most lamentable comedy and most cruel death of Pyramus and Thisby* demonstrates the dynamics of a unified society in which 'sundry subjects . . . communicate their works, artes and exercises together for common benefit.' As Stephen Orgel and others have taught us, such courtly interludes celebrate the established power structure,[4] and indeed, throughout the play the activities of Peter Quince and his fellows are directed towards the noble wedding. Unlike the amateur theatrical in *Love's Labor's Lost,* Peter Quince's production is a success because Duke Theseus magnanimously accepts it as an offering of 'simpleness and duty' (83) and because the audience's wit at the actors' expense consists of *sotte voce* jokes to each other rather than jibes intended to humiliate the actors. But although the characters gathered to celebrate the multiple weddings are animated by mutual goodwill and a common purpose, the barriers between groups remain. The actors of Pyramus' 'tedious brief scene' (56) retain their composure while those in the Pageant of the Worthies lose theirs, not simply because their audience is kinder but because they are protected by their incomprehension of sophisticated discourse. Bottom interprets literally and responds condescendingly to the ironic remarks he hears. The aristocratic audience is similarly limited. They show no grasp of the relevance to their own lives of the drama of tragic love. Theseus is incapable of imagining that Bottom, the workingman whom he patronizes so graciously, also has been loved by the Fairy Queen. Nor does he understand that the motives of love and duty he attributes to the tradesmen are actually subordinate to financial ambition. By honoring the Duke they hope to prosper, and by trying to prosper they honor the Duke. The wall that divides Pyramus and Thisby and courteously produces a chink for them to talk through is thus an apt image for the cultural differences between Athenians.

[4]Stephen Orgel, *The Illusion of Power: Political Theater in the English Renaissance* (Berkeley: University of California Press, 1975).

The barrier that separates also joins and can allow limited communication.

The performance in the last scene epitomizes the strategy used throughout the play. Just as the spectators who critically watch the play-within-the-play constitute a spectacle that the theater audience watches critically, so the text continually invites critical scrutiny of the social hierarchy and cultural traditions that its comic structure endorses. Finally, the audience, who have been in the position of privileged spectators aware of all the secret workings of fairy magic beyond the characters' comprehension, is reminded by Puck's epilogue both that their experience has been totally dependent on the efforts of the figures on stage and that as audience they have the power to judge. That is, the theatrical experience, like other social experiences, consists of sundry subjects communicating together.

SYLVAN BARNET

A *Midsummer Night's Dream*
on Stage and Screen

In the last few decades, the productions of *A Midsumme
Night's Dream* that have aroused the most interest are th
ones that have emphasized the dark aspects of the comedy
This concern with "the fierce vexation of a dream'
(Oberon's words in 4.1.72) makes a marked contrast witl
the sweet, opulent productions that from the middle of the
nineteenth century until the second decade of the twentietl
century prettified the play with butterfly-winged chil
fairies, gauzy sets, and Mendelssohn's music. When The
seus smoothly says to Hippolyta, "I wooed thee with m
sword," directors and spectators—heirs to Brecht, and t
Artaud's Theater of Cruelty—can easily perceive the vio
lence of rape. And so a play that a century ago was though
to be an airy trifle, full of high jinks and lovely sentiment
about love, is now seen largely as an image of brutality
Thus, in John Hancock's production (San Francisco, 1965
New York 1967), Hippolyta in leopard skins was brough
onstage as a captive, Hermia was a transvestite, Demetriu
wore an electrified codpiece; the emphasis was on th
malevolence of the fairies, and the cruelty and lust of th
humans. Mendelssohn's music was used—but ironically
since it blared from a jukebox.

It is not puzzling that our time should emphasize the eroti
cism and the violence of the play, just as it is not puzzlin
that the second half of the nineteenth century emphasize
the lyricism; what is puzzling is that *A Midsummer Night'
Dream*—Shakespeare's play as opposed to operatic ver
sions of it—was in effect banished from the theater from th
second half of the seventeenth century until 1840, whe

Madame Vestris staged a fairly full text at Covent Garden in London. For instance, J. P. Kemble's version, produced at Covent Garden in 1816, on the one hand was heavily cut and on the other hand was amplified with songs and with a good deal of spectacle. Further, Kemble's production changed the structure of the piece: the play of *Pyramus and Thisby* was given *before* the two pairs of Athenian lovers were united, so that Shakespeare's play could conclude with a pageant showing the "Triumphs of Theseus," which included "the Cretans, the Amazons, the Centaurs, the Minotaur, Ariadne in the Labyrinth, the Mysterious Peplum or Veil of Minerva, the Ship Argo, and the Golden Fleece." The assumption in the early nineteenth century was that Shakespeare's *A Midsummer Night's Dream* was a "closet drama," a play that could be enjoyed only when read in one's private chamber. On the stage, the imaginative poetry vanished, and all that was left was the mechanical trickery of carpenters. Thus, William Hazlitt said of the 1816 production:

> All that is fine in the play was lost in the representation. The spirit was evaporated, the genius was fled. . . .

And, still Hazlitt:

> Poetry and the stage do not agree together. The attempt to rec-oncile them fails not only of effect, but of decorum. The *ideal* has no place upon the stage. . . . That which is merely an airy shape, a dream, a passing thought, immediately becomes an unmanageable reality.

When *A Midsummer Night's Dream* was first published, in 1600, the text announced that the play "hath been sundry times publiquely acted." The assertion is probably true, but there are no records of these public performances. A letter of January 15, 1604, referring to the performance at court on January 1, 1604, of a "play called Robin good-fellow," is all there is before the Puritans closed the theaters in 1642.

Curiously, during the period when the theaters were offi-cially closed (1642–1660), *A Midsummer Night's Dream* seems to have led a surreptitious life in an extract entitled

The Merry Conceited Humors of Bottom the Weaver. The fact that this abridgment was made, and presumably performed under severely limited conditions, suggests that *A Midsummer Night's Dream* had a considerable prior reputation, but we cannot go much further. When the theaters reopened, after the restoration of Charles II, *A Midsummer Night's Dream* was staged in 1662. We do not know in what ways the text may have been cut or amplified, but we do know that Samuel Pepys recorded his impression of the production. He regarded it as "the most insipid ridiculous play that ever I saw in my life," but he also noted that he saw "some good dancing and some handsome women." The earliest Elizabethan spectators might also have commented approvingly on the "good dancing" and even on the "handsome women" (though these "women" would have been played by boys), but in view of the later history of operatic versions of *A Midsummer Night's Dream*, we can allow for the possibility that what Pepys saw was already some sort of musical adaptation of the play. In any case, in 1692 Henry Purcell's operatic version, *The Fairy Queen*, was given in London. Chiefly a series of masques, it retained only 750 lines of Shakespeare's 2,100. For instance, in the second act, Shakespeare's rustics and fairies are complemented by the spirits of Night, Mystery, Secrecy, and Sleep, who sing Titania to sleep; the Seasons appear in the fourth act, and in the fifth act, which concludes the opera, we get "Chinese men and women. A chorus of Chinese. A dance of six monkeys. An entry of a Chinese man and woman. A grand dance of twenty-four Chineses."

In the eighteenth century various operatic adaptations were made, but the original play was not staged. Even David Garrick, who did much to restore Shakespeare's texts to the stage, in 1755 produced a musical version called *The Fairies*, which used fewer than 600 of Shakespeare's lines. In 1840, however, Madame Lucia Vestris restored much of Shakespeare's text. Although she still left but some four hundred lines, retained some of the added songs, introduced to the London stage Mendelssohn's full score (the overture, written for a German production in 1827, had already been heard in a London production of 1833), cast women for

Oberon and Puck (she herself played Oberon, in a knee-length blue tunic), and put considerable emphasis on spectacle, her production nevertheless represented a serious effort to get back to Shakespeare's play. This version, enthusiastically received, seemed (at least to many critics) an ample refutation of Hazlitt's view that *A Midsummer Night's Dream* is a closet drama.

Madame Vestris's *A Midsummer Night's Dream* served as the basis for all productions of the play until Harley Granville-Barker's uncut version of 1914. Her immediate successors were Samuel Phelps, who, using Mendelssohn's music, staged *A Midsummer Night's Dream* in 1853, and Charles Kean, who staged it in 1856. Although Kean cut the text more heavily than did Vestris or Phelps—he reduced it to about 1,100 lines—his production is of some interest because he tried to represent Athens with an historically accurate set, though because he believed that the Athens of Theseus's time was too crude, his set showed the Parthenon.

Despite the importance of these mid-nineteenth-century productions, *A Midsummer Night's Dream* was not often staged in the second half of the century, or in the first decade of the twentieth, but such productions as there were (e.g. Augustin Daly's in 1888, Frank Benson's in 1889, and Beerbohm Tree's in 1900, 1905, and 1911) were chiefly praised for their spectacle. The live rabbits in Beerbohm Tree's forest seemed especially attention-getting. It was hard for a Victorian producer to resist the glories of stage machinery and especially of new techniques of lighting. The critic William Archer complained about Daly's Oberon: "When Oberon says 'I am invisible,' he seizes the opportunity to blaze forth like the Eddystone light." The spectacular conception of *A Midsummer Night's Dream* perhaps reached its height in the productions of Max Reinhardt, who staged it eleven times between 1905 and 1934 (at first in Germany, then in England, and finally in the United States), and whose 1935 film will be discussed later.

In 1914 Harley Granville-Barker produced *A Midsummer Night's Dream*, the third of his experimental productions of Shakespeare at the Savoy Theatre. In this, as in his earlier productions, Barker sought to keep the action moving, which means that he did not use cumbersome illusionistic scenery which would have delayed the play while sets were assembled and taken down. Instead, he relied chiefly on what he called "decorative" settings. Thus, the enchanted wood was not a world of real plants embedded in a mossy bank, Victorian style, but was represented by a grassy cloth, above which there hung, parallel to the ground, a floral wreath ten feet in diameter, with an inner wreath. A backcloth (green at the bottom, violet above) and broad bands of hanging cloth (green, blue, and violet) served to suggest (rather than to counterfeit) trees. Though some critics complained about the lack of illusionistic scenery, many found the sets attractive and recognized that these sets allowed the action to move without the usual long interruptions during which sets were changed; scene flowed into scene, and no scene had to be cut. Other departures from traditional productions of the *Dream* were Barker's use of males to play Puck and Oberon, his use of English folk tunes instead of Mendelssohn (this seems an obvious choice, but it was a novelty in 1914), and his use of actors who spoke in a natural rather than a declamatory style. Even more unusual was his text, an uncut version of Shakespeare's play. Perhaps most unusual of all, however, was his costuming of the fairies. Puck was a redheaded English hobgoblin, somewhat rustic and somewhat sinister; Oberon, Titania, and their followers were not the traditional butterflylike creatures, but were gilded and made to look somewhat like bronzed images (Barker pointed out that the text says they have "come from the farthest steep of India"). Furthermore, dressed and painted in gold, Titania and Oberon were played not by darling children but by adults who did not skip and flit about, but who, instead, moved somewhat mechanically, like marionettes. There was some talk about the influence of such Russian contemporaries as the designer Bakst and the dancer Nijinsky, and today we can see that Barker's production, however revolutionary it then seemed, was very much a product of its age. Yet this production was not simply of its age; in showing that Shakeapeare's play could be staged in an uncut text, Barker exerted a lasting influence.

One other point should be made about this production:

although the somewhat disconcerting metallic fairies may seem to anticipate the menacing bestial fairies of some productions of our own day, such as Alvin Epstein's Yale production of 1975, on the whole Barker's *Dream* was attractive rather than off-putting. The violent eroticism of recent productions was of course absent from the 1914 production, which was suitable for family entertainment.

Barker's version provoked divided critical opinion; the first production after his, W. Bridges-Adams's at the Stratford Memorial Theatre in 1919, restored Mendelssohn's music, and (returning to tradition) cast a woman in the role of Puck. And again the fairies were pretty children. For Bridges-Adams, Barker's production was sophisticated and arty, not at all what a country lad such as Shakespear would have wanted. Other post-Barker productions, too, have seemed to be pre-Barker in their use of a nineteenth-century style, but on the whole Barker left his mark on the play, and almost every production of the next fifty years was in one way or another a response to Barker's. For instance, when Harcourt Williams took over the direction of the Old Vic in 1929, he produced *A Midsummer Night's Dream* during his first season, with John Gielgud as Oberon. Williams, like Barker, required the actors to speak fairly rapidly, and, again like Barker, he used English folk tunes instead of Mendelssohn. His fairies, with lead-green faces, were dressed in seaweed rather than in the pretty costumes of the nineteenth century. In 1937 Tyrone Guthrie, however, reacting against what could now be thought of as the Harley Granville-Barker tradition, produced a rather Victorian and balletic *Midsummer Night's Dream*, with the dancer Robert Helpmann as Oberon, and with Vivien Leigh as Titania.

One production, however, neither echoed nor answered Barker: this was Louis Armstrong's and Benny Goodman's *Swingin' the Dream*, done in 1939 with a predominantly black cast that included Armstrong as Bottom, Butterfly McQueen as Puck, Maxine Sullivan as Titania, and the Dandridge Sisters as three fairies. The book was by Gilbert Seldes and Erik Charell, the locale was New Orleans in the late nineteenth century, and the scenery was indebted to Walt Disney. Despite all of this talent, it was unsuccessful, running for only thirteen performances.

The 1940s saw a good if rather traditional production directed by Nevill Coghill, with Peggy Ashcroft as Titania and Gielgud again as Oberon; the 1950s saw several productions, including George Devine's (1954) and Peter Hall's (1959). Devine's *A Midsummer Night's Dream*, though not especially well received, is interesting because of its birdlike fairies. These were not cute and fluffy, but were disturbing, beaky, rather reptilian things which foreshadowed the more sinister production of Michael Langham at the Old Vic in 1960 and the yet more sinister productions by John Hancock in San Francisco (1965) and by Liviu Ciulei in Minneapolis (1985). Hancock's has already been mentioned, and Ciulei's will be discussed in a moment.

When Peter Hall directed the play at Stratford in 1959 (he directed it again in 1962, and a film version in 1968), he sought to evoke something of the original production of the 1590s, whether it took place in a public theater or in an Elizabethan country house as part of a wedding ceremony. Hall used an apron stage with two balustraded staircases that led to a balcony at the rear. These constructions, which remained in view during the forest scenes, provided areas for the lovers and fairies to romp. And romp they did, in what was regarded as a clownish production, with Charles Laughton mugging as Bottom. Hall's 1962 version, with Judi Dench as Titania and Diana Rigg as Helena, used a fuller text, and was less farcical, more cynical, and better received.

In 1960, a year after Hall's first production, Benjamin Britten composed an operatic version that, unlike the eighteenth-century operatic versions, surely deserves to endure. Britten used only about half of Shakespeare's text, and he put almost all of the emphasis on the irrational behavior that takes place in the woods (the opera begins not with Theseus and Hippolyta in Athens, but with Puck and the fairies in the wood, and then shows Oberon quarreling with Titania), but he added almost no text. His opera is both a highly original work and a memorable interpretation of Shakespeare's play.

Of all the productions of Shakespeare's play since Barker's the most widely discussed was Peter Brook's Stratford version, given in 1970. Brook has said that he was influenced by Jan Kott's *Shakespeare Our Contemporary*, which emphasizes the night world of sex and violence. In the spirit of Kott, Brook said that Oberon furnishes Titania with "the crudest sex machine he can find"—though one might pedantically point out that Oberon doesn't choose Bottom, or anyone, for it is only by chance that Bottom enters Titania's line of sight. Curiously, given the stimulus of Kott, the production was in many ways attractive and elegant. The brightly lit box set, looking somewhat like a gymnasium, consisted of three white walls surrounded by a catwalk, with trapezes that allowed the actors to swing neatly through the air. The magic flower was not a flower but a plate spinning on a wand, passed from Oberon to Puck, and the whole evoked not only the world of gymnasts but of jugglers and circus folk.

The circus element was evident from the start; the entire company entered to a roll of drums, removed their white capes and revealed their costumes, with Theseus in purple, Hippolyta in green, and the lovers chiefly in white. The fairies wore gray pyjamalike garb, presumably to suggest their invisibility and their role as attendants. (Somewhat like roustabouts in a circus, they served as stagehands, for instance sweeping up confetti and agitating the metal coils that served as trees in the forest scene.) During the performance, actors who were not engaged in the action sometimes occupied the catwalk, observing what was happening below, again like performers in a circus. As early as 1948 Brook had criticized the tradition of associating *A Midsummer Night's Dream* with gauzes, ballet, and Mendelssohn. Later, in connection with his 1970 production, he said:

> Today we have no symbols that can conjure up fairyland and magic for a modern audience. On the other hand there are a number of actions that a performer can execute that are quite breathtaking. So we went to the art of the circus and the acrobat because they both make purely theatrical statements.

The theatricality was further emphasized by doubling: Theseus and Oberon were played by one performer, Hippolyta and Titania by another. (Oddly, this apparent innovation was used also in *Bottom the Weaver*, the mid-seventeenth-century abridgment of the play.) No effort was made to disguise the doubling; the costumes were changed onstage. The point of this doubling (which has become a convention in almost all productions after Brook's) apparently was to suggest 1) that the action in the wood was a fantasy of Theseus's and Hippolyta's, or, to put it a little differently, beneath the civilized exteriors of Theseus and Hippolyta are the irrationalities of Oberon and Titania: and 2) that the play is very much a play, a theatrical entertainment and not a realistic imitation of the real world.

Despite some critical grumbling about the strong sexuality of some scenes (at one point, when Bottom was carried off, one of his bearers thrust an arm out from between Bottom's legs, suggesting an enormous phallus), and despite the complaints that Kott's dark view inspired the production, there was much that was delightful and graceful. Even the joke of using Mendelssohn's wedding march while Bottom and Titania lolled in a hammock of ostrich feathers, as Puck and Oberon swung on trapezes, was good fun. At the end of the play, when the text calls for the fairies to bless the house, the entire cast left the stage, entered the aisles, and shook hands with members of the audience.

Most productions of *A Midsummer Night's Dream* are somewhat more traditional than Brook's, but the emphasis on anti-illusionism and on aggressive sexuality continue, and since 1964, when Kott's book was published in English, most productions have been influenced by Kott's vision of the play as a work concerned with violence and power. For instance, Liviu Ciulei at the Guthrie Theater in Minneapolis in 1985, and in Purchase, New York, in 1986, used a blood-red vinyl set in order, he said, to represent passion in a play about a society in which males dominate. His Hippolyta, a black woman, in an opening dumb show at first appeared in dark battle fatigues. Female attendants removed her clothes, tossed them onto a glowing brazier, and then wrapped her in white clothes taken from mannequins. (Thus Ciulei gave the play racial overtones too.) Theseus then entered and offered casual approval of the transformation of a passionate black into a tamed pseudo-white. Violence of a less subtle sort was provided by the switchblades of the lovers, which are more threatening to a twentieth-century audience than swords would have been.

The most recent production (1996–97) at the time of writing (1997), directed by Jonathan Miller at the Almeida Theatre, London, de-emphasizes the magic of the fairies, but in a way very different from Brook's. In Miller's production, the play was set in an aristocratic household in the 1930s. Theseus was the lord of the manner, the young women in love were debutantes, and the fairies were servants, costumed as butlers and bellboys in livery; Puck was a valet who wears white gloves. But if the fairies provided no magic, the set did. Entrances and exits were made through a wall of glass doors or panels that were sometimes transparent, sometimes translucent, and sometime reflecting, giving an air of uncertainty to the locale. At times, then, when a performer faced the audience one could also see the performer's back. The audience might well say with Hermia, "Methinks I see these things with parted eye, / When everything seems double" (4.1.192–93). Not surprisingly, "Smoke Gets in Your Eyes" was used for background music.

Two films of some importance have been made of the play, one by Max Reinhardt and William Dieterle in 1935, the other by Peter Hall in 1968. The Reinhardt-Dieterle version is especially distinguished for its ballet and its special effects in the Victorian tradition (Titania's attendants danced down a spiral moonbeam, and Oberon's disappeared into his cloak) and for its cast: the matinee idol Dick Powell played Lysander; other members of the cast included Olivia De Havilland (Hermia), Victor Jory (Oberon), Anita Louise (Titania), Mickey Rooney (Puck), Joe E. Brown (Flute), and James Cagney (Bottom). But despite Mendelssohn's score, the visual beauty (Reinhardt's emphasis), and the comedy, there is a good deal of darkness (usually attributed to Dieterle), especially in Jory's sinister Oberon and in Oberon's bat-winged attendants. The film in some ways is a remarkable precursor of the post-World War II productions, but in this it is not unprecedented, for something of the dark view can be found even as early as the end of the eighteenth century, in paintings of *A Midsummer Night's Dream* by Henry Fuseli.

Peter Hall's film, made with the Royal Shakespeare Company, is less distinctive but is far more faithful to the text. (Reinhardt and Dieterle omitted at least half of Shakespeare's lines.) Because it was made with an eye toward showing it on television screens as well as in movie theaters, it chiefly uses medium shots and closeups (long shots don't work well on television), though Hall did include a few attempts at spectacle. The interiors evoke an English manor house of the seventeenth century, and the exteriors evoke rural England rather than Athens. A rather bestial Oberon (goat-bearded and satyr-horned) and green-skinned fairies help to keep the film from sentimentalizing the play.

Although Hall's film was in part made for television, the television version most widely circulated is the one made by the BBC in 1981, directed by Elijah Moshinsky. It uses what has been dubbed the BBC house style: Jacobean sets and costumes (a seventeenth-century library for some interiors), but there is also some spectacle in the scenes in the woods. Even these spectacular scenes, however, have a twentieth-century (rather than a nineteenth-century) feel; there are pools of water, but these pools are places in which lovers are dunked so that they may emerge bedraggled. Three other points about the BBC version: 1) Theseus's speech on the power of the imagination (5.1) is trimmed a bit, and it has been moved so that it immediately follows Bottom's soliloquy (4.1) about his dream; 2) Oberon treats Puck roughly, in a manner that suggests to many viewers a sado-masochistic relationship; 3) closeups and middle shots are especially used, which work better on TV than long shots do. There are, of course, some long shots, which often are used for tableau-like effects. The result is that the production as a whole seems rather static.

Surveying the stage history of *A Midsummer Night's Dream*, then, one is somewhat surprised to find that a play so favored by the late twentieth century, and so prettified by the nineteenth, was almost unknown to the stage of the seventeenth and eighteenth centuries. One finds, also, to one's pleasure, that although dark interpretations are now most popular, other interpretations are not lacking. In certain moods we can delight in Pepys's characterization of the play of the rustics ("the silliest stuff that ever I heard"), but directors, and audiences, continue to find the play, again in Hippolyta's words, "strange and admirable."

Bibliographic Note: For a brief but useful survey of productions through the centuries, see Jay Halio, *A Midsummer Night's Dream* (1994), a short book in a series called Shakespeare in Performance. For an eighty-page survey of the stage history, followed by the text of the play with abundant annotations indicating how passages were handled in various productions, see *A Midsummer Night's Dream*, ed. Trevor R. Griffiths (1996). Part of a small book, Roger Warren's *A Midsummer Night's Dream* (1983), in a series called Text and Performance, is devoted to relatively recent stage productions by Peter Hall, Peter Brook, Robin Phillips, and to Elijah Moshinsky's BBC television version. Brook's version is the subject of David Selbourne, *The Making of "A Midsummer Night's Dream"* (1982).

Among the useful studies of earlier productions are Gary Jay Williams on music and the stage history of *A Midsummer Night's Dream*, in *Yale / Theatre* 4 (1973), and Williams's essay on Madame Vestris's production, in *Theatre Survey* 18 (1977). Also on Vestris see Trevor Griffiths in *Shakespeare Quarterly* 30 (1979). On Granville-Barker, see J. L. Styan, *The Shakespeare Revolution* (1977), and Eric Salmon, *Granville Barker* (1983). On Max Reinhardt, especially his *Dream* of 1905, see J. L. Styan, *Max Reinhardt* (1982). *Peter Brook's Production of William Shakespeare's "A Midsummer Night's Dream" for the Royal Shakespeare Company* (1974) includes comments by Brook. On film versions, see Roger Manvell, *Shakespeare and the Film* (1979), and, on Hall's film, Michael Mullin in *Educational Theatre Journal* 27 (1975) and 28 (1976).

Shakespeare Quarterly (since 1950) and *Shakespeare Survey* (an annual since 1948) are valuable sources of contemporary reviews, and both publications include occasional scholarly articles on stage history.

Suggested References

The number of possible references is vast and grows alarmingly. (The *Shakespeare Quarterly* devotes one issue each year to a list of the previous year's work, and *Shakespeare Survey*—an annual publication—includes a substantial review of biographical, critical, and textual studies, as well as a survey of performances.) The vast bibliography is best approached through James Harner, *The World Shakespeare Bibliography on CD-Rom: 1900–Present*. The first release, in 1996, included more than 12,000 annotated items from 1990–93, plus references to several thousand book reviews, productions, films, and audio recordings. The plan is to update the publication annually, moving forward one year and backward three years. Thus, the second issue (1997), with 24,700 entries, and another 35,000 or so references to reviews, newspaper pieces, and so on, covered 1987–94.

Though no works are indispensable, those listed below have been found especially helpful. The arrangement is as follows:

The titles in the first five sections are accompanied by brief explanatory annotations.

1. Shakespeare's Times

Andrews, John F., ed. *William Shakespeare: His World, His Work, His Influence,* 3 vols. (1985). Sixty articles, dealing not only with such subjects as "The State," "The Church," "Law," "Science, Magic, and Folklore," but also with the plays and poems themselves and Shakespeare's influence (e.g., translations, films, reputation)

Byrne, Muriel St. Clare. *Elizabethan Life in Town and Country* (8th ed., 1970). Chapters on manners, beliefs, education, etc., with illustrations.

Dollimore, John, and Alan Sinfield, eds. *Political Shakespeare: New Essays in Cultural Materialism* (1985). Essays on such topics as the subordination of women and colonialism, presented in connection with some of Shakespeare's plays.

Greenblatt, Stephen. *Representing the English Renaissance* (1988). New Historicist essays, especially on connections between political and aesthetic matters, statecraft and stagecraft.

Joseph, B. L. *Shakespeare's Eden: the Commonwealth of England 1558–1629* (1971). An account of the social, political, economic, and cultural life of England.

Kernan, Alvin. *Shakespeare, the King's Playwright: Theater in the Stuart Court 1603–1613* (1995). The social setting and the politics of the court of James I, in relation to *Hamlet, Measure for Measure, Macbeth, King Lear, Antony and Cleopatra, Coriolanus,* and *The Tempest.*

Montrose, Louis. *The Purpose of Playing: Shakespeare and the Cultural Politics of the Elizabethan Theatre* (1996). A poststructuralist view, discussing the professional theater "within the ideological and material frameworks of Elizabethan culture and society," with an extended analysis of *A Midsummer Night's Dream.*

Mullaney, Steven. *The Place of the Stage: License, Play, and Power in Renaissance England* (1988). New Historicist analysis, arguing that popular drama became a cultural institution "only by . . . taking up a place on the margins of society."

Schoenbaum, S. *Shakespeare: The Globe and the World*

(1979). A readable, abundantly illustrated introductory book on the world of the Elizabethans.

Shakespeare's England, 2 vols. (1916). A large collection of scholarly essays on a wide variety of topics, e.g., astrology, costume, gardening, horsemanship, with special attention to Shakespeare's references to these topics.

2. Shakespeare's Life

Andrews, John F., ed. *William Shakespeare: His World, His Work, His Influence,* 3 vols. (1985). See the description above.

Bentley, Gerald E. *Shakespeare: A Biographical Handbook* (1961). The facts about Shakespeare, with virtually no conjecture intermingled.

Chambers, E. K. *William Shakespeare: A Study of Facts and Problems,* 2 vols. (1930). The fullest collection of data.

Fraser, Russell. *Young Shakespeare* (1988). A highly readable account that simultaneously considers Shakespeare's life and Shakespeare's art.

————. *Shakespeare: The Later Years* (1992).

Schoenbaum, S. *Shakespeare's Lives* (1970). A review of the evidence and an examination of many biographies, including those of Baconians and other heretics.

————. *William Shakespeare: A Compact Documentary Life* (1977). An abbreviated version, in a smaller format, of the next title. The compact version reproduces some fifty documents in reduced form. A readable presentation of all that the documents tell us about Shakespeare.

————. *William Shakespeare: A Documentary Life* (1975). A large-format book setting forth the biography with facsimiles of more than two hundred documents, and with transcriptions and commentaries.

3. Shakespeare's Theater

Astington, John H., ed. *The Development of Shakespeare's Theater* (1992). Eight specialized essays on theatrical companies, playing spaces, and performance.

Beckerman, Bernard. *Shakespeare at the Globe, 1599–1609* (1962). On the playhouse and on Elizabethan dramaturgy, acting, and staging.

Bentley, Gerald E. *The Profession of Dramatist in Shakespeare's Time* (1971). An account of the dramatist's status in the Elizabethan period.

————. *The Profession of Player in Shakespeare's Time, 1590–1642* (1984). An account of the status of members of London companies (sharers, hired men, apprentices, managers) and a discussion of conditions when they toured.

Berry, Herbert. *Shakespeare's Playhouses* (1987). Usefully emphasizes how little we know about the construction of Elizabethan theaters.

Brown, John Russell. *Shakespeare's Plays in Performance* (1966). A speculative and practical analysis relevant to all of the plays, but with emphasis on *The Merchant of Venice*, *Richard II*, *Hamlet*, *Romeo and Juliet*, and *Twelfth Night*.

————. *William Shakespeare: Writing for Performance* (1996). A discussion aimed at helping readers to develop theatrically conscious habits of reading.

Chambers, E. K. *The Elizabethan Stage*, 4 vols. (1945). A major reference work on theaters, theatrical companies, and staging at court.

Cook, Ann Jennalie. *The Privileged Playgoers of Shakespeare's London, 1576–1642* (1981). Sees Shakespeare's audience as wealthier, more middle-class, and more intellectual than Harbage (below) does.

Dessen, Alan C. *Elizabethan Drama and the Viewer's Eye* (1977). On how certain scenes may have looked to spectators in an Elizabethan theater.

Gurr, Andrew. *Playgoing in Shakespeare's London* (1987). Something of a middle ground between Cook (above) and Harbage (below).

————. *The Shakespearean Stage, 1579–1642* (2nd ed., 1980). On the acting companies, the actors, the playhouses, the stages, and the audiences.

Harbage, Alfred. *Shakespeare's Audience* (1941). A study of the size and nature of the theatrical public, emphasizing the representativeness of its working class and middle-class audience.

Hodges, C. Walter. *The Globe Restored* (1968). A conjectural restoration, with lucid drawings.

Hosley, Richard. "The Playhouses," in *The Revels History of Drama in English*, vol. 3, general editors Clifford Leech and T. W. Craik (1975). An essay of a hundred pages on the physical aspects of the playhouses.

Howard, Jane E. "Crossdressing, the Theatre, and Gender Struggle in Early Modern England," *Shakespeare Quarterly* 39 (1988): 418–40. Judicious comments on the effects of boys playing female roles.

Orrell, John. *The Human Stage: English Theatre Design, 1567–1640* (1988). Argues that the public, private, and court playhouses are less indebted to popular structures (e.g., innyards and bear-baiting pits) than to banqueting halls and to Renaissance conceptions of Roman amphitheaters.

Slater, Ann Pasternak. *Shakespeare the Director* (1982). An analysis of theatrical effects (e.g., kissing, kneeling) in stage directions and dialogue.

Styan, J. L. *Shakespeare's Stagecraft* (1967). An introduction to Shakespeare's visual and aural stagecraft, with chapters on such topics as acting conventions, stage groupings, and speech.

Thompson, Peter. *Shakespeare's Professional Career* (1992). An examination of patronage and related theatrical conditions.

———. *Shakespeare's Theatre* (1983). A discussion of how plays were staged in Shakespeare's time.

4. Shakespeare on Stage and Screen

Bate, Jonathan, and Russell Jackson, eds. *Shakespeare: An Illustrated Stage History* (1996). Highly readable essays on stage productions from the Renaissance to the present.

Berry, Ralph. *Changing Styles in Shakespeare* (1981). Discusses productions of six plays (*Coriolanus, Hamlet, Henry V, Measure for Measure, The Tempest,* and *Twelfth Night*) on the English stage, chiefly 1950–1980.

————. *On Directing Shakespeare: Interviews with Contemporary Directors* (1989). An enlarged edition of a book first published in 1977, this version includes the seven interviews from the early 1970s and adds five interviews conducted in 1988.

Brockbank, Philip, ed. *Players of Shakespeare: Essays in Shakespearean Performance* (1985). Comments by twelve actors, reporting their experiences with roles. See also the entry for Russell Jackson (below).

Bulman, J. C., and H. R. Coursen, eds. *Shakespeare on Television* (1988). An anthology of general and theoretical essays, essays on individual productions, and shorter reviews, with a bibliography and a videography listing cassettes that may be rented.

Coursen, H. P. *Watching Shakespeare on Television* (1993). Analyses not only of TV versions but also of films and videotapes of stage presentations that are shown on television.

Davies, Anthony, and Stanley Wells, eds. *Shakespeare and the Moving Image: The Plays on Film and Television* (1994). General essays (e.g., on the comedies) as well as essays devoted entirely to *Hamlet*, *King Lear*, and *Macbeth*.

Dawson, Anthony B. *Watching Shakespeare: A Playgoer's Guide* (1988). About half of the plays are discussed, chiefly in terms of decisions that actors and directors make in putting the works onto the stage.

Dessen, Alan. *Elizabethan Stage Conventions and Modern Interpretations* (1984). On interpreting conventions such as the representation of light and darkness and stage violence (duels, battles).

Donaldson, Peter. *Shakespearean Films/Shakespearean Directors* (1990). Postmodernist analyses, drawing on Freudianism, Feminism, Deconstruction, and Queer Theory.

Jackson, Russell, and Robert Smallwood, eds. *Players of Shakespeare 2: Further Essays in Shakespearean Performance by Players with the Royal Shakespeare Company* (1988). Fourteen actors discuss their roles in productions between 1982 and 1987.

————. *Players of Shakespeare 3: Further Essays in Shake-*

spearean Performance by Players with the Royal Shakespeare Company (1993). Comments by thirteen performers.

Jorgens, Jack. *Shakespeare on Film* (1977). Fairly detailed studies of eighteen films, preceded by an introductory chapter addressing such issues as music, and whether to "open" the play by including scenes of landscape.

Kennedy, Dennis. *Looking at Shakespeare: A Visual History of Twentieth-Century Performance* (1993). Lucid descriptions (with 170 photographs) of European, British, and American performances.

Leiter, Samuel L. *Shakespeare Around the Globe: A Guide to Notable Postwar Revivals* (1986). For each play there are about two pages of introductory comments, then discussions (about five hundred words per production) of ten or so productions, and finally bibliographic references.

McMurty, Jo. *Shakespeare Films in the Classroom* (1994). Useful evaluations of the chief films most likely to be shown in undergraduate courses.

Rothwell, Kenneth, and Annabelle Henkin Melzer. *Shakespeare on Screen: An International Filmography and Videography* (1990). A reference guide to several hundred films and videos produced between 1899 and 1989, including spinoffs such as musicals and dance versions.

Sprague, Arthur Colby. *Shakespeare and the Actors* (1944). Detailed discussions of stage business (gestures, etc.) over the years.

Willis, Susan. *The BBC Shakespeare Plays: Making the Televised Canon* (1991). A history of the series, with interviews and production diaries for some plays.

5. Miscellaneous Reference Works

Abbott, E. A. *A Shakespearean Grammar* (new edition, 1877). An examination of differences between Elizabethan and modern grammar.

Allen, Michael J. B., and Kenneth Muir, eds. *Shakespeare's Plays in Quarto* (1981). One volume containing facsimiles of the plays issued in small format before they were collected in the First Folio of 1623.

Bevington, David. *Shakespeare* (1978). A short guide to hundreds of important writings on the subject.

Blake, Norman. *Shakespeare's Language: An Introduction* (1983). On vocabulary, parts of speech, and word order.

Bullough, Geoffrey. *Narrative and Dramatic Sources of Shakespeare*, 8 vols. (1957–75). A collection of many of the books Shakespeare drew on, with judicious comments.

Campbell, Oscar James, and Edward G. Quinn, eds. *The Reader's Encyclopedia of Shakespeare* (1966). Old, but still the most useful single reference work on Shakespeare.

Cercignani, Fausto. *Shakespeare's Works and Elizabethan Pronunciation* (1981). Considered the best work on the topic, but remains controversial.

Dent, R. W. *Shakespeare's Proverbial Language: An Index* (1981). An index of proverbs, with an introduction concerning a form Shakespeare frequently drew on.

Greg, W. W. *The Shakespeare First Folio* (1955). A detailed yet readable history of the first collection (1623) of Shakespeare's plays.

Harner, James. *The World Shakespeare Bibliography.* See headnote to Suggested References.

Hosley, Richard. *Shakespeare's Holinshed* (1968). Valuable presentation of one of Shakespeare's major sources.

Kökeritz, Helge. *Shakespeare's Names* (1959). A guide to pronouncing some 1,800 names appearing in Shakespeare.

———. *Shakespeare's Pronunciation* (1953). Contains much information about puns and rhymes, but see Cercignani (above).

Muir, Kenneth. *The Sources of Shakespeare's Plays* (1978). An account of Shakespeare's use of his reading. It covers all the plays, in chronological order.

Miriam Joseph, Sister. *Shakespeare's Use of the Arts of Language* (1947). A study of Shakespeare's use of rhetorical devices, reprinted in part as *Rhetoric in Shakespeare's Time* (1962).

The Norton Facsimile: The First Folio of Shakespeare's Plays (1968). A handsome and accurate facsimile of the first collection (1623) of Shakespeare's plays, with a valuable introduction by Charlton Hinman.

Onions, C. T. *A Shakespeare Glossary*, rev. and enlarged by

R. D. Eagleson (1986). Definitions of words (or senses of words) now obsolete.

Partridge, Eric. *Shakespeare's Bawdy*, rev. ed. (1955). Relatively brief dictionary of bawdy words; useful, but see Williams, below.

Shakespeare Quarterly. See headnote to Suggested References.

Shakespeare Survey. See headnote to Suggested References.

Spevack, Marvin. *The Harvard Concordance to Shakespeare* (1973). An index to Shakespeare's words.

Vickers, Brian. *Appropriating Shakespeare: Contemporary Critical Quarrels* (1993). A survey—chiefly hostile—of recent schools of criticism.

Wells, Stanley, ed. *Shakespeare: A Bibliographical Guide* (new edition, 1990). Nineteen chapters (some devoted to single plays, others devoted to groups of related plays) on recent scholarship on the life and all of the works.

Williams, Gordon. *A Dictionary of Sexual Language and Imagery in Shakespearean and Stuart Literature*, 3 vols. (1994). Extended discussions of words and passages; much fuller than Partridge, cited above.

6. Shakespeare's Plays: General Studies

Bamber, Linda. *Comic Women, Tragic Men: A Study of Gender and Genre in Shakespeare* (1982).

Barnet, Sylvan. *A Short Guide to Shakespeare* (1974).

Callaghan, Dympna, Lorraine Helms, and Jyotsna Singh. *The Weyward Sisters: Shakespeare and Feminist Politics* (1994).

Clemen, Wolfgang H. *The Development of Shakespeare's Imagery* (1951).

Cook, Ann Jennalie. *Making a Match: Courtship in Shakespeare and His Society* (1991).

Dollimore, Jonathan, and Alan Sinfield. *Political Shakespeare: New Essays in Cultural Materialism* (1985).

Dusinberre, Juliet. *Shakespeare and the Nature of Women* (1975).

Granville-Barker, Harley. *Prefaces to Shakespeare*, 2 vols. (1946–47; volume 1 contains essays on *Hamlet, King*

Lear, Merchant of Venice, Antony and Cleopatra, and *Cymbeline*; volume 2 contains essays on *Othello, Coriolanus, Julius Caesar, Romeo and Juliet, Love's Labor's Lost*).

―――. *More Prefaces to Shakespeare* (1974; essays on *Twelfth Night, A Midsummer Night's Dream, The Winter's Tale, Macbeth*).

Harbage, Alfred. *William Shakespeare: A Reader's Guide* (1963).

Howard, Jean E. *Shakespeare's Art of Orchestration: Stage Technique and Audience Response* (1984).

Jones, Emrys. *Scenic Form in Shakespeare* (1971).

Lenz, Carolyn Ruth Swift, Gayle Greene, and Carol Thomas Neely, eds. *The Woman's Part: Feminist Criticism of Shakespeare* (1980).

Novy, Marianne. *Love's Argument: Gender Relations in Shakespeare* (1984).

Rose, Mark. *Shakespearean Design* (1972).

Scragg, Leah. *Discovering Shakespeare's Meaning* (1994).

―――. *Shakespeare's "Mouldy Tales": Recurrent Plot Motifs in Shakespearean Drama* (1992).

Traub, Valerie. *Desire and Anxiety: Circulations of Sexuality in Shakespearean Drama* (1992).

Traversi, D. A. *An Approach to Shakespeare*, 2 vols. (3rd rev. ed, 1968–69).

Vickers, Brian. *The Artistry of Shakespeare's Prose* (1968).

Wells, Stanley. *Shakespeare: A Dramatic Life* (1994).

Wright, George T. *Shakespeare's Metrical Art* (1988).

7. The Comedies

Barber, C. L. *Shakespeare's Festive Comedy* (1959; discusses *Love's Labor's Lost, A Midsummer Night's Dream, The Merchant of Venice, As You Like It, Twelfth Night*).

Barton, Anne. *The Names of Comedy* (1990).

Berry, Ralph. *Shakespeare's Comedy: Explorations in Form* (1972).

Bradbury, Malcolm, and David Palmer, eds. *Shakespearean Comedy* (1972).

Bryant, J. A., Jr. *Shakespeare and the Uses of Comedy* (1986).

Carroll, William. *The Metamorphoses of Shakespearean Comedy* (1985).

Champion, Larry S. *The Evolution of Shakespeare's Comedy* (1970).

Evans, Bertrand. *Shakespeare's Comedies* (1960).

Frye, Northrop. *Shakespearean Comedy and Romance* (1965).

Leggatt, Alexander. *Shakespeare's Comedy of Love* (1974).

Miola, Robert S. *Shakespeare and Classical Comedy: The Influence of Plautus and Terence* (1994).

Nevo, Ruth. *Comic Transformations in Shakespeare* (1980).

Ornstein, Robert. *Shakespeare's Comedies: From Roman Farce to Romantic Mystery* (1986).

Richman, David. *Laughter, Pain, and Wonder: Shakespeare's Comedies and the Audience in the Theater* (1990).

Salingar, Leo. *Shakespeare and the Traditions of Comedy* (1974).

Slights, Camille Wells. *Shakespeare's Comic Commonwealths* (1993).

Waller, Gary, ed. *Shakespeare's Comedies* (1991).

Westlund, Joseph. *Shakespeare's Reparative Comedies: A Psychoanalytic View of the Middle Plays* (1984).

Williamson, Marilyn. *The Patriarchy of Shakespeare's Comedies* (1986).

8. The Romances (*Pericles, Cymbeline, The Winter's Tale, The Tempest, The Two Noble Kinsmen*)

Adams, Robert M. *Shakespeare: The Four Romances* (1989).

Felperin, Howard. *Shakespearean Romance* (1972).

Frye, Northrop. *A Natural Perspective: The Development of Shakespearean Comedy and Romance* (1965).

Mowat, Barbara. *The Dramaturgy of Shakespeare's Romances* (1976).

Warren, Roger. *Staging Shakespeare's Late Plays* (1990).

Young, David. *The Heart's Forest: A Study of Shakespeare's Pastoral Plays* (1972).

9. The Tragedies

Bradley, A. C. *Shakespearean Tragedy* (1904).

Brooke, Nicholas. *Shakespeare's Early Tragedies* (1968).

Champion, Larry. *Shakespeare's Tragic Perspective* (1976).

Drakakis, John, ed. *Shakespearean Tragedy* (1992).

Evans, Bertrand. *Shakespeare's Tragic Practice* (1979).

Everett, Barbara. *Young Hamlet: Essays on Shakespeare's Tragedies* (1989).

Foakes, R. A. *Hamlet versus Lear: Cultural Politics and Shakespeare's Art* (1993).

Frye, Northrop. *Fools of Time: Studies in Shakespearean Tragedy* (1967).

Harbage, Alfred, ed. *Shakespeare: The Tragedies* (1964).

Mack, Maynard. *Everybody's Shakespeare: Reflections Chiefly on the Tragedies* (1993).

McAlindon, T. *Shakespeare's Tragic Cosmos* (1991).

Miola, Robert S. *Shakespeare and Classical Tragedy: The Influence of Seneca* (1992).

———. *Shakespeare's Rome* (1983).

Nevo, Ruth. *Tragic Form in Shakespeare* (1972).

Rackin, Phyllis. *Shakespeare's Tragedies* (1978).

Rose, Mark, ed. *Shakespeare's Early Tragedies: A Collection of Critical Essays* (1995).

Rosen, William. *Shakespeare and the Craft of Tragedy* (1960).

Snyder, Susan. *The Comic Matrix of Shakespeare's Tragedies* (1979).

Wofford, Susanne. *Shakespeare's Late Tragedies: A Collection of Critical Essays* (1996).

Young, David. *The Action to the Word: Structure and Style in Shakespearean Tragedy* (1990).

———. *Shakespeare's Middle Tragedies: A Collection of Critical Essays* (1993).

10. The Histories

Blanpied, John W. *Time and the Artist in Shakespeare's English Histories* (1983).

Campbell, Lily B. *Shakespeare's "Histories": Mirrors of Elizabethan Policy* (1947).

Champion, Larry S. *Perspective in Shakespeare's English Histories* (1980).

Hodgdon, Barbara. *The End Crowns All: Closure and Contradiction in Shakespeare's History* (1991).

Holderness, Graham. *Shakespeare Recycled: The Making of Historical Drama* (1992).

————, ed. *Shakespeare's History Plays: "Richard II" to "Henry V"* (1992).

Leggatt, Alexander. *Shakespeare's Political Drama: The History Plays and the Roman Plays* (1988).

Ornstein, Robert. *A Kingdom for a Stage: The Achievement of Shakespeare's History Plays* (1972).

Rackin, Phyllis. *Stages of History: Shakespeare's English Chronicles* (1990).

Saccio, Peter. *Shakespeare's English Kings: History, Chronicle, and Drama* (1977).

Tillyard, E. M. W. *Shakespeare's History Plays* (1944).

Velz, John W., ed. *Shakespeare's English Histories: A Quest for Form and Genre* (1996).

11. *A Midsummer Night's Dream*

For bibliography concerning the stage history of the play, see page 147. For the play in general, in addition to the titles listed above in Section 7, The Comedies, see the following:

Briggs, K. M. *The Anatomy of Puck* (1959).

Fender, Stephen. *Shakespeare's "A Midsummer Night's Dream"* (1968).

Howard, Skiles. "Hands, Feet and Bottoms: Decentering the Cosmic Dance in *A Midsummer Night's Dream*." *Shakespeare Quarterly* 44 (1993): 325–42.

Levine, Laura. "Rape, Repetition, and the Politics of Closure in *A Midsummer Night's Dream*." *Feminist Readings of Early Modern Culture*. Ed. Valerie Traub (1996), pp. 210–28.

Montrose, Louis Adrian. *The Purpose of Playing: Shakespeare and the Cultural Politics of the Elizabethan Theatre* (1996).

Price, Anthony, ed. *Shakespeare's "A Midsummer Night's Dream": A Casebook* (1983).

Young, David. *Something of Great Constancy: The Art of "A Midsummer Night's Dream"* (1966).

The Signet Classic Shakespeare Series:
The Comedies
extensively revised and updated to provide more enjoyment through a greater understanding of the texts

The Signet Classic Shakespeare Series:
The Histories

*extensively revised and updated to provide more
enjoyment through a greater understanding of the texts*